FAITH

BEYOND

BELIEF

FAITH
BEYOND
BELIEF

Stories of Good People Who
Left Their Church Behind

Margaret Placentra Johnston

Theosophical Publishing House
Wheaton, Illinois • Chennai, India

Quest Books
Theosophical Publishing House
P. O. Box 270
Wheaton, IL 60187-0270

www.questbooks.net

Cover design by Mary Ann Smith

Typesetting by EDX Electronics

Library of Congress Cataloging-in-Publication Data

Johnston Margaret Placentra
Faith beyond belief: stories of good people who left their church behind / Margaret Placentra Johnston.—1st Quest ed.
   p.   cm.
Includes bibliographical references and index.
ISBN 978-0-8356-0905-0
1. Spiritual biography.   I. Title.
BL72.J54 2012
204.092'2—dc23
[B]   2012009272

5   4   3   2   1   *   12   13   14   15   16

Printed in the United States of America

Dedication

While there are many to whom I could have considered dedicating this book, in the end I realized I owe the most to the story contributors themselves. These ten people trusted me with protecting their identity (to the degree they each needed me to) and diligently stuck with me over several years of first developing their stories, then through writing the manuscript in various stages. They patiently cooperated through several revisions and reconsiderations as to whether real names or pseudonyms should be used. But along with the various other interviewees whose stories were not chosen, these people showed great faith in being willing to bare some of their most private moments with countless strangers, all in the belief that some greater cause was being served. For their immense generosity, I dedicate this book to them.

Contents

CONTENTS

Acknowledgments

There is no way to include everyone to whom I owe a debt of gratitude for their part in this book. Attempting chronological order, I could begin with my parents for an upbringing that included religion but never restricted independent thought and for countless other gifts too numerous to list here. Deserving of mention are the priest—whose name I do not recall—who taught my freshman high school religion class, and the entire Catholic University Theology Department from forty-some years ago, for their honesty, even when they must have known their open-ended pedagogy risked leading so many young minds away from the church.

From my more adult life, the people of the Northern Virginia Ethical Society probably most helped open my eyes to wider ways of seeing the world. And a special thanks goes to Marilyn Miller, whose gift to me years ago, I am certain, stands behind my strength and commitment in putting this message out there.

I would thank all the theorists upon whose work this book is based, and the members of my various writing groups who helped me clarify my words and intent. While *all* the members of *all* the groups contributed deeply to this work, the most notable among them is Beverly Fourier, who generously opened her home to one small group over the course of nearly five years. This book owes much to her commentary.

Acknowledgments

I would thank the people at Quest Books for understanding what I was trying to do before this book took its current form. I would especially thank Sharron Dorr for her direction and my editor, Phil Catalfo, for his ideas and corrections. My agent, Lisa Hagan, offered an amazing level of support and love, for which I am most grateful.

I would thank certain friends, certain family members, and my two sons for their support, lively discussions, and interest in this crazy idea of mine. Developing this book has made up for the religious education I never forced my children to get. But most of all, I would thank my husband, Bill Johnston. Over the course of a very few years, I went from being a full-time income producer in a completely non-controversial job to a very part-time practitioner, spending most of my time delving into an unrelated field, planning to expose a concept full of risk to conventional thought. For not being threatened by what could only have been a most perplexing metamorphosis, for not worrying about what "other people" might think, for allowing me the freedom to grow—without risking your love—into someone I was not when you married me: thanks, Bill!

Introduction

Are you tired yet of the warring between religious believers and non-believers? (Have you noticed how some, especially in our political arena, fan the fires of this battle?)

Did the "New Atheist" writers, Sam Harris, Richard Dawkins, and Christopher Hitchens, speak clearly to your rational mind, yet leave your heart still yearning for some greater spiritual reality?

Does the challenge of a more sophisticated understanding than either the religious believers or the nonbelievers typically put forth excite you?

Readers of this book who are merely inquisitive about people's spiritual decisions can sit back and just enjoy the entertainment value of these stories. But readers seeking something more—those responsive to the three questions above—will also gain the opportunity to view religious and spiritual maturity in a different light. This new complexity will open fresh ways of appreciating our shared humanity and arm these readers against some particularly short-sighted outlooks that are threatening to insinuate themselves into our general culture.

Anyone paying attention can see how winning out over the other guy has become way too important in our society. In much of the business world, little thought is given to what might constitute "right conduct" beyond what brings the most monetary benefit. Reckless behavior on Wall Street has caused millions of dollars in personal losses and has led many to lose their homes. In healthcare, major decisions are made by "bean counters" at huge insurance conglomerates whose primary allegiance is to corporate profit motives. Often those motives supersede concern for the medical well-being of those they were established to serve. Where money is concerned, the welfare of customers, clients, and patients receives far less consideration than it deserves.

When winning becomes too important, it blurs concern for the way our actions affect others; it necessarily sets up someone on the opposing side who must "lose." The win/lose mentality prominent in our society is a symptom of a much larger problem—a *spiritual* problem, in fact. A contagious societal myopia blinds us to the ways that strictly self-serving actions harm the overall society. As the most spiritually developed humans are aware, we are all part of a greater whole. What is done to the least member of that whole harms everyone. The short-sighted, spiritually myopic actions of ruthlessly determined "winners" have a far-reaching effect that goes little noticed; they also harm the winners themselves.

This spiritual myopia is even more evident in the political arena, where the need to win has been distorted entirely out of proportion. Contenders particularly desperate for power have reduced the concepts of truth, honor, and dignity to their most superficial meanings. Pundits and political rivals hijack terminology to their advantage and misinterpret events in a frantic effort to place opponents in a bad light. They twist truth to fit their convenience, at great cost to civility—and with no concern for how their actions might harm the larger society.

How is it that our culture has allowed this spiritual myopia to progress uncorrected to this extent in the political arena? How is it that even some otherwise sophisticated citizens fall prey to their tactics? The most desperate contenders have enlisted the aid of a special weapon: God. They call upon the Bible, God, and *their own* particular religion to fight their battles for them. Their spiritual myopia consists in the fact that they invoke these entities only in their most superficial connotations. Does their sense of righteousness *really* only extend as deep as following the Bible? Does the God they invoke really only support the efforts of *Christians*? Gullible listeners fall prey to these religious simplifications only because we, as a nation, suffer from a similar myopia. However sophisticated we may be in other aspects of life, our spiritual views are stunted by literal connotations that keep us focused at the provincial level. We remain unaware of a well-defined process of spiritual development; many in the general public do not recognize what constitutes spiritual maturity.

But this is not a book about politics, or even the spiritual myopia that pervades the general culture (as portrayed in our mass media). It concerns only the one form of myopia that lies at the base of so many of the others. At the individual level, good, honest people are doing their best to live a meaningful life. Necessary to a meaningful life is the opportunity to live in truth. If our would-be leaders are distorting our reality by spouting mistruths, we must detach ourselves from their influence.

Treatment for the political, religious, and spiritual myopia of our society entails a perspective-broadening pair of glasses disclosing a wider truth. The spiritual-development process leads us away from such divisiveness and the winner-take-all mentality. The truth it delivers is one that works for *all* people.

Using very plain terminology, this book discloses a particularly paradoxical form of religious truth. It is one that is easily missed without careful attention and study. Amid the win-or-lose attitudes of our society's messages, it has been missed by all but the most diligent. If political groups claiming religious authority are showing the divisiveness and self-protecting, winner-takes-all symptoms of a pervasive cultural and spiritual myopia—*and if our culture condones this*—it must be that we have all contracted the disease. We must find a cure.

In this book, ten real-life stories, of two very different kinds, address the above questions. They illuminate steps in a faith journey that is well known in certain circles but receives little attention in our larger culture.

Though not saying it in so many words, various experts have described a surprising and counter-intuitive set of steps that lead a person away from the winner-takes-all stance and the divisiveness and triumphalism most of us fail to recognize as spiritual immaturity. The spiritual-development process leads people toward a maturity founded on a deeper appreciation of the goodness values; it *unites* rather than divides.

I am not a professional theologian, nor is my training in the academic fields of psychological, sociological, or theological research. I am merely a life-long seeker of truth, and nearly everything I have written here is founded on the immensely difficult work of many thinkers more intellectual, more spiritually developed, and more schooled than I.

My contribution has been to analyze selectively the core of these works and translate them for the general reader into a perspective that I hope will ease a discomfort many feel about religious belief. That I have not conducted my own research on this subject is actually an advantage. The topic crosses several disciplines; no one field covers it all. Furthermore, lacking an academic reputation to protect, I can afford to make connections among the works of the theorists that are evident in the reading but which are impossible to show according to proper academic method. *Faith Beyond Belief* synthesizes for the layperson a perspective that appears elsewhere only in complex and abstract form—scattered across many various documents from different disciplines and written in heavily coded language—perhaps waiting to be discovered by the greater society. I believe the time for this discovery is now. Global communications have broadened awareness that our community is not defined by our nationality or our religion; we are not just Americans or Christians but citizens of a much larger universe.

Hints are popping up all over that society is ready for the message *Faith Beyond Belief* aims to simplify. With this book, I hope to cast a clear, bright light on a viewpoint that otherwise remains shrouded in shadow by those too polite to discuss such topics openly, those afraid to face bold truths, and those who benefit from others remaining dependent upon the religious institution.

By now the huge "spiritual, but not religious" movement has clarified that spirituality need not involve belief in religious dogma. But *Faith Beyond Belief* takes this discussion one step further. While anyone can *claim* to be spiritual, when arrived at through a *specific process* of development, a stance by that name may actually be more authentic and more mature than traditional religiosity. Though the spiritual endpoint I describe in no way specifically *excludes* traditional religious participation, it does necessarily reach far beyond the typical religious endpoints explicitly embodied by our religious institutions.

A lot of what I have written here about the spiritual stages is not *strictly* true. Surely any critic could tear apart the four distinctions I make (between Lawless, Faithful, Rational, and Mystic stages) and come up with hundreds of exceptions and reasons why the stages are not valid. But that should not prevent the general concept from illuminating something useful.

While no given person is either one hundred percent optimistic or pessimistic (or entirely introverted or extroverted), we still recognize the validity of those distinctions. We allow optimism versus pessimism (and introversion versus extroversion) to teach us something interesting and important about human nature. Similarly, we should not allow the fact that no actual, complex individual could exist entirely at any one stage to prevent the spiritual development stage *concept* from offering a better understanding about ourselves—and about the nature of religious belief. Taking a bird's-eye view, I think it becomes obvious that the stages are at least true in general. From this generalization we can learn to see patterns that will help us better understand the exceptions.

The main thesis of this book is that much of traditional religion promotes a spiritually immature message, saying that only people who believe as it does are right. Just about anyone with enough nerve to question such beliefs honestly will realize this cannot be true in a literal sense. But rejecting everything about religion just because we cannot accept the literal message is also not the most mature position. Our complex humanity is capable of much greater sophistication. Just as our human brains are equipped with skills that take us far beyond the black-and-white reasoning of the believer versus nonbeliever controversy, our spirits are equipped to encompass far broader perspectives than our traditional religious institutions explicitly articulate. *Faith Beyond Belief* aims to point out avenues by which one might access this more sophisticated reasoning and these broader perspectives.

While this introduction will acquaint readers with the main text, the "Personal Letter to My Readers" below allows me, as the author, to introduce myself personally. Besides explaining a bit about who I am, it details a significant event in my own spiritual story.

Part 1, "Religion—Who Needs It?" contains real-life stories from four contributors who found greater personal authenticity outside the dictates of traditional religious authority. Each contributor began with a different kind of question, but all went through a similar process and all arrived at a similar point. The *Faith Beyond Belief* stories were written by cooperative effort between the contributors and me, often with many drafts passing back and forth between us to be sure I had represented the experiences accurately. The stories in both parts 1 and 3 are true to the extent that what the contributor told me was true. I have attempted to maintain something of the individual voice of each contributor, but the reader will understand that to some degree my own conceptual bias must unavoidably have crept into each narrative. Most of the names have been changed, as were some incidental details, depending on the individual needs of each contributor to maintain anonymity.

Part 2, "Are They Right?" discusses the wisdom of the decisions made by the part 1 contributors, contains a little more of my own story, and points the way to the larger narrative about spiritual maturity to which the rest of the book is devoted.

The six stories in part 3, "Who is a Mystic?" are more complex and involve more of the contributor's life history than those in part 1. They sample ways in which a person might arrive at a mature stance that includes spirituality, and how the traits and values of such a stance might play out in ordinary lives.

Part 4, "Toward an Understanding of Post-Critical Faith," further clarifies spiritual development theory in the light of the theorists' work, while part 5, "What Does It All Mean?" discusses the implications that can be drawn from the stories and from the larger narrative about what it means to mature spiritually.

Taken together with the surrounding discussion, the stories offer an overarching explanation for the atheist/believer controversy itself. This explanation disallows dividing people up into good versus bad, right versus wrong, or even right versus left. It shows how any such black-and-white distinctions deny the complexity of which human reason and spirituality are capable and are necessarily inadequate when applied to humanity itself.

This book may not be for everyone. If the questions at the beginning of this introduction and the ensuing discussion threatened your view of reality or made you feel defensive, then this book—especially the discussion parts—may not be for you. If your religion brings you needed comfort against a world filled with fear, if your specific religious beliefs are holding your world together, please read no further. Similarly, if your atheism defines your existence, you may want to do the same.

On the other hand, if you welcome a challenge that takes you past the typical believer-versus-nonbeliever divide—if the questions on the first page left you curious to know more—I invite you on a tour through the *Faith Beyond Belief* perspective. I point the way to a common human faith process by which religious (and atheistic) righteousness, divisiveness and triumphalism, are replaced by the "higher" goals of inclusiveness, unity, and love. It is an endpoint available to us all.

I have used the plainest language possible to render the road as smooth as possible. But *Faith Beyond Belief* is only a sample trip. My hope is that this broad overview of spiritual development theory will spur further reading of the more detailed works by the theorists mentioned—which could, in turn, eventually lead to an even broader understanding of spiritual maturity in our society as a whole.

Personal Letter to My Readers

I agonized over the decision to write this book. In particular, I worried for sake of potential readers who may be drawn to it, not because of the topic, but solely on the basis of their affiliation with me. My most genuine concern was that some people might wind up seriously confused. Not for the world would I disrupt the belief system of those whose religion is holding their world together.

But I have not curtailed my involvement in a profession I love to devote five years of my life writing something intended to cause harm. There are many for whom this book will serve as an integrating force delivering a welcome, peace-bringing perspective that may help them make better sense of the world. For such people, *Faith Beyond Belief* will not harm, but help. I believe such messages have a way of falling mainly on the right ears—or in the case of a book, before the right eyes and into the right hands. I offer this book fully trusting that the universe will guide it into the right hands and let it slip right through the wrong ones.

As a Doctor of Optometry, I have spent the last thirty years prescribing glasses and contact lenses, improving my patients' sight in the physical world. For most of those years, I owned and managed my own private practice and found joy in helping people in an enjoyable, comfortable setting. As a result of my diagnostic skills, just about every patient walked out of my office seeing noticeably better than when he came in. Challenging as it was, there was nothing controversial about this work.

In recent years, I have found myself driven toward a mission fraught with far more controversy. Having accepted a call from some unknown place to promote sharper sight of a different sort, I have had to push myself beyond the comfortable and the pleasant. In hope of promoting clearer vision outside the bounds of the physical world, I have had to expand my comfort zone to address a wider audience on a thorny, less concrete issue, thereby exposing myself to the risk of being seriously misunderstood.

Some twenty years ago, I ran across a passage in M. Scott Peck's *The Different Drum* that turned my rather pat view of the world upside down: "Stage IV men and women will enter into religion in order to approach mystery."[1] (This stage is introduced in chapter 5.) The intervening years between that reading and the production of this book have been filled with an internal tug-of-war between two opposite reactions. Years of avoidance would alternate with months of avidly reading every bit of related material I could get my hands on. I was caught between the conscious struggle to dismiss the spiritual-development stages as nonsense and the power of that model to captivate me as Truth at the subconscious level. Before long, I realized that the concept of spiritual growth had permeated my being in a way that would forever color my understanding of the world and my place in it.

Over time, I noted that few others interpret world events through the lens of spiritual development theory. In fact, it seems no one else even calls it by that name yet. But a solid theory with numerous contributing theorists it seems to be. Reading just one or another of the theorists, the concepts are easy to dismiss. Each of the theorists has a bias that may appeal to some readers but be misunderstood or rejected by others. But from a bird's-eye view, one can see that they all have said more or less the same thing; each describes a different facet of the same gem. The more of them I read, the greater understanding I gained about what true maturity in spirituality means (which is quite a different thing from saying I will ever attain that goal myself).

Some will say that we need not dissect religion as specifically as I do in this book. Like a beautiful painting, if you analyze it in too technical a manner, it detracts from one's appreciation of its beauty. In general I would agree. And were it not for the divisive and untruthful imposition of religion in its least mature expressions into our political and economic arenas, I would not have written about religious belief in this way. But given the viciously contentious factors in action today, hijacking religious belief as a political weapon, it is time we get down off our high horse about the sanctity of religion and talk about it in an intelligent manner—one that respects our rational intellect but also acknowledges the unknowable aspects of our existence. In my heart, I can feel our fractured society crying out for this message.

Though committing to write *Faith Beyond Belief* was not an easy decision, eventually I saw that someone with my particular set of experiences and situation in life had no excuse *not* to share that viewpoint. So, driven as I am to provide clearer vision wherever possible, I have placed my neck on the proverbial chopping block to present this message..

Just as it was not an easy book to write, *Faith Beyond Belief* may not be an easy book to read. It may initially cause disquiet in readers from almost every spiritual level. Rather than offer the immediate comfort of new glasses that are essentially the same prescription as the last pair, *Faith Beyond Belief* challenges the reader to adapt to something new.

Occasionally we in the eye-care field have to encourage a patient to "get used to" the better vision afforded by a new pair of glasses gradually. In particularly difficult cases, we may ask her to wear the new ones for just an hour or two a day at first, alternating with the old pair, until she can manage the new ones full time. In a similar vein, I recommend flexibility on the part of readers in approaching the perspective offered in this book. It is probably best read slowly, perhaps one story at a time or one section at a time.

Often when we are most challenged and manage to stretch ourselves to look most honestly at the source of that discomfort, we reap the most substantial rewards. In expanding our horizons beyond the comfortable, we learn the most about ourselves.

After careful reflection, successful adapters will come to agree that a broader vision than that offered by our traditional religions and our mainstream society is possible. *Faith Beyond Belief* calls us not to comfort, but to vigor.

In *The Interior Castle*, Saint Teresa of Avila begged the God of her understanding for assistance in the very difficult task of explaining her "Mansions," only "if there is any advantage to be gained from its being done, but not otherwise."[2] In the same spirit, I hope the spiritual development concept will become clear through my efforts in this book only if it will offer an "advantage" to society, but not otherwise. Likewise with my readers—I hope that those for whom there is advantage in seeing the connections I am trying to make will see them. To those for whom there is no such advantage, I trust *Faith Beyond Belief* will appear as nothing more than a collection of interesting stories. I begin by recounting a personal experience of my own from about forty years ago.

Rational Beginnings

From the back seat of the rusty, faded-gray *Deux Chevaux*,[3] my very American ears were starting to ache. Over the roar of the noisy engine, I had been working hard to follow the repartee. Just three months into my Junior Year Abroad program in Avignon, France, and still getting used to the language and the culture, it seemed I was dating this French guy, Michel, our driver. His younger sister, Annette, serving as our "chaperone" for the day, sat next to him in the front seat. The two were sparring verbally in colloquial French, a typical brother-and-sister thing. But I had faded from their awareness; they weren't even showing off for me anymore. Before long, I gave up any hope of participating in the pointless conversation. The old car was so noisy that they would not have heard me anyway.

Looking out the window, the beauty of the lovely country scenery was dulled by darkish clouds looming overhead. Withdrawing from this generally dreary atmosphere, my thoughts turned inward—and to religion as I had come to know it in my short twenty years of life. Never did I suspect how far my personal musings during this forty-minute car ride to Mont Ventoux, the local attraction I was to be shown that day, would take me.

I had been raised Catholic in a nominally religious family. Tuition at the Catholic school was always paid, and we followed all the church's rules, foremost among them the one that required attendance at Mass every Sunday. Missing Mass was a mortal sin, and if you died without going to confession to get rid of that sin on your soul, you would go immediately to Hell. As I understood it, religion was largely a rote matter: Follow the rules and you will be rewarded in Heaven. Break the rules and you will be punished.

For eight years in elementary school, we were required to memorize three or four catechism questions a night. By eighth grade, everyone could supply a perfect rote answer to any one of hundreds of questions in that little book. But just like little kids saying the Pledge of Allegiance with lots of mispronounced words, we had no idea what it all meant. We just got that you had to be sure you got to confession every week so there would be no mortal sins on your soul in case you died. I never thought of religion as connected to anything exciting or glorious. Though my home life and schooling (Catholic grammar school, Catholic high school, and Catholic college) contained rich and satisfying experiences, none of them were connected with religion. The unspoken message was that, once we were adults, religion could be stored away in a "Sunday only" compartment in our minds.

In high school, things took a really interesting turn. In the freshman-year religion classes, we were let in on the secret that all the "facts" we had memorized from the catechism over the years were not *literally* true. We were told that Heaven and Hell were not real, physical places; they were merely "states of being." We were also taught that Jesus Christ was not literally the Son of God, either. It was just what they called "anthropomorphic" language—terminology conjured up so common folks could better understand the church's teachings.

Furthermore, we were taught that the Bible was not based in actual fact. Much like Aesop's Fables, the Bible contained useful stories from which we could learn. But just as no one actually believes that Aesop's animals actually talked, many accounts in the Bible could be seen as allegorical.

At first I was indignant at having been forced, in elementary school, to memorize teachings that were not, strictly speaking, true. But more importantly, I was delighted to finally be let in on the truth! I still remember, from the end of freshman year, my excitement and wild anticipation that "next year, they will surely teach us the *real* truth."

To my extreme disappointment and confusion, however, the next year's religion classes contained only courses on family life, comparative religion, and the like. No Catholic truths were ever disclosed.

By the time junior year rolled around and we were supposed to be choosing a college, I knew my eleven years of religious education had left me seriously in the lurch. I had been stripped of all I had been taught to believe, and what was left in its place was woefully insufficient to sustain me for the rest of my life. I realized that if I were ever to gain a solid religious foundation, I would need to study religion in college.

What better place for this than the Catholic University of America? The high school guidance counselor demanded that my parents appear in his office to discuss my choice of college. "I want you folks to realize," he told them, "that your daughter is choosing a *radical* institution!" This was the late sixties, and I suppose my parents assumed he meant politically radical. He didn't elaborate further, and, as my parents were confident I was not at risk for *politically* radical behavior, I set off for Washington, DC and Catholic U with their full approval.

In my choice of college, I was looking at religious study solely as an intellectual and philosophical issue, not as a source of moral guidance or inspiration. I don't remember giving much thought to moral issues in those days. At Catholic U, my religious education proceeded according to plan. The required theology and philosophy courses, numerous enough to make up the equivalent of a college minor, absorbed most of my energy.

Strikingly, all the theology and philosophy courses encouraged us to question. In one course, regular weekly essays were assigned on such broad topics as "Who is God?" and "Who is Jesus?" Ready in my rote memory were predetermined answers to these questions—but alas, providing catechism answers, we had been warned on the first day of class, would merit us a grade of "F"! The professor made it clear we would be graded on the quality of *our own original thought*. Well, this was the whole reason I had chosen this college in the first place, so I threw myself into these exercises with a zeal I had never put into anything else before.

Another course, entitled "The Phenomenology of Religion" introduced us to various renegade theories. One of these was Sigmund Freud's book, *The Future of an Illusion,* where Freud argued that all religions are constructs invented by man to explain phenomena he could not otherwise understand. As further scientific discoveries were explaining a lot of prior mysteries, the need for supernatural explanations was becoming unnecessary. Soon, Freud felt, there would be no further need for religion. I dutifully studied and considered these concepts, but only on an intellectual level, at the time not applying them to my own belief system.

During these years I had come to recognize some examples of extreme hypocrisy among the traditionally religious people I had known—women I remembered from my hometown who would walk piously down the aisle from Communion each Sunday and yet, come Monday morning, tear a fellow member of the local "Mothers' Club" to pieces behind her back. Meanwhile, the people I genuinely admired most, those who would help others just because it felt good, for example, or those whose behavior was more consistent with their stated ideals, often seemed to feel no need for church or doctrine at all.

Between these personal observations and the theoretical questioning in the theology courses, there was reason enough for me to discard my religious beliefs. But, convinced as I was of the validity of my religion, I held on to my traditional beliefs, sealing away the cognitive dissonance in some far distant corner of my brain. After two years of active, intellectual theological questioning, I still held tightly to my original Catholic beliefs.

And so I arrived in France for my junior year of college—and stepped into Michel's Deux Chevaux for that gloomy trip to Mont Ventoux—with no serious doubts about my religion, at least not at the conscious level. As the tedious banter between the two siblings dragged on, my silent personal musings continued. I had been surprised to note that not too many French people actually went to church. Good, simple, honest, salt-of-the-earth people, with solid family values, just got up on Sunday morning and went hiking in the mountains or had a bunch of folks over for a fancy breakfast. This would have been scandalous back home in New Jersey.

The college program in France was my first experience with an educational institution not affiliated with the Catholic Church. In this program, religion wasn't even mentioned, so theological thoughts and concepts had a chance to gel, undisturbed by further teachings. That day in the car, I reflected on the whole arc of my religious education: the endless elementary school catechism questions; the demolition, in high school, of all the grade-school religious concepts; the college courses where questioning was rewarded; the hypocrisy of many of the supposedly religious people I had observed in my youth. As they all paraded through my mind in sequence, I allowed logic to take me wherever it might. And somehow, that day, I logically linked all those observations together and came to the startling realization that, not only did I lack a solid basis on which to form a belief in God, but also that, for many, God was nothing but a crutch! And I decided I really did not need any such crutch in my life.

To my amazement, as the clouds gave way to a bright sunny sky, I stepped out of that car at the base of Mont Ventoux essentially an atheist. In less than an hour, reason had trumped fourteen years of religious training. There was and could be, I now saw, no such creature as the God of my catechism classes. No angry, punishing God would condemn me to eternal damnation if I were accidentally hit by a car on my way to confession. I decided that no such God was necessary. No such God was possible. And if there *were* a Supreme Being, he or she could not possibly harbor such petty, human emotions as the God I had been taught about. That God—the catechism God—could only have been a figment of human imagination. Indeed, it would be a colossal disappointment if I were to learn that that God *did* exist.

Most of all, I decided that if I were to live a good life, it would be up to me to figure out how; morality was not a matter of confessing my sins in time. How about if I just lived by a higher standard and didn't do wrong things? What if I avoided doing the things that I knew in my heart were wrong simply because it felt better to do the right thing? Living this way, I would not need to concern myself with eternal punishment or reward. I didn't even believe there was any life after death anyway.

I also decided that the only thing that counted was the here and now. Life right here on earth was an incredible gift, and if I took every opportunity to make this life the best I possibly could, then no possible God "up there" (if by chance, there was an afterlife) could fault me for the use I had made of that gift. I would determine my life's course and, as long as I followed my own conscience, I would always know I had done my best.

I knew immediately that this was a very serious move. Being responsible for running my own life would apply to adverse circumstances as well as good ones. There would be no God to fall back on in times of strife. I knew this decision was going to require great strength and determination on my part. With a grave sense of the magnitude of my decision, I proceeded ahead.

In the days that followed, I felt uncommonly liberated. I no longer had to fear eternal punishment for unintentional transgressions against the exacting rules of the church, no longer needed to fear that the devil was watching my every move. It was empowering to know that this decision meant I would have to figure out right from wrong in each situation I encountered. I could no longer rely on the rules of the church. This felt good! It was scary, but I was ready. No longer waiting for God to show me the way, I plowed full speed ahead.

While I was still in that car, there had been a pivotal point just after I assembled all the logic in which I knew I could collapse the argument in either direction. I could either say no—all my reasoning would be pointing me away from belief in God, but I could choose to believe anyway—or I could follow the reasoning to its logical conclusion.

On the one side sat tradition: everything I had been taught, everything almost everyone I knew believed, the support of a God who would answer prayers, and the comfort of "knowing" what happens after we die. On the other side sat a thrilling level of personal responsibility, freedom from the fearful parts of religion, the devil, the threat of eternal punishment for unwittingly violating one of the minor laws of the church, and a certain sadness at giving up all that my religion had promised—the fairy tales, the answers about our existence, the hopeful creed.

My decision that day was the more ambitious one. The step that took me from believer to nonbeliever is the same one that took me from child to adult. I felt empowered, happy, excited—but sad, for the fairy tale was over. What had started out as a boring car trip on that long ago fall day in Avignon turned out to be an event that formed the framework of a life philosophy that served me well for many years to come.

Perhaps some will point fingers at me for the false pride and audacity of the conclusion I reached that day. But that decision was a first step in taking an adult measure of responsibility for my life. The stories that follow feature some people who made similar choices and others whose life pointed them toward a very different path. Though for some these choices came at a price, each case is meant to show how eschewing the comforts of conventional belief in favor of a more vigorous and more truthful path can lead to greater spiritual authenticity and a fulfilling life.

Author's Note

I would like to take this opportunity to clarify several random points. While some texts make a very great deal over the difference between a *stage* and a *level*, I have chosen to use the terms interchangeably.

Given the lack of proper gender-neutral English pronouns, my editor and I agreed to alternate randomly between the use of she/her/hers and he/him/his. We tried to split the references evenly but very much hope no one is actually counting.

As I was reared in Christianity, some terms are natural to me but are not meant to exclude those from other traditions. For example, the word *church* in my title is meant as a generic place of worship. It is not meant literally to exclude temples, mosques, chapels, and shrines.

Lastly, though a disproportionate number of *Faith Beyond Belief* stories are from ex-Catholics, this book is in no way meant to be a book against Catholicism. In fact, it is the interface with the more fundamentalist belief stances and the inappropriate imposition of the religious voice in the political arena from the (mostly Protestant) religious right that inspired this book.

Despite its continuing, ludicrous, unrealistic injunctions against birth control, and despite its not offering an explicit liberal or less literal faction, I find Catholicism richer and more nuanced—and feel it may better allow for the complex interpretations of spiritual maturity—than other forms of conservative Christianity. Despite my continued, and perhaps stubborn, lack of religious participation, I remain deeply grateful for the truth process for which my Catholic education prepared me.

Part One

Religion—Who Needs It?

Each story in this part illustrates an intense struggle between continued acceptance of traditional beliefs and the doubts arising from within the person's own reasoning. Despite these contributors having come from several different religions, their concerns are similar. The person enjoys the comforts of belonging to a group in which everyone believes the same things and hesitates to give up that certainty. The religion provides moral structure and rules about behavior without which the person may be at risk of falling into a life of chaos. Readers will note how, in each story, the person resolves these issues to emerge stronger, more grounded, and more self-reliant. In later chapters, I will suggest an explanation for this phenomenon that is obviously common, but rarely discussed.

Chapter 1

The Surprise behind Door Number Two (Valerie)

Valerie, a young southwestern mother of three, speaks with a very tangible excitement in her voice, demonstrating the enthusiasm she holds for life. As discrepancies in the logic of church stories began to bother her, so did the seemingly naïve acceptance of these concepts by her fellow church members. Valerie's process of letting go entailed four years and several valiant attempts to hold on. Eventually, reason won out over the teachings of her church. The reader will note how the stronger sense of self that emerged opened new doors in Valerie's life.

—∾∾—

Warm, Welcome, and Safe

I was born and reared in a family firmly steeped in the Mormon faith and am a graduate of Brigham Young University. My religion always felt right to me; inside the walls of my church, I was warm, welcome, and safe. A strong church provided a rich sense of community, laid out a set of predetermined rules for good living, and promised answers to questions about my existence. I grew up with all the blessings of one convinced that her religion offered the One and Only True Set of Beliefs. My life was rich; my faith was its own reward.

Never could I have imagined that I would one day find it necessary to pry open "Door Number Two," behind which lurked realities completely at odds with the teachings of my youth. But as an adult, I would spend a full three years pacing in front of that closed door, pretending it was stuck shut. I would spend another year hovering in front of it with my hand poised uncertainly on the knob before I finally summoned the nerve to fling that dark, heavy door wide open. To my great surprise, what I found inside was . . . myself.

In my teen years and early twenties, I had completely accepted the Mormon faith—and not merely because my parents had handed it to me on a silver platter. I had sought answers on my own in the form of what the Mormon religion calls a "witness" from the Holy Ghost. One of the foundational beliefs of Mormonism is that if you have sincerity in your heart as you ask God in prayer whether something you are questioning is true, he will give you an answer. Typically, this answer will come in the form of a burning sensation or a sort of peaceful feeling in your heart. I believe one of the reasons the Mormon Church has such devoted followers is that all church members are encouraged to assure themselves of the validity of their faith by seeking out this type of spiritual experience on their own.

I was fourteen when I sought my first witness from the Holy Ghost. I had read the entire Book of Mormon and then set about praying for my own answer as to whether or not it was true. Sure enough, I got the wonderful response I had hoped for! It was a sweet but powerful burning sensation in my heart, like when a song would inspire me, or like the time when I first realized a certain teenage crush might actually develop into a relationship.

After that first witness from the Holy Ghost, I became a sort of spiritual junkie. Seeking out ever more of these witnesses, I asked about Joseph Smith, the Bible, and even our new prophet. Every time I asked, the expected answer would come. Every witnessing I experienced deepened my conviction about the validity of church doctrine—and about the fact that God himself was supplying the answers. The power of these witness experiences formed a very strong basis for the passion I held in my heart for my religion.

Throughout the next decade or so, I had ongoing conversations in my head with God. He would advise me of his wishes on this or that issue and provide inspiration for my daily activities. This would include serving on a mission for the church in the Philippines and holding many leadership positions. Along the way, I allowed a personal passion for performance dance to languish by the wayside in favor of serving the needs of my church. I was certain that I was a member of the one and only true church of Jesus Christ—the Mormon Church. I was content to know that I had the real truth and created a life that revolved around my religion.

Pacing in Front of the Dark and Dangerous Door Number Two

Given the level of my commitment to the church, I was shocked when, in my mid-twenties, soon after I became a mother, the first inkling of doubt crept into my being. I had joined an internet Bible study group and, though I had studied other religions while growing up, this was the first time my studies included input from people of the other Christian religions and non-Mormon interpretations of the Bible.

There had always been points of doctrine and verses in the scriptures that didn't make sense to me. But that hadn't bothered me, because I always figured God would explain it someday. Plus, I already knew that my church considered certain parts of the Bible to have been translated erroneously. But once I heard those issues discussed in more depth by people from other religions, I realized the discrepancies were much larger than I had thought.

Although I was accustomed to studying the Bible every year, I now feared that if I read it any further, I would jeopardize my beliefs. For the first time, I had moments of actual skepticism. This scared me. Up to that point, I had been graced with certainty about nearly everything regarding my religion, so a life that included doubt was hard to fathom.

Moreover, I felt ashamed to question, so I shut those lurking doubts out of my mind and refused to think about them. Life continued as usual.

Also, around this time I started to notice how the demands of church activities could interfere with duty to one's family. For example, in each congregation the bishop was a man whom the church fathers had summarily nominated to this position—a choice supposedly dictated by God. This person would suddenly be expected first to accept the position without hesitation (since he was, after all, chosen by God) and then to devote countless hours to running the local church, all without pay. Meanwhile, he would also have to maintain a full-time job outside the church to support his family.

It suddenly dawned on me what that position would cost this man in terms of time for his family. If my husband were called to be the bishop, I would want him to refuse. I knew that my children needed time and attention from both their parents; to sacrifice their needs to anything or anyone at all during this crucial time in their lives just felt wrong.

Also, I was not pleased with some of the people the Church leaders were putting in charge of the children's groups. There was one particular individual in whose care I simply could not bear to leave my children, even for a few minutes. Though this person was supposedly designated specifically to this position by God through the bishop, it was a choice I knew in my heart I could not trust.

All at once I began to sense that my duty to my family exceeded my duty to the everyday needs of my church. This dampened my religious commitment a bit and paved the way to my eventually opening Door Number Two. However, for the time being I managed to push my concerns down beneath the surface, said nothing to my husband or anyone else about this, and continued my full church participation as before.

Later that same year, I was called to be the leader of the women's organization in our church. Our belief system maintained that God would provide inspiration and guide the actions of those in such leadership positions. As the leader, I was expected to accept his inspiration in choosing the direction this group would take.

Coincidentally, both my mother and my mother-in-law held similar positions in their respective local congregations at the same time. We occasionally got together and shared our stories and experiences. My mother, my mother-in-law, and I are all very different people, and it soon became apparent to me that we were each being "inspired" to act in ways that were typical of our own personality. At this time we also had a fairly new prophet leading the church, and I could see how much his decisions were being determined by his personality.

Why, I wondered, if we were all receiving inspiration directly from God, were all our choices such direct expressions of ourselves? I thought, Are we actually being called by God—or are we each really just doing our own thing? This question caused yet another inkling of doubt. Yet, frightened and ashamed to be questioning everything, once again I told no one of my doubts and plugged away, ever firm in my commitment to the Mormon Church.

Turning the Knob

The next turning point occurred a year later, when my husband went through his own crisis of faith. He phoned me on his way home from work one day, delivering the almost-worst possible news: "Valerie, I no longer believe that our church is true." Shocked and fearful, I got him to promise that he would spend two weeks reading scriptures and praying before making a final decision. I just knew that as long as he tried to get an answer by praying, he would receive that blessed witness from the Holy Ghost, the heart and soul of Mormonism. It had always worked for me. I was certain Mark would receive his witness. Then he would believe again, and things would return to normal. I was not worried.

For the next two weeks, I watched Mark read scriptures and search for an answer. To my shock, after that time was over, he was more certain than ever that he no longer believed. I never imagined he would not get the answer he was supposed to! God had promised to answer prayers about the truthfulness of his church—but it didn't happen this time.

As it turned out, my husband's leaving the church gave me the emotional permission I needed to finally face my own questions. One by one, my doubts from earlier years began creeping out of their hiding places. The doubts I had to face were about scriptures: the more I read, the more contradictions I saw. For example, I wondered, "Why does the Book of Mormon make clear references to God as the Trinity, when it is key Mormon doctrine that God the Father, the Holy Ghost, and Jesus are distinct individuals?" I had always trusted that this inspired key doctrine was absolute, so I was confused by the blatant contradiction of the wording I found right there in black and white in the Book of Mormon.

While in the past I had been able to compartmentalize each inconsistency into its own individual place in my brain, they now all seemed determined to come rushing out at the same time.

The various people in the Book of Mormon were beginning to feel more like flat characters of a poorly written story rather than real, complicated people. Could there really be any such thing as a person who is "all good," like Nephi, or "all bad," like his evil brothers, Laman and Lemuel? Could their dark skin really be a punishment from God for their bad character? Could an all-loving God really be responsible for this racist concept?

Fighting the tide of all these doubts, I began a serious effort to receive an answer from God that the church was true. I wasn't about to throw everything away just because a few things didn't make sense. I continued to go to church every Sunday and participate fully. I maintained all the standards of the Mormon religion. I prayed and read scripture daily. But each reading made the scriptures appear more problematic and cut deeper into that wedge in my once rock-solid faith.

Six months into this process, I was losing hope. I went to the temple, the holiest place. You were more likely to get an answer from God there than anywhere else, and I told God I was staying until he gave me one. I begged him for just the slightest seed of hope. All I needed was to feel that warm glow in my heart, one more witness from the Holy Ghost.

Three hours went by, and the temple was closing. I had felt nothing and was forced to leave without an answer. I returned home in shock.

"The church isn't true," I declared to my frowning, bewildered husband as we sat on the bed. He was dumbfounded. I cried and cried.

Still, losing faith in the church was a conclusion I was not yet ready to accept. The following Sunday found me back in church as usual. For the next six months I continued with full involvement in church activities. Even though my hours-long quest in the temple had left me with little hope, I fought desperately to hold on to my traditional beliefs. During this time, I read the Bible and took every opportunity to deepen my understanding of other forms of Christianity. I searched frantically for an answer in other Christian religions, but found none.

Then, in my adult Sunday-school class, we began a new round of studying the Old Testament, as we did every year. We got to the story where Balak, a Moab king, wants the prophet Balaam to curse the Israelites so they could be driven out of his land. Balaam refuses the king's first request but, at the second request, agrees to accompany the king's messengers to the Israelites' camp. But on the way, his donkey refuses three times to follow Balaam's directions because of an angel he sees blocking the road. So Balaam beats him with a stick. At the third instance of such abuse, the donkey speaks up, asking Balaam, "What have I done to you? Why have you beaten me these three times?"

Well, that talking donkey finally blew it for me. Why, in this single incidence, was this donkey able to speak up and protect himself from his evil master's abuse , when down through the ages so many babies and other beings have remained unable to speak up for themselves against similar violence or mistreatment? I felt embarrassed to be in a room full of adults, who held not the slightest question about the supposedly literal truth of this talking donkey! I was getting tired of crazy, supernatural beliefs.

After this incident, I realized I would leave every church meeting angry about something. I was continuing my attendance not from belief, but from a desire for spiritual sustenance. Instead, the church was becoming a spiritual vacuum. I even allowed myself to become tired of the *idea* of God. Ever since I had visited the temple, praying for confirmation that the church was indeed true, yet experiencing only more doubt, I watched my relationship with a Being that I thought was my Heavenly Father slip away. I grew very distant from that God, who up to then had always been at my side.

Flinging that Door Wide Open

One year after I allowed myself to begin questioning my faith, I made a final, desperate attempt to find Truth in the church I had once so fervently loved. Every day for two weeks, I spent two solid hours in uninterrupted scripture study and prayer. Just as with my husband, over those two weeks the Holy Ghost sent me no witness, and no warm glow filled my heart. I lost any remaining hope I may have had and finally had to admit that I could find no truth in our church teachings.

For an entire year I had stood with my hand posed lightly on that Door Number Two—the one marked "It's Not True!" After I finally got the nerve to pry that door open, there was no going back—just as there is no way to pretend Santa Claus is real once you've seen your father putting the shiny new bicycle next to the Christmas tree.

When at last I opened that door, it was not demoralizing but liberating. I revisited my time as the leader of the church women's organization, when God was supposedly inspiring my actions and I had questioned why his inspirations sounded so much like they were coming from my own personality. Suddenly I realized: all that inspiration, all those ideas, had *not* come from God—they had come from within *me*! All those conversations when I thought God was telling me what he wanted me to do—all of that was actually coming from me. All the strength I'd thought I had derived from this imaginary God-partner throughout my whole life had really come from within myself. This was empowering! Once I finally flung Door Number Two wide open, what I found behind it was my own self.

Now that I have chosen not to accept the Bible, the Christian God, or any other God, life is much more exciting. Every part of the world is open and undecided, available for exploration. I have so many new questions and take such delight in seeking their answers. Everything about my life has become better. My husband and I are closer than we've ever been.

Initially my parents rejected my decision to leave the church, alternating accusations and veiled threats with begging for my return. The key to regaining their respect was that I was always truthful and clear about how I saw things when they challenged my beliefs, and I never attempted to change theirs. Over time, they began to see that I love who I am and that I am passionate about my new worldview. We can once again enjoy a healthy, honest relationship.

I was once a happy Mormon who thought all the important answers were found safely behind Door Number One—in the beliefs I had been taught all my life. Now that I have finally added the prefix "ex-" to my identity as a Mormon, I am even happier. Finding the courage to open Door Number Two let me experience a joy and inspiration that could only come from within my own being.

—◦◦◦—

Valerie's story is particularly interesting for the way other people play into her decision. Some of her initial problems arose out of her strong sense of responsibility to her children. She didn't trust the person in charge of the children's group. She didn't want her husband to sacrifice family time to the church. Interactions with her mother and mother-in-law let her realize that inspirations that were supposed to be coming from an external God actually came from within her own being.

Valerie was lucky to have the support of her husband in opening that very heavy Door Number Two. It is evident that if she had handled her parents' initial disapproval in a weaker or less mature way, they may have rejected much more than just her new worldview. If we are to uphold healthy personal relationships with those who still hold traditional views, a very fine line must be walked between personal honesty and maintaining respect for those who disagree.

Chapter 2

Reason . . . or Blind Faith? (Abu Ali)

Although Abu Ali's Islam is very different from Valerie's Mormonism and my Catholicism, the reader will note similarities in the emerging deconversion pattern. When a firm believer first notices a fault in the logic of his or her faith, a very circuitous process of trying to hold on tends to follow. But all the while, the forces of reason continue to urge the person to let go. In Abu Ali's case, questions arose about whether he could live a moral life without his religion. He worried about abandoning his community, about his personal safety, and about the safety of his family. In the end, his view of truth eventually won out over group conformity, convenience, and even the threat of a hell worse than most of us could imagine.

───∽∾∿───

I was born a Muslim and spent roughly the first fifty years of my life in faithful practice of all that my religion entailed. I worked tirelessly to promote Muslim values as a devout, active, and prominent member of my religious community. I conscientiously taught my children to believe all the tenets of our faith, to say their prayers, and to become devout Muslims themselves. Interactions with my family, my wife, and my brothers and sisters were all tied into the practice of our faith. The feeling of belonging to a unified group with homogenous values brought me security and an identity I could bank on.

As the Muslim faith had taught me, I took for granted that there are moral absolutes—unchanging standards of good and evil, dictated by God. Adhering to this framework of absolute moral rules allows Muslims to lead lives as good, decent human beings and is considered crucial in keeping them from becoming corrupt and sinful. Islam teaches that without these absolute standards, people will drown in a sea of moral relativism in which "anything goes." In the face of such moral chaos, Islam's moral rules brought me comfort and a sense of security.

In addition, by not questioning the tenets of my religion, I enjoyed the certainty that I had the "right" faith. By continuing participation in the Islam community, I could be sure I was "saved." In the Muslim mind, being saved is a huge deal if it is Hell you are being saved from. Hell is described very graphically in the Qur'an—the sacred scripture of Islam—as a place of eternal torture, where "we shall burn them in Fire. As often as their skins are roasted through, We shall change them for other skins,"[1] and "boiling water will be poured down over their heads. With it will melt what is in their bellies, as well as their skins."[2] And those who did not believe will be made to eat from the tree of Zaqqûm, a tree in Hell so horrible that "the shoots of its fruit-stalks are like heads of Shayâtîn [devils]."[3] So the fear of eternal damnation is not something any Muslim can easily shake off. It serves as a powerful motivation for adhering to Islam.

I had never been a proponent of the more narrow-minded and hardline versions of my religion, however. Never a fanatic, I viewed God as a loving being and always had a problem with the angry, punishing God my religion sometimes presented. Until about age fifty, my Muslim faith provided me a comfortable community of shared values in which to rear my family and a belief system that gave coherence to my world. It also provided me assurance of attaining Paradise on the Last Day of Judgment, as explained in the Qur'an,[4] if only I obeyed the rules laid out by my religion.

But the events of September 11, 2001 triggered a turning point in my life. Suddenly, I had to face the conflict between my religion and the way Muslims were being viewed by much of the non-Muslim world. Was our image as unpardonable aggressors one of our own making, or was the West at fault for provoking the situation?

At first, I tried to suppress these thoughts and reacted to criticism of Islam with denial, anger, and blame. I denied there was anything wrong, felt hypersensitive to any criticism, and blamed the West for creating and exacerbating problems. But eventually, I had to accept that Muslims must take responsibility for the problems we faced. Since so many Muslims I know (myself included) are peaceful and good, it pained me to face the fact that my own people had planned and carried out those horrible acts in New York, Pennsylvania, and Washington DC on 9/11. Still, I could not accept that Islam itself was to blame: the problem was the way Islam was being interpreted by some of its own followers. I started arguing among my Muslim friends for a reinterpretation and reform of our traditional views. But instead of easing my conscience, this seemed only to highlight the futility and dishonesty of the views many insisted upon upholding.

This dilemma of Islam's relationship to the rest of the world then caused me to begin questioning other things about my religion that I had previously taken for granted. Little by little, doubts crept in about some of our beliefs. I tried to tell myself that although my rational mind found it difficult to believe certain things in Islam, there must be explanations beyond my capacity to understand, and I should be content to trust that God knew best. But these efforts were in vain. Slowly, over time, my formerly unshakable faith began to waver. Serious doubts about the validity of Islam in general began to set in.

Certainly I had nothing to lose and everything to gain by "holding fast to the rope of Allah."[5] My whole family, my community, and the very life I had created for myself depended upon my remaining a believer. Moreover, without the divinely ordained moral absolutes Islam provided, I would lose my yardstick for determining right from wrong.

Lacking those comforting boundaries, I would be at risk of moral confusion; my behavior choices could, over time, become slowly corrupted.

But eventually, I allowed myself to notice that, despite the divinely ordained absolute standards of right and wrong, Muslims do differ on some moral opinions—such as whether it was right or wrong to slaughter thousands of innocent people in the World Trade Center. At the same time, I noticed that most people of various faiths agree on some general principles of behavior. For example, just about everyone agrees that it is wrong to murder, steal, or commit adultery. It is not the threat of Hell that causes good behavior. Most principles of goodness can be arrived at without the assistance of God, and my own ethical behavior did not merely derive from the rules of my religion. These musings helped me realize that I am equipped with a solid moral compass within my own conscience. I could safely make my own moral decisions without the need for pre-set rules laid out by Islam.

For a while after having this realization, I went through all the motions of being a good Muslim. I fervently hoped that one day my faith would return. Eventually, though, the futility of pretense became apparent. I found I could no longer make myself believe the tenets of my birth religion; it was not possible to choose belief as the easier alternative. It dawned on me that no God would want anyone to pretend to believe in something falsely.

Obviously, leaving the faith I had known was not a step to take lightly. I was quite shocked the first time someone mentioned I might be an apostate (someone who has abandoned belief in his or her religion). I had not thought of myself that way—*apostate* was such an evil word! In Islam, apostates are considered enemies of God, people who have sold their souls to the devil. They are hated and attacked by Muslims everywhere. Was I really an apostate? I didn't like the label, nor do I like the label of ex-Muslim. I just wanted to be *me*. Admitting to myself that I no longer believed in Islam was extremely difficult, but finally I was forced to face the truth: I was indeed an apostate. The feeling of freefall, with nothing to grab onto, was terrifying. Though my rational mind told me that the Hell Islam promised for my defection was nonsense, the internal fears I suffered over this were excruciating. Meanwhile, I knew that the isolation I would face from my community was literal and real. The punishment, if my apostasy were to be discovered, was complete. As you may know, some forms of Islam require that a male apostate be put to death.

And yet, no matter how painful the effects of leaving Islam, I could not live a lie. When I could no longer stand the discrepancy between my sincere beliefs and those of my religion, I was forced to move away from my job, my family, and my community. I had been well known in that community, and what I feared most was that someone would seek retribution against my children. I started a new life in a new town where, at least, I enjoyed great relief at no longer needing to live a double life or needing to express in public beliefs that I no longer held in private.

In stepping away from Islam, I knew I was becoming something other than a Muslim. Finally I was free to be myself—even though I wasn't sure who that was. Having lost the religious label that had been a huge part of me for all my life, I went through a period of groping for an identity. I had no idea who I was in the process of becoming, yet I had to allow myself to live in the truth.

I was haunted by the thought that I was betraying my community in its time of need. Muslims were being stigmatized and branded as evil people—something that I knew was not true. I knew most Muslims were decent, hard-working, law-abiding individuals. I did not want to align myself with their enemies, but I was in no position to do any good by remaining among my people. Islam is such an ingrained part of who they are that there was no authentic life for me among them.

The fear of Hell and isolation from my community were not the most painful parts of losing my faith. It was the effect on my family that hurt the most. In my new town I have kept very much to myself, corresponding regularly only with my two brothers. I have five sisters whom I was not able to tell because I knew they would be very upset. Losing my faith played a major part in the break-up of my marriage, though my ex-wife still does not know that I have left Islam completely. By now my two older children know where I stand about religion. But all my children are confused by the fact that the father who brought them up as devout Muslims no longer adheres to the faith that he himself taught them. When I was a Muslim, I felt it was my duty to pass on my own beliefs about God and religion to them. Now I tell my children that they must find out for themselves what they believe, and if they are happy being Muslims then that is what they should be.

But I do feel one should have the courage to honestly examine his beliefs—fully embracing the ones he can accept and discarding the ones that do not stand up to scrutiny. Life is too short to allow it to be dictated by beliefs one does not truly accept.

In fact, I now feel that if there is a God, it would be his doing that we were created as self-aware beings. This God would expect us to make use of the reasoning tools we were given and to take responsibility for making our own decisions—about religion, about what is good and evil, and about other things as well. It is this ability to reason that makes us human and different from animals.

—◦◦◦—

In Abu Ali's deconversion process, we note a broadening of his worldview. He noticed that most people of various religions do generally agree on the same behavior principles: as he says, "Just about everyone agrees that it is wrong to murder, steal, or commit adultery." It became obvious that it is not threat of the Muslim Hell that keeps people in other religions from "sinning." At the same time, in approving the "slaughter [of] thousands of innocent people in the World Trade Center on 9/11," some people within Abu Ali's religion had gone against some of these general behavior principles.

To reach this realization, Abu Ali had to allow his mind to stray outside an essential teaching of his religion: that the Qur'an is the final revelation from God and therefore that Islam is the most right religion. He had to allow himself to realize that some Muslims thought their religion was so right that humanity's behavior rules against murder did not apply to them.

But this insularity is not limited to Muslims. Fundamentalist Christians have been known to blow up abortion clinics, also in the thought that their beliefs are so right that humanity's behavior rules do not apply to them.

The discrepancy between what Abu Ali's religion taught and what his mind was telling him is called cognitive dissonance. He chose to resolve the dissonance by expanding his worldview to accommodate a broader perspective. This growth cost him dearly; he was forced to revamp his entire life for the sake of living in this truth. But his choice showed a deeper integrity than if he had ignored the first inklings of religious doubt or chosen to relieve the cognitive dissonance in a less vigorous way.

I found Abu Ali (and one other contributor) through a 2007 article entitled "Leaving Faith" in the International Humanist News, where a very different version of his story first appeared. Abu Ali's original version had been revised by Diana Brown, who was then IHN's editor. For the purpose of further developing his story for this book, Abu Ali agreed to communicate with me only through Ms. Brown. Every question to him had to be directed through a third party, so Abu Ali is the only contributor with whom I have not discussed his experiences directly.

Chapter 3

Fear, Superstition, God, Religion (Jim)

Jim is probably the most avowedly atheist of the people in these stories. Readers can trace a path similar to that in the prior stories. In Jim's case, a single, logical discrepancy from his traditional religion weighed heavily on his mind all through his youth. He made many attempts to hold on to his religion, but his ultimate deconversion occurred at a much younger age than Abu Ali's and thus was less disruptive.

—◈◈◈—

My earliest childhood days were colored by the influence of my maternal grandmother, whom I called Nana, and who had brought the many superstitions typical of her background when she immigrated from Italy. A common theme in these superstitions was fear of bad luck. One didn't walk under a ladder or let a black cat cross his path for fear of it. If someone broke a mirror, she or he was in for a long seven years of bad luck.

As a young boy, I often wondered what was behind these superstitions. What exactly could be the *cause* of this ever-looming bad luck? If no one saw the black cat cross your path, where would the bad luck come from? Was there something out there that saw and knew everything that happened? Why would this entity, whatever it was, want to give you bad luck for some innocent happening that wasn't even your fault? Why would fault even be assigned?

Nothing in my world could explain what might be behind these superstitions; nothing in nature was all-seeing, all-knowing. Whatever might be causing all this bad luck had to be supernatural.

Of course, we never took Nana's superstitions seriously. I, for one, would just respond as if what she was describing were true, while inwardly doubting that this supernatural force would direct random episodes of vaguely-defined "bad luck" into my life for crossing some arbitrary boundary about behavior.

In my elementary-school days, I began to notice similarity between the teachings of the Catholic Church and the superstitions of my maternal grandmother. "What," I wondered, "is the difference between the supernatural entity that Nana believes is at the root of these superstitions and the supernatural force we learn about in church?" This God supposedly saw and judged our every action, even if no one else saw us do it, just as in Nana's superstitions. Was there really any difference between the bad luck she warned us about and the punishment that threatened us if we broke the church's rules?

I found myself making ever more mental comparisons between the church God and the unmentioned, but obviously crucial, supernatural force presumably behind Nana's superstitions. If I were to break a mirror, some supernatural force would see to it that I would be punished. Likewise, if I were to tell a lie, a different supernatural force—God— would see to it that I went to Purgatory or to Hell. Each belief system relied on a separate mysterious force as the cause and on some adverse human event as the effect.

I was supposed to understand that there were two very different kinds of supernatural force: one that supported superstition and one that supported religion. But the two were similar in my mind; I could find no plausible distinction between them. I slowly discerned an essential conflict: we were supposed to believe in the supernatural God of the church just because someone said so, but we were not supposed to believe the superstitions, because someone said we shouldn't. What proof was there for either belief? This left me very confused.

When I was about ten years old, my questions came to a head. One Sunday, as my mother, my two sisters, and I stepped out of the church, I looked up at Mom and asked: "What is the difference between superstition and religion?" A momentary frown and a nearly imperceptible shrug later, she vaguely mumbled something to the effect that "religion is real," then rushed off to speak to an acquaintance. However unsatisfied I was with her answer, I knew I could not expect further discussion from her on this matter.

Meanwhile, I could not figure out my own beliefs one way or the other. From my position in a kind of religious limbo—"Is God real, or just another form of superstition?"—I went through the motions of being a good Catholic boy all through grade school. Just to be on the safe side, I even became an altar boy. But, in truth, the only thing I ever really liked about my religion was the singing at Mass. And still the same question nagged me: was either or both concepts of the supernatural real?

My rational mind told me I could dismiss God as no different from Nana's superstitions. But my irrational side could not release the fear of the threatened punishment. I tried hard to believe in God, because I didn't want to wind up burning in Hell. Would God really punish me forever if my mind kept telling me he wasn't real? I thought about this endlessly but could not find an answer of which I could be certain.

This lingering dilemma weighed me down for years. By high school, I badly needed to find a way out of it. Trying to push the decision in the safer direction, I went through a period where I tried very hard, even harder than I had in grade school, to believe God was real. I went to church every morning before school and prayed every night—and in between, I said the rosary. I felt that if I immersed myself in religion, I would one day learn to believe in God. Despite all these efforts, however, I found no certainty in religious faith.

I was finally able to resolve my religious dilemma in the early sixties—after I made love for the first time while in college. I won't say

I didn't enjoy this event, but all during that act of lovemaking I felt the lingering fear that I might be suddenly struck by a bolt of lightning for doing something I had been taught was sinful. Would God bring retribution upon me now, or wait until I got to Hell? The relieving conclusion came the next day. I was talking with a group of friends in the middle of campus, thoughts of the previous day's sexual adventure—and the associated guilt—still on my mind, when I casually looked up into the sky. All I saw was a clear, beautiful blue expanse—no bolts of lightening threatened to strike me, not even a cloud. Suddenly I knew: I would not be killed for my "sin" of the prior evening, nor would I ever be punished in Hell. I was safe!

At that moment, I realized that there was no supernatural force—neither religious nor superstitious. Both existed solely in the imaginations of others and were, in fact, one and the same. My relief was boundless; fears and doubts that had filled my thoughts up to that point vanished in an instant. On that day, the religion of my youth went the way of Nana's superstitions. "There is no God," I was finally able to say with certainty.

After that, I felt so much better. I could finally put an end to the doubt that had clouded my younger days and live without fear of a supernatural being constantly looking over my shoulder. No capricious God was going to punish me for this or any of the other sins of the Church— eating meat on Friday, missing Sunday Mass, failing to believe. In addition, I could now enjoy sleeping in on Sunday mornings!

What freedom to know that what had really kept me from doing anything truly wrong all my life was my own conscience and the general rules of my society, with roots going back thousands of generations before any church existed. Fear of punishment from the supernatural was simply not a factor after that.

Why had others felt the need to inflict all that fear? If they could not let me rely on my conscience, what did that say about theirs? I felt so relieved to know that I would be the one to determine what was right for me to do—not a God whose laws often did not make sense in the modern world.

All through college and my subsequent military career, I held fast to my atheism, though at that point I didn't really do much with it. I knew the difference between right and wrong, with or without God. I made my decisions based on common sense and a desire for fairness toward my fellow man.

During my stint in the army I read many history books, including ones on the history of religions. After leaving the military, I worked at a civilian job, and in that period I read many books on ancient cultures and ancient religions. Both the books on religious history and the ones about ancient cultures lent depth to my understanding of religions, their beginnings, the historical settings in which they were founded, the beliefs many of them held in common, and their mutual interdependence. Among the things I learned was that religions were created to explain natural phenomena that could not be explained scientifically at the time.

I also learned that moral rules about behavior were not the basis on which religions were formed. The basic concept of right and wrong developed out of the experience of people living together and establishing societal norms. As societies advanced, these norms became laws. Thus, moral codes existed long before the founding of today's organized religions. Religions merely incorporated these norms into their doctrines. Then they went about using threats and fear of punishment to try to make people follow their rules.

One book that profoundly affected me was Bishop John Shelby Spong's *Resurrection: Myth Or Reality?* Here was a man of the cloth who questioned the literal truth of the Resurrection. If the Resurrection was not to be taken literally, what other miracles could we dismiss as well? Another influential book was Hyam MacCoby's *The Mythmaker: Paul and the Invention of Christianity*. This book helped me see how some of the religious traditions in which I was brought up were recreations of older stories told in pre-Christian religions, notably Judaism.

The film, *Zeitgeist: The Movie*, gives many examples of traditions from pre-Christian religions that were incorporated into Christianity. The

Annunciation, the Holy Ghost, the birth of a Savior on December 25, the Virgin Birth, the Three Kings, the Twelve Apostles, baptism, miracles, crucifixion, being buried for three days, and the Resurrection—all these elements on which Christianity is supposedly founded appeared in myths and stories from the pre-Christian era.

This information supported my conclusion that there is no God. As I understand it, God is the result of people having a need for a supernatural force to provide explanations about the world and their existence and to guide their actions through life.

What most religious believers have in common is fear. Fear of the unknown breeds anxiety. Belief in God or gods fills that void and therefore mitigates the fear. Whether it is real or not, these people need something to lean on—and for them, God serves as a crutch.

In 1980, Ronald Reagan was elected president. I had been out of the army for four years. Until then, I had no reason to speak out about my atheism, no need to share my beliefs with anyone else. I believed what I believed, and my convictions gave strength to my daily life. But Reagan's attempts to mix politics and religion really bothered me. In protest, I started speaking out against this inappropriate commingling. I spoke not necessarily as an atheist, but as one convinced of the importance of separation of church and state.

While the Reagan era inspired me to become vocal about the separation of religion and politics, it wasn't until the George W. Bush years that I took this issue on as a sort of mission. Bush and his cronies on the religious right really scared me. Doing my best to deflate their influence, I joined Americans United for Separation of Church and State (aka Americans United; www.au.org) and soon attained a position on the board of the Houston chapter. I also became involved with a Houston atheist group. In the 2004, 2006, and 2008 political campaigns, I opposed every way I could what I saw as the Republican takeover of my country. But it was not even so much Republican politics that fueled my fire; it was that the party had aligned itself with the religious right and was trying to justify its actions by bringing God into the mix.

Marie, my late wife, was an atheist and an extremely intelligent person, a self-made woman with many and varied accomplishments. At an early age, and without a college degree, she worked for several newspapers. Later, as a single mom caring for two young daughters, she obtained her bachelor's and master's degrees in English with honors. She then worked as an editor and eventually taught college English.

Marie was someone who had truly taken responsibility for her own life, and the results were magnificent. Her atheism was a comfort to me, because we were always able to discuss the irrational motivations behind organized religion and why people chose to follow it. In reference to the existence of God, Marie would often quote Hemingway's line, "It's pretty to think so."[1]

As atheists, Marie and I knew we had to be accountable to ourselves for our actions, self-correcting where necessary and constantly seek to improve ourselves. We knew the importance of forgiving ourselves and others. We did so not out of fear of a supernatural being but for our own and others' sake. We felt compelled to make every day of our life on earth mean something in a way that did not depend upon the existence of God. As we saw it, belief in God would have led us to see life on earth as some sort of test, rather than the gift that it is. Our days would have been wasted trying to follow a bunch of rules in hopes of gaining a prize at the end—Heaven—as opposed to making each day count, as we always tried to do.

I am so glad we shared our approach to life because, sadly, in 2001, Marie passed away. This was before I began my activist efforts, and I am sorry she never got to see them. But her funeral was a beautiful event. A local atheist group helped me plan a lovely ceremony where we celebrated the beauty of the life she had lived. Today I'm a member of several atheist groups and am never afraid to express my thoughts about atheism.

I am at peace with myself and with my worldview. There are no gods to account to, and I suffer no fear of punishment. I base my actions on morals that existed long before today's religions came into being. For my actions I am accountable only to myself and to the people around me.

I do not need any mythical supernatural being or rules from a church to govern my behavior. In my faith journey so far, I have come to equate religion with the superstitions my grandmother brought from the old country. Just as I overcame the superstition-based fears of my childhood, as a young adult I was able to overcome the fears generated by organized religion. By this time in my life, I can clearly state that religion is mere superstition and nothing more. Now nature is my religion, and science is my god.

———

Jim mentions how religious people seem to need religion to fill a knowledge void about what happens after death. Living without religion, as Jim and Marie did, took more courage than grasping at the ready answers waiting at the local church; *they had chosen a more vigorous path. This issue of religious certainty will also figure into the later discussion of the form of faith that can arise beyond the constraints of religious belief.*

As with some of the prior stories, Jim's deconversion brought him to an increased reliance on self; he adopted a morality motivated by his own conscience. This represents an increase in personal responsibility, acting in the most authentic, effective way possible and making the most of the opportunities that this life presents.

Ability to live without religious certainties and a drive to make the most of one's current life are all important steps in personal growth. They are also important factors in developing the type of faith that can arise beyond belief. Despite Jim's (and some of the other part 1 contributors') atheism and the possibility that they might not like my use of the term, they have all undergone important steps on the road to spiritual maturity. Parts 3 through 5 of this book will show how the issue of atheism versus religious belief becomes almost a moot point in the spiritual-development process.

Chapter 4

Animals . . . Vegetables . . . Ethics . . . Truth (Kevin)

Kevin is a veterinarian in Canada in his early fifties. It was his deep connection to animals that inspired the path he describes in this story. Soon after adopting a vegetarian diet for health reasons, Kevin became intrigued with the dietary restrictions of various religious traditions. Then questions in his church about whether animals have a soul pushed him to realize he could not envision an afterlife for humans unless animals also had an afterlife. As his religious convictions slipped away, his circle of concern expanded from just humans to one where animals are included.

———∞∞———

Though born in Kenya, I am of Indian ancestry and was raised as a Roman Catholic. My dad was born in Uganda but completed most of his schooling in Goa, a Portuguese colony on the west coast of India. The numerous Catholic converts there took their religion very seriously, which deeply impressed my father. In fact, he spent many years in a Jesuit seminary there before changing his mind, leaving the Jesuit order, and returning to Africa. His family arranged a marriage with a suitable woman and sent her to him. This is how I came to be born in Africa and to spend my early years there with my parents.

As far as I know, my mother was always devout, but one major experience from my childhood surely served to deepen her faith. When my younger sister was about ten years old, she contracted a serious case of tetanus. She spent nearly a month in the hospital intensive care unit and at one point was given up for dead. My mother vowed that if my sister's life were spared, Mom would say a rosary on her knees every day for the rest of her life. My sister did survive, and my mother's faith was reinforced; her devotion would influence our family life from that point forward.

We always noticed that my father remained aloof from all family devotions; he didn't seem to care if he went to church or not. We always worried about his spiritual well-being and were encouraged to pray for his soul. But for some reason we never thought to question him about his actual beliefs. It was only many years later that we learned about the seminary and how he had been just short of ordination when doubts about his calling and his beliefs surfaced. He began to see how the Jesuits' notion of humility and blind obedience failed to mesh with his own view of goodness. In the end he realized his true calling was not in service to God but to his fellow man. When as an adult I confessed my own crisis of faith to him, he encouraged my religious questioning, adding, "You are on the right track in your thinking, but keep your ideas to yourself and don't talk about it much as not many people will understand you . . . religious people will think you are crazy!"

As I was growing up, my parents had wanted me to pursue a career in medicine or dentistry. But by my teen years, we had moved back to Goa and I soon felt a certain nostalgia for my childhood years in Kenya, where a variety of wild and domestic animals and pets had always graced our home—budgies, chickens, ostriches, several *dik-diks* (a small antelope that lives in the bushes of East Africa). I realized that I had inherited my dad's love of animals and saw that veterinary medicine was a natural fit for me.

At age twenty-five, after completing a masters in veterinary science, I married my childhood sweetheart from Kenya, who was then living in

Canada. We settled in Guelph, Ontario, where I earned a second veterinary degree that would allow me to practice my profession in Canada. Over the next decade or so, I built a solid foundation for my life. As a veterinarian, I loved being able to heal so many animals—or relieve them of their terminal suffering. My practice, which I subsequently established in Mississauga, was flourishing; my wife was responsible for a large part of the business end of my practice. Our family life was also going great: we were graced with two wonderful children, and together we formed a close-knit family who still enjoys spending time together.

If anyone had asked me about my faith during my youth or during the early years of my marriage, I would have said I was a devout Catholic. I never really questioned my beliefs; I went to church regularly and followed what I had been taught. In my forties, however, I found myself in the throes of a midlife crisis. I began to feel the effects of age and became concerned with my excess weight. I started to suspect that there was more to life than what I was experiencing.

Then, on that fateful Tuesday morning of September 11, 2001, I realized that anything could happen to anyone at any time. This realization served as a turning point for me. Since some things are completely out of our control, I decided that I would take control of those aspects of my life that I could and make the best possible use of the gifts I have been given. Always trying my best would free me from worry about things I could not control. I joined a local men's weight-loss program where the teachers encouraged us to figure out why we were turning to food for satisfaction that should be gotten elsewhere. After introducing us to strategies for countering that impulse—eating more healthfully, getting more exercise—they pointed us toward deeper issues. We were encouraged to find ways in which we could, to some degree, control our own destiny.

Seeking a healthier lifestyle and further weight loss, I decided to eliminate meat from my diet. I came across Frances Moore Lappé's *Diet for a Small Planet*, which opened my eyes to the health and ecological value of a vegetarian diet and heightened my awareness of the ethical issues surrounding the humane treatment of animals. Then I read *The Pig Who Sang to the Moon: The Emotional World of Farm Animals* by Jeffrey Moussaieff Masson. It was his final chapter, "On Not Eating Friends," that finally convinced me to become a vegetarian. That single decision set the stage for many of my spiritual and ethical realizations and discoveries from that point forward.

I continued to reevaluate my priorities and came to realize that, outside of family and work activities, I hardly did anything else. I decided to join a Catholic men's charitable organization, the Knights of Columbus. This was fun for me because of the camaraderie with other men, similar to what I had experienced in the men's weight loss club.

I realize now that up to that point in my life, my involvement with religion was more lukewarm than fervent, more rote than inspired. Perhaps, in a subconscious effort to correct this, I began spiraling into a sort of spiritual high. I went to Mass every day, and I encouraged my kids to go with me. I started wearing a wooden cross around my neck. Many Catholic men would wear a hidden crucifix, or wear one only during religious activities, but I felt, "If I am going to be a Catholic, I should be willing to wear this cross on my sleeve." So I wore that cross to work, to dances, and in other social activities. I made sure my tie didn't cover it up. I don't know if I was trying to emulate a priest or what. I do believe there was a priest-like aura about me in those days.

I also became the leader of the Knights of Columbus youth group, the Columbian Squires. We built a very good program and attracted lots of new members. In many of the activities I was able to introduce an element of spiritual education. For example, in leading the rosary, I would try to make the lesson more interesting by encouraging the kids to contemplate the mystery related to each part of the rosary

So here I was, a life-long, lukewarm Catholic suddenly picking up interest in a dramatic way and getting involved with the faith at deeper levels. I look back at that time and wonder why I took that spiritual plunge so suddenly. Some religious friends and colleagues say this is typical when your children are growing up: the kids are starting to have questions about their existence on which to form their own beliefs, and the parent wants to set a good example for them. I don't know if that was my reason, but in the long run it backfired. Maybe I got to know my faith too closely and asked too many questions. I was about forty-five when lots of problems started showing up with my belief system that I couldn't reconcile with my scientific knowledge.

Through the Knights of Columbus, I had started a Yahoo! group to announce our meetings and other activities. I was tasked with maintaining the calendar, and I began adding in the feast days of the saints. I would research the life of each saint as their feast day came up and put an announcement with a little summary on the online calendar that would show up every year after that. As I researched the lives of the saints, over time I realized I found them depressing—especially the martyrs. Here were all these wonderful people who seemingly had been somehow duped into giving up their life for their religion. Who knows what wonderful things these men and women could have accomplished if their lives had not been sacrificed? Rather than appreciate their contributions, I began to wish these folks had focused on more practical matters that could benefit mankind. It seemed to me they had wasted their lives on what I was coming to see as delusion.

Through my interaction with the Knights, I was involved with Pope John Paul II's visit to Toronto during the 2002 World Youth Day celebrations. This was a special privilege; I knew I could get no closer to Heaven than being in the presence of the Pope. However, my involvement also exposed me to the *business* of the church and supplied my first hint that the church's internal workings might leave something to be desired.

Thinking it important to create a spectacular show, the committee in charge of the pope's visit decided to stage his arrival in such a way as to have it appear that he was majestically descending among the people from out of the heavens. They would need not just one helicopter, but three, for this performance! Though I had been assigned to a different committee, it was great fun being part of a group licensed to spend the church's money this way. However, the superficiality of it diminished my enthusiasm. Why did the pope need such pompous theatrics and extensive entourage when he was supposed to be a humble servant of God?

So while this involvement with the church was very exciting, it also felt hollow. In my heart, despite all the religious activities—Knights of Columbus, mentoring in the youth group, church group, and everything else—something just didn't ring true. Unbeknownst to me, at the time a new perspective was forming that would emerge later all at once.

That fall, I tried to generate interest at my church for a Blessing of the Pets ceremony. But the parish priest was averse to this idea. There had been an incident at another church where a pet owner wanted her poodle to partake in the Eucharist and receive Holy Communion after the blessing. Somehow our priest could not separate this unlikely (not to mention bizarre) occurrence in another parish from the simple blessing we were seeking in ours. As a veterinarian, I took a particular interest in this issue and engaged the priest, a good friend, in an informal discussion. "Of course, communion for an animal is inappropriate," I agreed, "but you have to admit that only a very passionate pet owner would want the similar blessings of communion for her closest companion!"

The priest countered: "A dog cannot benefit from the Sacrament of Holy Communion in any tangible way, because it does not have a human soul!" A discussion ensued as to the difference between animal souls and human souls, which left me more confused than before. Up to that point, I had never questioned that animals—at least those we keep as pets—had an afterlife similar to that of humans. I assumed both animals and humans would all meet up again one day, whole and healthy as described in the comforting poem "The Rainbow Bridge":[1]

Just this side of heaven is a place called Rainbow Bridge.
When an animal dies that has been especially close to someone here,
that pet goes to Rainbow Bridge.
There are meadows and hills for all of our special friends
so they can run and play together . . .

The animals are happy and content,
except for one small thing;
they each miss someone very special to them,
who had to be left behind.
They all run and play together,
but the day comes when . . .

you look once more into the trusting eyes of your pet,
so long gone from your life but never absent from your heart.
Then you cross Rainbow Bridge together.

—Author unknown

Thus began my quest to understand the afterlife of animals. Through my professional training, I had learned humane animal husbandry techniques, but I never made the connection between domestic pets and the food I ate before I became a vegetarian. I began to notice the inconsistency of my attitudes toward different classes of animals based on their utility for humans. I wondered, "Shouldn't the animals we breed and slaughter for food be entitled to the same privileges in eternity as the pets we treat with such love and compassion?"

While I had effectively compartmentalized my knowledge of evolution from my religious beliefs, I now felt the need to reconcile the two. I felt there could only be one truth: either all animals, including the ultimate primate, *Homo sapiens*, have souls—and thus equally significant afterlives—or none do. Which was it?

Turning again to books for answers, I found the work of author and animal-rights attorney Steven M. Wise. In *Rattling the Cage,* he makes a serious case for redefining the legal status of our closest relatives, the chimpanzees and bonobos (pigmy chimps), from thinghood to personhood. In another book, *Drawing the Line: Science and the Case for Animal Rights,* he presents a taxonomy that allows us to consider whether an animal possesses self-awareness and has mental abilities, desires, and intentions that resemble those of humans. Wise's books blurred the line for me between sentience and intelligence in primates and other species, respectively.

I concluded that we are not much different from Wise's "nonhuman animals," except for the size and complexity of our brains. As for our soul, I pondered, "When, exactly, during evolution or gestation, would the eternal human soul become infused into our bodies?"

As the concept of the uniqueness of the human soul began to unravel, so did many others from my faith, leaving me bewildered and lonely. I think I now understand what motivated the spiritual high I was on just around the time these doubts were cropping up. The religious medals I wore, the attendance at Mass every day, the preaching to my children—all were just ways I was grasping harder to cling to the religion of my upbringing. But these efforts could only mask for so long the religious low that was lurking inside me. I finally had to acknowledge that it was only humankind's ability to think abstract thoughts that allowed people to create a god for themselves. I had no choice but to admit to myself that the religion I had so tried to hold onto had not been handed down by God to man, but rather had been made up over time by men seeking answers about their existence. I was now a nonbeliever.

With no God standing in judgment to determine my afterlife, I became more interested in following an ethical life in the here and now. Roger Walsh's book entitled *Essential Spirituality* opened my eyes to the universality of religious traditions. Over the centuries, Walsh wrote, "countless people have fought, tortured, and killed over the differences between the world's religions."[2] But now, through the use of modern global communications, certain scholars have discerned that all major religions contain a central core called the *perennial philosophy*. "The words differ from one tradition to another, but their central message is the same: You are more than you think . . . your true Self is intimately linked to the sacred, and . . . you share in the unbounded bliss of the sacred."[3] If this is the case, how can any religion be the *only* correct one?

Furthermore, Walsh showed, you don't even need to practice a religion or believe in a Supreme Being to be a good person—or even to be spiritual. He outlines seven practices that help develop spiritual virtues in us all—virtues endorsed by all the world's great religions. This was a new concept to me. Until that point, I had never questioned my early teaching that being good meant living my life true to the Catholic faith—following the church's rules. For example, morality was largely seen as being about whether a person held to certain tightly defined religious rules about sexual behavior, all the while virtually condoning certain forms of dishonesty, cruelty, and even stealing. After reading Walsh, my idea of being good took on an entirely different meaning. Interpersonal ethics—acting toward others in a way that is consistent with our beliefs—became my predominant ideal.

Roger Walsh taught me how I could be a good person and live ethically without having to believe in anything other than the here and now. It seemed that many of the principles he delineated were similar to those of Christianity. For an example, the virtue of charity that the Catholic Church endorses—embrace generosity and the joy of service—sounded a lot like Walsh's seventh practice—express spirit in action. In my enthusiasm for my new discovery, I voiced some of Walsh's concepts on the Knights of Columbus online Yahoo! group with which I was still involved. To my surprise, my friend the priest demanded I stop posting that stuff. I suppose he was unable to see the forest for the trees: how many of Walsh's concepts were simply more general expressions of the same values Catholics endorse.

Once I made the mental leap toward nonbelief myself, I was faced with the prospect of acknowledging publicly that I had no interest in the external, omnipotent power residing as a figment of most people's imagination.

Religious belief is a prerequisite for membership in the Knights of Columbus, so I was morally obliged to submit a letter of resignation. This left me the odd man out in our social circle, as all the other men were (and still are) in the Knights. My wife is still religious, and I still go to church with her once in a while. I try to tune out the homily as

I find it a disturbing reinforcement of dogma rather than an enlightening discourse. My wife still calls my deconversion a midlife crisis. At least I didn't go off and have an affair or buy a fancy sports car!

I have not spelled out my atheist stance in so many words to my children. Instead, I speak to them about issues like evolution, hoping it will encourage them to think more independently and, eventually, decide their own beliefs.

I want to explain something about nonbelief. Atheism or humanism is often seen (by believers) as a rudderless ship. I always get the questions: "Where do you get your moral compass?" and "How do you know what is right and wrong if you don't believe in God or an afterlife?" Well, there are so many good things I do that are not necessary to my survival, not designed to assure my salvation. I just feel I have to get out there and make a difference in the lives of others. I don't need a religious imperative to motivate me; unlike in my religious days, when morality was central to my religion, now I just see it as the proper way to live.

For me it all boils down to the word *empathy*. It is all about the golden rule: do unto others as you would have them do unto you. If you can empathize, you don't want to steal from a person, because you realize how badly you would feel if they stole from you. Morality does not really require religion or a set of commandments. Most of us have it ingrained in us to be good. Most normal people have a built-in moral compass they can rely on if they make the proper effort. The problem is that many people become lazy and let the rules of religion take over instead of reasoning things out. It is much more difficult to figure out for oneself what is right and what is wrong—and more challenging to figure out on one's own how to live life more fully.

Given all this, I don't feel that *atheist* is the right term for me. While I didn't personally know too many atheists, the atheist websites I have found sound angry and bitter toward religion. I don't feel that way at all. Since my deconversion, I have maintained many friendships originally formed on the basis of common religious beliefs. Now they are based on our mutual respect for the right of each person to make up his or her own mind.

I call myself a secular humanist rather than an atheist. Secular humanism, for the most part, is about learning to live your life with reason and intent but without having to rely on deities, promises of eternal reward, threats of punishment, or concern for the next life. The secular humanist manifesto pretty much mirrors what I feel. I have served two years as president of the Halton-Peel Humanist Community, a local Secular Humanist Community, and am now on the board of directors of our national association, Humanist Canada.

—◦◦◦—

Kevin's story illustrates a reason-based deconversion that, like Jim's and some of the others, emphasizes personal ethics and what good can be done in this life, as opposed to focusing on salvation in an afterlife for which no proof exists.

A circle of concern that expands beyond one's own group is a big factor in spiritual maturity. For most of us, it is probably more about including people of a different religion, nationality, or sexual orientation. But Kevin's interesting connection to animals brought him to an even broader circle of concern. (In the part 3 stories, watch for people whose circle of concern also includes all of nature, an even broader perspective.)

Kevin's reference to Roger Walsh's Essential Spirituality *hints at the content in the rest of this book. He mentions Walsh's description of the perennial philosophy, a common core that underlies all major religions. What this common core does not contain are specific beliefs. Once a person has expanded his perspective beyond his own group, beliefs that apply only to one religion while excluding everyone else no longer work.*

Part Two

Are They Right?

Chapter 5

Are They Right?

The stories in part 1 illustrate how several obviously sincere, good people from different religions went about questioning their religion. In a similar process, they all reasoned themselves out of religious belief altogether.

Traditionally religious people often claim we need religion, and the rules it provides, to behave ethically—that without the threat of punishment from God, we would degenerate into a morally ruinous lifestyle. The four people in the part 1 stories would disagree. As they would now be labeled atheists, or at least agnostics, let's revisit how they measure up ethically and morally.

Valerie became continually more sensitive to the need to address her religious doubts. Hiding within the Mormon religion, for her, would have meant running away from logic and reason. There is nothing ethical about turning one's back on the truth. For Valerie, going it alone was a harder path than staying in her church would have been. But her personal integrity and dedication to the truth led her to choose the more difficult way.

Abu Ali's religion taught that without the rules and structure, he would risk falling into moral relativism, where any behavior can be justified through a process of rationalization. Instead, over time he came to rely on his own *internal* moral compass, by which he could determine right from wrong. Moreover, he noticed that the most important moral points were not particular to Islam but were common to all religions.

Jim was very explicit in the ways he had freed himself from the need for outer authority in determining his behavior.

As a result of Kevin's choices, which expanded his circle of caring and awareness to include animals, his sense of morality and ethics deepened. Also, his decision to leave his religion meant he had to quit the Knights of Columbus, forcing him to stand apart from everyone in his social circle. He had to tolerate his wife attributing his defection from the church to a midlife crisis. Despite these hardships, Kevin chose allegiance to his view of the truth over the benefits of remaining a regular member of his group.

All these people were deeply concerned with ethics and truth. All were bold enough to directly address some of life's most difficult questions about God and religion. All were willing to brave personal risk in order to maintain allegiance to what they saw as the truth. All rated living truthfully of higher importance than the convenience and safety of remaining in the religious community to which they belonged. Once they decided against the teachings of their church, it took strength to follow their convictions. The decisions they made and the actions they took required far more personal integrity than if they had swept their religious doubts under the carpet. In other words, all these people discovered their own internal moral compass and learned to trust that over external religious rules.

Surely these people are not the ones fundamentalists refer to as weak sinners condemned to Hell, simply because they do not believe in God. We will not find these people committing heinous crimes simply because their behavior is not governed by church rules or because they are not "saved" by the Lord. Thus we have to wonder what certain types of religious people mean when they say atheists are bad or that people must belong to a church in order to lead a good life. We must also question what they mean when they say that only those who believe as these religious leaders do are saved. What kind of God would condemn the earnest folks in our part 1 stories, who tried their best to know him but found no one answering the door when they knocked?

Furthermore, these are stories of intelligent, principled, reasonable people, living fruitful, satisfied lives, not chaotic losers who would commit ethical transgression to get what they want out of life. Though some preachers would have us believe otherwise, it is obviously possible to lead an ethical, reasoned, fulfilling life without subscribing to traditional religious beliefs.

But we also have to ask: are they *right*? In rejecting their birth religion and concluding that no God exists, did the people in the part 1 stories reach the "right" conclusion?

An emerging group sometimes referred to as "the New Atheists" and their followers would answer that question with a resounding "Yes!" Richard Dawkins, Sam Harris, Christopher Hitchens, and others of their persuasion would have you believe that human reason is the highest god and that the atheist stance is the last word in the believer-versus-nonbeliever controversy. These three authors each wrote a highly reasoned treatise against religion or God, each of which hit the best-seller list around the middle of the last decade.

In *God Is Not Great: How Religion Poisons Everything*, Christopher Hitchens claims that religion is a man-made imposition, grounded on wishful thinking, and that religion has misrepresented the origins of man and the cosmos and has subsisted through the ages upon man's fears. To Hitchens, the foundational books of most religions are but transparent fables, and the common concept of God is something man created in his own image rather than the other way around. "[I]f triangles had gods, their gods would have three sides," he quips.[1]

Showing how "ethics and morality are independent of faith"[2] and cannot be derived from it, Hitchens thinks that religion has outlived its usefulness and it is time for science and reason to take its place as dominant forces in society. This will do away with unneeded violence, unwise health practices, and the blind submission advocated by some religions, thus improving civilization, he argues.

In *The End of Faith: Religion, Terror, and the Future of Reason*, Sam Harris posits what all professed nonbelievers and most believers must feel is self-evident: that whatever we believe, it must correspond to an actual, literal reality. Unlike most believers, though, he elevates the faculty of human reason to the level of religion itself, saying it is reason that inspires deeper ethics and brings order into the world while religious faith detracts from it. "[O]ur religious traditions are intellectually defunct and politically ruinous," he writes.[3] Even in the final chapter, when discussing spirituality, consciousness, meditation, and even mysticism, Harris insists that these concepts must be kept free of any supernatural connotations. He would lead us to a world where reason, spirituality, and ethics come together to form a strictly rational approach to our deepest concerns. Using the word *faith* as almost synonymous with *religion*, he claims such a world would mean "the end of faith."

In *The God Delusion*, Richard Dawkins claims that religion and morality are both by-products of something else. Religion, he says, is a by-product of memes. The term *meme* is attributed to Richard Dawkins (who is an evolutionary biologist) and refers to units of cultural inheritance, like genes. But where genes carry on biological traits, memes pass cultural beliefs, attitudes, and habits down through the generations. So according to Dawkins, religion is a by-product of societal memes. It keeps getting passed down from generation to generation because of its own ability to fulfill the wishes and drives of normal human psychology.

Morality, Dawkins claims, may be a by-product of natural selection. Because the forces of natural selection favor those who do good, moral behavior may develop independent of religion, a possibility that invalidates the claims of fire-and-brimstone preachers. Dawkins quotes a study that showed no significant difference in morality between atheists and believers.

Regarding scripture, Dawkins gives his readers many examples of why we would not want to derive our morals from Old Testament scripture, and shows that modern morality does not come from the Bible. He finds appalling the story of Noah, wherein God was so displeased with mankind that he drowned everyone except for one family (and animals as well, except for one pair from each species). Despite the fact that few modern theologians take such stories literally, Dawkins laments that many regular people, including approximately 50 percent of the US electorate (according to a Gallup poll), *do*. Dawkins points out another deed attributed to God in the Old Testament that modern moralists would consider evil: God ordering Abraham to sacrifice his son, Isaac. Despite an angel having stayed Abraham's hand at the last minute, what would ever justify the psychological damage done to Isaac or the emotional trauma inflicted upon Abraham by such a God? "What makes my jaw drop," he writes, "is that people today should base their lives on such appalling role models as Yahweh."[4]

And from the New Testament, Dawkins finds the principle of atonement "morally obnoxious." Here he refers to the "sin" of Adam eating a forbidden fruit in the Garden of Eden and the supposed need for Jesus to live and die thousands of years later in atonement on behalf of all humanity for this seemingly minor infraction on the part of one man. After establishing that Adam and Eve surely never existed in the literal sense, and that the bite of forbidden fruit was symbolic of the sins of mankind in general, Dawkins offers this acerbic comment: "So, in order to impress himself, Jesus had himself tortured and executed, in vicarious punishment for a *symbolic* sin committed by a *nonexistent* individual?"[5]

Dawkins claims that the zeitgiest has shifted in the direction of improved social consciousness and insists that this has nothing to do with religion. He uses the phrase "the American Taliban" to describe factions of the religious right that would lead us toward a Christian fascist state. In sum, *The God Delusion* aims to show how religion and the concept of God fill a gap in human psychology—a gap that Dawkins himself fills with science.

These three New Atheist authors and their numerous followers would like us to believe, as they do, that religion is nothing but hogwash, that human reason is the last word, that science will one day present us with the ultimate truth of our existence, and that the visible reality we enjoy on earth is all there is. Are *they* right?

In a sense, we can say they are. For these authors, the word *God* evokes the Supreme Being they learned about in Sunday school and later rejected. For many religious people, and probably all nonbelievers, the word *God* calls up some version of that same Being. Most people reading a book with a title such as this one would probably agree that *that* God—to borrow a few words from Dawkins, the jealous, petty, unforgiving, homophobic, racist, judgmental, "sky" god men have created in their own image—is better left denied.

But there is another approach to spirituality that allows for faith but does not require us to turn a blind eye to reason. This brand of faith goes beyond the literal, childlike belief in a parent-figure God who requires our worship through a specific traditional religion and who rejects the sincere attempts of all others who try to reach him by different means.

Though many others before me have tried to explain it, the concept of spiritual growth as it applies to movement toward faith—*beyond belief* in a literal "sky" god among everyday people—is still poorly understood and barely acknowledged in society. I suspect that broader appreciation of the opportunities that exist for this kind of spiritual growth is being drowned out by some of our most vociferous religious leaders. Though I certainly claim no expert status, the rest of this book represents my attempt to provide yet one more way to access this information.

I will begin this discussion by continuing the story of my own personal experiences. It serves only as an introduction to parts 3 through 5 and is as far as my own personal journey can take us. Additional understanding of spiritual maturity will have to come from the experiences of others who have traveled farther—and the work of those who have studied them.

Begrudging Wisdom

The fearsome, yet somehow oddly thrilling words jumped right off the page, crept stealthily past the obviously snoozing hogwash detector in my brain and spoke directly to my heart: "Stage IV men and women will *enter into religion* in order to approach mystery."[6] I grasped the book more tightly, reread the words, and then threw it down. A prickly sensation worked its way up my spine. My heart rate kicked up a notch.

"Stage IV indeed! What nonsense!" *If* this Stage IV thing was valid—and if it involved religion—it meant I had been wrong, very wrong for almost my entire adult life. For years I had said too much, too loudly, without having the full picture. My rational mind frantically sought to reject this assault on my certainty and my long-held atheism. But, to my dismay, there was no way to push the budding truth back down once it had poked its way up to the surface.

At the same time, a certain respect lay just barely detectable at the edge of my awareness. An odd sense of gratitude was surfacing through my anger and embarrassment. My conflicting emotions were directed at the now-deceased M. Scott Peck and his book that lay in my hand that day in the early nineties: *The Different Drum: Community Making and Peace*.

My confused reaction to Peck's words was the culmination of a process that had begun a few years earlier. One weekend I had accompanied my family on a short vacation to Deep Creek Lake, Maryland. As a professional woman, business owner, and mother of two small children, I was used to having little or no time of my own. Hence, personal reading material was the last thing I thought to bring when packing for that trip. But, once installed in the large lakefront house with space enough for four small families to coexist for those few days at least, I quickly realized that my children were busy exploring with their cousins while my husband and other family members busied themselves with other activities. To my surprise, I had time on my hands.

Above the rustic fireplace sat a row of perhaps thirty books, from among which I selected a dog-eared, ragged volume with an intriguing title by an author of whom I had never heard: M. Scott Peck's *The Road Less Traveled: A New Psychology of Love, Traditional Values, and Spiritual Growth*. I was fascinated with the insights and wisdom Dr. Peck shared from his years of psychiatric practice and his own studies.

My interest was piqued by a concept Peck summarized in just a few paragraphs. He had just made the point that we are each responsible for figuring out what we believe about religion, as opposed to merely accepting as a complete package the religion in which we were brought up.

Next, Peck explained how, in his practice of psychiatry, he had initially been puzzled by a certain finding. In some cases, the only way he could help patients out of their psychological difficulties was to lead them *away from* their religion. But in other cases, the only way he could help people heal was to point them *toward* religion. The explanation Peck offered for this puzzle was *spiritual growth*, adding that people go through various stages in their spiritual development. They were, therefore, not all starting out at the same place when they came to him. But there was a common pattern: people would actually discard religious belief for a time, only to return to it in a deeper, more meaningful way. "A skeptical atheism or agnosticism," Peck wrote, "is not necessarily the highest state of understanding at which human beings can arrive. To the contrary . . . behind spurious notions and false concepts of God there lies a reality that is God."[7]

Well, *that* was curious. All my adult life, I had been feeling superior for having no need of organized religion. I was proud I had figured out that all the religious dogma I'd been taught for all those years of Catholic school was untrue. And I surely did not believe there could be a God up there who would reward only those people who believed or did certain things when there were some—in other parts of the world, for example—who would never get the same chance.

But Dr. Peck was saying that, after a period of not believing, people sometimes *return* to religion. Furthermore, he said, when people return, their faith is of a different, deeper type than it was before they stopped believing—*and* it has an actual basis in reality! My reaction at the time was, "Oh well, perhaps this guy is just one more religious nut like all the others!"

The vacation was soon over, and I quickly resumed my normal busy life. But a small yet nagging doubt about my atheist stance lingered at the back of my mind, to be dealt with at a later time.

Other parts of Peck's book made a lot of sense to me, though, so over the years, when time allowed, I would occasionally pick up some of his other writings. Before long, I came across *The Different Drum*. Here Peck expounded further on the spiritual growth concept, outlining some very specific stages a person might go through on the road to spiritual maturity. While he gave some credit to Dr. James Fowler, who published extensive research on the matter in his book *Stages of Faith: The Psychology of Human Development and the Quest for Meaning*, Peck shared stages he developed himself out of his own experiences with his psychiatric patients. While Fowler had outlined six stages, Peck condensed his model into four.

In Peck's scheme, the lowest stage—which we all supposedly pass through as children, but which sometimes persists as a stage of arrested development in an adult—is the Chaotic, Antisocial Stage I. Here the individual is basically manipulative and self-serving, unprincipled and governed only by his or her own will.

The person who has grown to Peck's Formal, Institutional Stage II has, often by means of a sudden and dramatic conversion, submitted himself to the governance of a formal institution or "church." People in this stage are very attached to the outward forms of their religion—to, for example, saying certain prayers at certain times in a certain way. These people need stability and do not deal well with changes in the structure of their religion. Their God is a legalistic, punitive person-like figure, completely external to and separate from the believer's own being.

If a person reaches Peck's Skeptic, Individual Stage III, she or he has likely asked the hard questions about religion and may have become a nonbeliever. The Stage III person is self-reliant and will not likely accept religious truths proffered by others. Individualistic and independent, deeply committed to principle (such as truth or justice), this person has completely internalized such values and thus has no need of a formal belief system or rules and structures that limit behavior. Generally self-governing and taking a scientific approach to life and philosophy, the person in Stage III is an active seeker of truth.

So far, Peck's explanation of these stages was a huge hit with me. I had moved to the Skeptic, Individual Stage III at age twenty and had been a card-carrying, flag-waving atheist for most of my adult life. I now sensed the truth in everything Peck said. I could even recall elements of my life that corresponded well with Peck's descriptions of Stages I and II. I was sure of my superiority over those "weak" folks in the "lower" stages, who depended on organized religion to define their life, needed a certain explanation about where they came from and what happened after death, and used God as an excuse for what went wrong in their life—or to gloat over what went right.

Oddly, it had been my Catholic school education that led me to Stage III. In elementary school, we had been handed all the facts of our religion in a neat little book called the catechism. We were led to believe that everything about our religion had already been figured out by others and that we had only to memorize it—and then, of course, to follow the rules. In high school we were let in on the secret that a lot of the catechism we had so rigorously memorized was not literally true and that there was no actual place up in the sky where people were rewarded and no place beneath the earth where a fiery devil lurked to administer eternal punishment.

But for me, without all those facts and rules, I didn't know what the Catholic Church was all about. So I chose to study religion at a higher level in college. At the Catholic University of America, all the theology classes encouraged us to question church tenets and reason out our beliefs on our own.

For me, the end result of all the questioning was that most Catholic teachings, as I understood them at the time, did not stand up to rational examination. I finished college as a confirmed, proud atheist. I was certain that all the effort people expended in assuring their salvation through church participation could be better spent focusing on the practical aspects of the here and now, and in helping others where possible. In fact, I was very happy to be freed from some of the really scary parts of the Catholic religion—the devil and the threats of eternal punishment in Hell.

By the time I got through Peck's Stage III in *The Different Drum*, all I could think about was how valid this concept of religious stages was. Everything Peck said made perfect sense. How grateful I felt that he had explained it all so clearly! Why, I wondered, had I never heard about these stages before?

But then I turned a page and read what happens when the truth seeker in Stage III keeps seeking. "[T]he more pieces [of the puzzle of life] they find," Peck wrote, "the larger and more magnificent the puzzle becomes. Yet they are able to get glimpses of the 'big picture' and to see that it is very beautiful indeed—and that it strangely resembles those 'primitive myths and superstitions' their Stage II parents or grandparents believe in. At that point they begin their conversion to Stage IV, which is the mystic, communal stage of spiritual development."[8]

Aaaarrrgh! Stage IV!! Could there really be a group more spiritually "mature"—and so more "right" about belief in God—than I was? I could see through the motivations of most of the religious people I knew and could sense that they approached religion to deal with their own fears and the need for definite answers. I *knew* that having dismissed that type of religion was a growth step for me. And now this guy Peck was saying some religious people had grown beyond the stage I was at?

The Stage IV person, Peck said, had dispensed with the need for definitive answers and had emptied herself of the "dogmas of skepticism such as, anything that can't be measured scientifically can't be known and isn't worth studying."[9] Rather than entering into religion to obtain answers, like the Stage II person, or rejecting religion because it can't be proven, like the Stage III person, the Stage IV individual would enter religion to further embrace an ongoing Mystery. Stage IV people, Peck said, see an invisible fabric connecting everyone and everything in the universe into the same whole. They have also emptied themselves of the notion of our separateness—from other people, from whatever view of God they might hold. This person sees the universe as one community to which we all belong, God included (!), and realizes that it is precisely the lack of this awareness among other people that "divides us into warring camps."[10]

A nagging feeling prevented me from dismissing this notion of Stage IV spirituality as the nonsense my rational mind wanted me to think it was. Resentment mounted. I had been so happy with my lack of belief. Life was so full. Who needed anything more than the here and now? And now, what? I had more work to do? Stage IV indeed! Why did I ever pick up this troublesome book? If only I could turn the clock back to the moment before I started that chapter. But it was too late now. Darn that Dr. Peck! I regretted the day I ever heard of him!

Just when I thought I had everything figured out, I realized—oh no!—my journey was not over. I had further to go, and it would not be an easy trip. Suddenly, my world was no longer as certain and definite as it had been, and, if Scott Peck was correct, I had a steep climb ahead of me. Despite the pain this new knowledge caused, and the numerous attempts of my rational mind to dismiss the concept, Peck's first three stages corresponded clearly with my own experience. In my heart I knew I would need to learn more about this fourth step and the spiritual-growth process.

I bought James Fowler's challenging *Stages of Faith* and struggled through it. Though based on solid research, Fowler's stages were less tangible than Peck's, and he wrote on a far more academic level. Moreover, he seemed to expound on spirituality from a plane most of us will never reach. It took me ten years to get through that text, but in the end, I was astonished to discern general ways in which Fowler's stages correlated with Peck's.

I finally realized, much as I was loathe to admit it, that a Stage IV person might have something to teach me. But where were my Stage IV role models? Surely I had never met one. They must be very rare, I thought. And I didn't really get how their acceptance and inclusiveness meant they had a better answer about the existence of God! If they were into seeking Mystery, did that mean they were not sure who God was? *Was* there a God or not? Neither Peck's nor Fowler's works really made this clear.

Over time, I began to understand that the godless world I thought I had all figured out was not nearly as neat and simple as I had believed it was. To my surprise, the more I studied the issue, the more intriguing it became.

Over the years between first picking Peck's book off that shelf and my decision to write this book, I discovered many works by other experts suggesting this same progression in spiritual growth, but using different terms. Some defined explicit stages numbering from as many as twelve to as few as two. Others delineated a simple dichotomy: *mature* faith versus *immature* faith. The commonalities in the spiritual growth path described by each of these writers from different academic fields, different faith traditions, and in some cases even different centuries, were truly captivating.

Of course, there is no such thing as four neat stages that fit all people, but Peck's framework resonated most intuitively for me and stood as a gauge against which I was able to compare the work of other theorists. Nineteen years later, I can look back and see where that one chance event of choosing an unknown book from a shelf that wasn't mine began a process that has lent unimaginable richness to my existence, however confusing and painful it was at first. And, thanks to Drs. Peck and Fowler, it has led to a project—my own spiritual development—that will keep me happily occupied to the end of my days.

Chapter 6

Spiritual-Development
Theory Simplified

What is the spiritual growth Peck and Fowler wrote about? First, let us consider common ways the term is used in the popular culture and rule out the ones we are *not* using here.

In this book, we are not speaking about spiritual growth in terms of developing the ability to have paranormal experiences or extrasensory perception, communicating with the dead, seeing past lives, or having visions. Whether these abilities are a sign of, or lead to, higher spiritual levels is not the point here. Some may consider these activities a part of "mysticism," but they are not necessarily characteristic of the Mystic (or Peck's Stage IV) level as we are using that term in this book.

Similarly, we are not speaking of the spiritual growth that may arise as a result of dedicated spiritual practices such as meditation. These may in fact lead to greater spiritual development, but there are other paths to such growth. The people in the stories in this book arrived at their growth through the rough-and-tumble experiences of life, mostly without the benefit of a strict meditation practice.

So what *is* spiritual growth? Jean Piaget, the famous developmental psychologist, focused his work on *cognitive* development only and implied that such growth ends at age fifteen. But many others, inspired by his work, have since explored human development in other areas and have shown that some types of growth do continue into adulthood. One of these is *spiritual* development.

The most well-known researcher in this line is Dr. James Fowler, who detailed results of his most extensive research project in the above mentioned *Stages of Faith*. In that book, he outlined six stages using a definition of faith that correlates very closely (if not perfectly) with spiritual development. Showing that people do continue to develop and mature in faith well past their entry into adulthood, Fowler claimed that his fifth stage (more on which later) is rarely reached before midlife, if at all. And Fowler's sixth stage is one that most people never reach. Since Fowler, others have taken the spiritual growth theory further. And an examination of writings that greatly predate him uncovers correlations with his theory going back as far as Saint Teresa of Avila in the sixteenth century.

I have found plenty of researchers and spiritual writers who have authoritatively described ways in which people develop spiritually. They may have used different terminology, and the number of stages they list may vary. But a meta-analysis shows a great deal of commonality among their works. I may be the first actually to lump all their works together under the term *spiritual-development theory*. Because the authorities upon whose work spiritual development theory depends come from various disciplines, I have chosen merely to call them "theorists."

I present spiritual-development theory not so much as fact but rather to inspire consideration as to whether this structure of belief stages has a place in our modern world. Does it make sense? Could it help us better understand ourselves versus others? Could it help explain some of the crazy conflicts that are escalating between believers and nonbelievers?

I have tried here to introduce the simplest possible overview of spiritual development to increase awareness of the concept and to inspire further study of the more detailed works referenced in the later chapters. Admittedly the spiritual-development-stage typology is initially uncomfortable to almost everyone, because it forces each one of us to stretch. No matter where we are on the spiritual path, stage theory implies that none of us has the final answer; we could all undergo further growth if we remain open to possibilities.

I challenge my readers to consider objectively whether an understanding of spiritual development can lead to a broader perspective and a kinder world. I invite them to ask whether awareness of the spiritual-development levels can lead them to a more comprehensive understanding of themselves—and of themselves in relation to others. And would such an understanding lead to greater compassion for those who believe differently?

To simplify the stages, I will be presenting a sort of layman's nomenclature, with the understanding, of course, that there are no strict lines of demarcation between them. As with any system of categorizing people, no one person exists wholly in one stage or another.

All the stories in part 1—about people reasoning themselves out of the traditional beliefs of their birth religion—describe the mindset of what we will call the **Rational** stage. This is roughly equivalent to Pecks' Stage III, which he called the Individual, Skeptic stage. To be sure, it is insulting to reduce anyone to a category like this, and it would be presumptuous of me to claim that I can judge another person's stage of spiritual development, especially on the basis of a simple story. So I use these categories only for the purpose of illustration. While I cannot claim necessarily that the contributors in part 1 are actually *in* the Rational stage, their stories do illustrate how someone at the Rational stage might think.

To arrive at the Rational level, a person must have individuated. Her concept of herself as an individual must have become stronger than her identity as part of a certain group. This does not mean she is selfish. It does mean if the values or beliefs of her group—her faith community, for example—no longer make sense to her, she has the strength to branch out. Confidence in one's own reasoning power takes precedence over loyalty to and dependence upon one's "tribe." The individual's view of the truth becomes more important than membership in the faith group or even the family. People in this stage have assumed personal responsibility for their beliefs and thus have taken a significant step toward their own spiritual maturity. In some cases, the period of questioning is very brief; the person barely notices it before moving past the Rational stage and thus never actually leaves the faith community. In other cases, the Rational stage lasts most of a lifetime and leads the person away from religious belief altogether.

Valerie, Abu Ali, Jim, and Kevin each began to note discrepancies in the "truths" of their respective religions while they were still fully engaged in them. If they had not been ready to move to the Rational stage, they could not have allowed themselves to notice those discrepancies. You can see the tug-of-war that took place as they wavered back and forth, trying desperately to cling to the comfort and safety of the group. But questions kept arising. Eventually, each of these people demonstrated readiness to face life without the support of a religious community. Their own views of the truth became more real to them than the tenets of their religion. In Abu Ali's case, this decision meant moving away from his family, his job, and his town. Had he not been ready to brave this storm, his mind would have closed down against the first discrepancy, and he would barely have acknowledged its existence.

Willingness to apply reason in determining one's beliefs and live with the moral, social, and philosophical consequences is a sign of growth, a mark of individuation, a measure of personal strength and maturity. In general, movement to the Rational level tends to lead a person toward certain traits or values. Reason outweighs comfort and safety. Science is trusted more than tradition or scripture. Truth is valued over conformity. Claiming salvation for—or extending worldly privilege to—only one's own religious group begins to sound selfish and limited; the walls of social justice are extended to include those outside one's own group. In this sense, a person in the Rational stage is more mature—personally and spiritually—than the person who has not critically reflected on the validity of her or his religion. See the chart below for characteristics typical of people at the Rational stage.

Though some preachers would have you believe otherwise, the critical reflection typical of people in the Rational stage is a necessary step in

Chart 1: Rational-stage traits

ISSUE	RATIONAL TRAIT
RELIGIOUS ATTITUDE	Skeptical Seeks truth over comfort
INTERPRETIVE STYLE	Reason/Science-based
LOCUS OF AUTHORITY	Conscience authority Principled
CIRCLE OF CONCERN	All Humans/Social justice (Worldcentric)
IDENTITY	Individuated, but **not** selfish
RELIGIOUS COMMUNITY	Questions/May reject
VALUES	Truth/Integrity
VIEW OF "GOD"	Science/Reason/Truth
OTHER	Critical Seeking Involved in social causes

moving toward spiritual maturity. Nonbelievers in this stage are not the crazed and amoral atheists fundamentalists denounce. For the most part, they have instead found a source of moral guidance within their own conscience that allows for more flexibility than the rules of their faith group in determining right from wrong. This is not the moral relativism traditional religionists warn against; rather, it is a function of the "higher authority" situated within the individual, the discerning sensibility that acknowledges that in some situations, traditional rules do not apply.[1] Being governed by the authority of his own conscience, the Rational level person does not need the rules of the church to control his behavior.

Again, while none are perfect examples, each part 1 story shows some characteristic of the Rational level of spiritual development. The stage all those people were moving out of was the **Faithful** stage—or

Peck's Stage II, which he called the "Formal, Institutional" stage. Peck said this group includes most people in most forms of organized religion, which may have been correct at the time he wrote it, but may be changing (for reasons we will discuss later).

In the Faithful stage, identity as part of a certain group is more important than the concept of self as an individual. So, if someone were to point out an incongruity in the religious tenets, rather than calmly consider both sides of the issue the Faithful person would turn away and might even label the person pointing out the incongruity "evil."

If a logical discrepancy regarding religion were to arise for someone at the Faithful stage, he or she would not be able to address it because of the difficulty in facing the consequences of an answer that might lead away from the group. Thus, Faithful-level people either do not even perceive such discrepancies or they dismiss them out of hand, for they are not sufficiently individuated to face life without the support of religious authority and their group.

Traditional forms of most organized religions supply answers about the purpose of existence and what happens after we die. These answers bring a welcome certainty to the Faithful-level person. In great need of this type of certainty, Faithful people will not ask "Does God exist?" or "Is my religion true?" in an objective manner, because they cannot accept a "no" answer. They cannot engage such questions with completely open minds; they cannot allow their reasoning to take them away from the safety of their group, the rules that order their world, and certainty about the purpose of their existence and what happens after they die.

Peck called this group "Formal, Institutional" because such people rely heavily on the forms (the rituals, rules, and beliefs predetermined by others) of the church or institution to which they belong. Its rituals are considered crucial and immutable; its rules must be followed to the letter; its tenets tell them what to believe. Thus Faithful people accept a prefabricated religion they can join and embrace in toto instead of having to figure everything out on their own. This kind of faith is like following a recipe in a cookbook: if you stick to the directions, you can be pretty sure you will get a dish that is close to the desired result. In the same way, the Faithful person follows the rules of her church in "cookbook fashion" because she wants to be "sure" to get into Heaven (or whatever the goal of her particular belief system might be).

Why do those at the Faithful stage hold on to the forms and rules so tightly? For one thing, they are uncomfortable with ambiguity. It threatens the certainty they need. Anything that is "other" threatens the stability of their world. Thus they readily accept proclamations by religious authorities that perspectives differing from their own faith group are wrong—misguided or even evil. People at the Rational stage, on the other hand, need less certainty. Most Rationals have done away with the need to know the reason for our existence and what happens next or have deliberately chosen to believe that nothing happens next. But some Rationals still exhibit the need for a different kind of certainty. They need to know they are right—that God definitely does not exist, or that science is the absolute reality. Some of the contributors of the part 1 stories show that kind of certainty. For my part, I definitely shared this type of certainty when I first made my own Rational step. But some Rationals, supposedly the ones ready for the next step, can dispense with that need for certainty. They are comfortable saying, "I just don't know." In this sense one might consider an agnostic to be more evolved spiritually than an atheist, since the agnostic allows room for doubt.

As mentioned earlier, at one time the average churchgoer in most congregations was more or less in the Faithful stage. Most people in this group were probably brought up in a religion and never questioned it much. Without reflecting on the reasons, they observed the routines and attended church or whatever just because it was expected. Others were converted by means of a sudden, profound experience—such as being "born again"—that brought them certainty as opposed to the chaos of the prior, Lawless stage (see below).

Just as there are traits associated with the Rational stage, a different set of traits is typical in the Faithful stage. The Faithful-level person has a tendency to hold a literal view of God and of scriptural texts. His God is external to him and judges his actions. In general, a Faithful person is less self-regulating than those at the later stages, so he really needs to follow church rules to the letter. He cannot imagine how anyone could behave with integrity without the threat of punishment, whether by authorities here on earth or by a judgmental Father God. The Faithful person is pre-critical, in that her faith has never been examined in an open-ended, objective manner. Perhaps because her preacher has suggested it, the Faithful person often holds an ethnocentric worldview where "only my church is right."

But in general, not trusting his own conscience, the Faithful-level person is always at risk of descending into chaos without externally imposed rules. Thus, rather than the authority of personal conscience, the Faithful person must subject himself to an "oracle authority"[2]—in most cases provided by his religious institution—taking literal guidance from scripture and the literal word of the religious authorities.

Faithful-stage people leave themselves open to an almost naïve acceptance of the tenets and rules of their churches because they need that religion for the security and order it brings into their lives. Chart 2 contrasts the traits typical at the Faithful stage against those at the Rational level.

Generally, those at the pre-critical, Faithful level accept the beliefs put forth by their church in a *literal* sense. Heaven is a sublime place in the sky where the good souls can be found contentedly milling about from cloud to cloud; Hell is a hot place under the earth where a horned, pitchfork-wielding devil rains terror upon those who transgressed against the rules of their religious institution; and God is an anthropomorphic being who spies on humans' every action from the sky, displaying many traits of human weakness, including anger and jealousy, and who—worst of all—*plays favorites*. Faithful-level people tend to accept whatever oracle authority tells them, be it their church, the government, or the leaders of their particular political party, because they like and need the rules and the structure. Because they do not question authority in a critical manner, they can be easily led (or misled) by their leaders, be they political or spiritual leaders.

Chart 2: Comparison of Faithful- and Rational-stage traits

ISSUE	FAITHFUL TRAITS	RATIONAL TRAITS
RELIGIOUS ATTITUDE	**Needs definite answers** **Won't question directly**	Skeptical Seeks truth over comfort
INTERPRETIVE STYLE	**Literal**	Reason/Science-based
LOCUS OF AUTHORITY	**Oracle authority**	Conscience authority Principled
CIRCLE OF CONCERN	**One's own group (Ethnocentric)**	All Humans/ Social justice (Worldcentric)
IDENTITY	**Defined by group Divisive against outsiders**	Individuated, but **not** selfish
RELIGIOUS COMMUNITY	**The only "right" one**	Questioning/May reject
VALUES	**Security/Certainty/ Comfort**	Truth/Integrity
VIEW OF "GOD"	**External, separate Being**	Science/Reason/Truth
OTHER	**Naïve (pre-critical) Fear-based**	Critical Seeking Involved in social causes

Security, certainty, rules, immutable answers, and the authority of leaders of their own group are the traits to which people at the Faithful level of spiritual development adhere tightly. They are easily threatened by change—and by those who do not agree with their beliefs.

But another reason the Faithful hold so tightly to the forms and rules is that, without those constraints, they risk falling back to the prior level—the **Lawless** level, or Peck's Stage I. Most texts describe this stage as one people pass through in a normal childhood, but Peck described it as an arrested development in an adult who never matured sufficiently from childhood.

Unlike the Faithful, who rely on the rules of their religion to govern behavior, or the Rationals, who have internalized rules similar to the ones dictated by the religions, the Lawless are governed only by their own will. The only criterion determining behavior is, "What I can get away with?" Please remember that the Rational level person is not led by the rules, because she is adequately governed by a conscience authority. Her conscience may lead her into an action that is not immediately pleasurable or compel her to make an uncomfortable decision when some sort of greater good requires it; she can make good ethical decisions on her own. The Lawless person, on the other hand, has no conscience—or, at least, a poorly developed one—and will not make good ethical decisions on her own.

Lawless-level folks are spiritually undeveloped. There may be some who actually attend church—or even run their own churches—but their participation would only have some superficial ulterior motive. They would go only because they personally have something to gain by it: for example, being seen in church helps strengthen an image they wish to promote, or perhaps they can make business contacts there. Religious beliefs would not be driving their actions. Everything a Lawless person does is self-serving.

Because they are unprincipled, adults at the Lawless stage generally live in some sort of chaos or a life filled with difficulty. Governed only by their own will, no overriding principles guide their behavior. If their will shifts from day to day, so do their priorities. They lack integrity because there are no principles, whether internal or external, guiding their choices in life.

People at the Lawless stage may be addicted to drugs or alcohol or may be in and out of trouble with the law. Peck applied the term *antisocial* to this group, but this word throws people off from recognizing its members. Occasionally, one of them with a strong will and focused ambition is able to summon the discipline to become very successful—in outward ways involving money, power, or social status. Some of these people can be well liked and may rise to positions of great prestige.

Whether an outward success or social failure, deep inside the Lawless person lacks integrity, because any goodness she can muster is based on pretense. Most of her interactions with others are manipulative in purpose. But the Lawless-level person may not see it that way. She may believe she is kind and loving because she cannot appreciate the depth those feelings reach in others who experience them genuinely. For the most part, she probably is not capable of realizing that other people have higher-level motivations than she does.

When a Lawless individual suddenly undergoes a conversion experience, he is catapulted up to the next stage in an inspiring instant (such as being "born again"). People who have had such an experience as an adult often make for some of the most ardent and vociferous Faithful.

On my website (www.exploring-spiritual-development.com/The-Lawless.html) I describe in detail a story from my own Lawless stage from my kindergarten years. It involved my stealing some medicine bottles with candy inside from a friend's toy doctors' kit. I mention it here because it is the only example I can give from the heart about the Lawless stage. A quote from the point just before I stole the bottles sheds light on the Lawless mentality:

Now, I had had enough moral training to realize it was wrong to steal. But . . . at that moment it just seemed that was my only choice. I wanted those bottles so badly that leaving them there at Gail's house was simply *not* an option for me that day. My conscience tried to step in and do its job, but, weakly developed as it was in those days, my only strong concern was, "Will I get caught?" And "If I get caught, just how much trouble will I get into?" Surely, these bottles had little or no monetary value.

But, in my relatively powerless state as a kid, I just could not think of a way to obtain bottles like that honestly through my own resources.

At no point did I consider that stealing those bottles was in some way harming my friends. I only wondered how long it would take them to realize the bottles were missing. Would they remember that we had played with them the day I was over there? Would it occur to them to accuse me of stealing them? Would the bottles be a serious enough loss that my friends would cause trouble about it?

I believe the motivations and feelings I had about my actions then mirror those of persons who persist into a Lawless adulthood: The rules didn't matter; my friends' welfare didn't matter. I wanted those pill bottles and nothing was going to stand in my way of getting them. I felt small and powerless. I saw no other way of obtaining the coveted medicine bottles through my own honest efforts. I viewed my friends as being "haves" while I was a "have not." Most importantly, my own strong desire to own those bottles overpowered all other considerations. There was no guilt over taking what I wanted if I could get away with it.

But I was brought up in a relatively stable home that allowed me to grow beyond that Lawless stage in a graceful, hardly noticeable way. By my teen years, I had certainly moved beyond it. But you can see how in a person with a different set of life experiences the "small and powerless" sense of being a "have not" and the condition of having a hugely underdeveloped conscience could persist far into adulthood. This would be your "Lawless" or Stage-One person—a victim of his own will.

The stories in part 1 showed examples of a normal step in human development—people questioning, doubting, and ultimately moving away from the Faithful to the Rational stage regarding their religion. (To be sure, not all Rational-stage people abandon their religion, but the dramatic shifts in the part 1 stories do clearly illustrate the process of this phase of spiritual development.) However counterintuitive it might seem, stage theory implies that people ready to question religion rigorously, relying more on reason than on external authority, experience spiritual growth and become more spiritually mature.

Chart 3. Lawless-stage traits (far left) compared to those at the Faithful and Rational stages

ISSUE	LAWLESS TRAITS	FAITHFUL TRAITS	RATIONAL TRAITS
RELIGIOUS ATTITUDE	**Disinterested or superficial interest only**	Needs definite answers Won't question directly	Skeptical Seeks truth over comfort
INTERPRETIVE STYLE	**Self-centered**	Literal	Reason/Science-based
LOCUS OF AUTHORITY	**One's own will Unprincipled**	Oracle authority	Conscience authority Principled
CIRCLE OF CONCERN	**Self (Egocentric)**	One's own group (Ethnocentric)	All humans/ Social justice (Worldcentric)
IDENTITY	**Selfish**	Defined by group Divisive against outsiders	Individuated, but **not** selfish
RELIGIOUS COMMUNITY	**May join for own needs**	The only "right" one	Questioning/May reject
VALUES	**Personal pleasure**	Security/Certainty/ Comfort	Truth/Integrity
VIEW OF "GOD"	**Self**	External, separate Being	Science/Reason/Truth
OTHER	**Undeveloped Manipulative, insincere Chaotic lifestyle**	Naïve (pre-critical) Fear-based	Critical Seeking Involved in social causes

Articulate arguments against God and religion advanced by the New Atheist writers Richard Dawkins, Sam Harris, and Christopher Hitchens also contribute significantly to our understanding of the Rational stage. All three of the "atheist manifestos" put forth by these authors are clear examples of Rational-level thought. With all due respect, we may even say the New Atheists caricaturize the Rational level.

But we must return to the question: Are they *right*? Is all religion based on false precepts that can be rationalized away once one no longer needs the support of a religious institution (and the social benefits that go with it)? Is the institution of organized religion so prominent in our culture based on falsehoods? Could it be that there really is no God? If this were the case, why has every society down through the ages, no matter how underdeveloped, always devised some degree of spiritual understanding? Could all these different cultures have been wrong?

In spiritual development theory, the Rational stage is not the final or most mature level one can reach. The eloquently rational theses of Dawkins, Harris, and Hitchens against God and religion may not be the last word—at least, if those studying spiritual development know anything.

If a Rational-level person keeps an open mind and continues questioning, he may find himself transitioning to a quite different form of spirituality, though he may or may not exactly reengage with organized religion per se. As my story showed, I was not pleased to hear about this supposedly higher level of spirituality the first time I heard of it. Fully (and somewhat arrogantly) engaged as I was in my Rational-stage beliefs, the thought of any spiritual reality was a nuisance. It was not easy to admit that there could be anything beyond the understanding I took such pride in having reached. I knew that I would never be returning to the literal Word, submission to an oracle authority, and the need for definite answers about salvation. But for some reason, I could not dismiss the possibility of a genuine faith that would come after the stage of critical reflection. What if the type of faith that followed Rational-level reasoning was something I just could not yet understand? If I had never met a person with that type of faith, how would I ever come to understand it?

Some kind of grace was apparently acting back then that at least allowed me to stay open to this other type of spiritual understanding. Over time the needed correlations and connections began to appear. By now I have just enough grasp of what this level is about to identify likely candidates for Peck's Stage IV—what we will, in this book, call the post-critical or **Mystic** level—by hearing snippets of their spiritual stories and naming the traits they embody. As most of them are unaware of this stage structure, they cannot identify themselves to us. But the more I learn about their intriguing stance, the more urgently I feel the need to share news of their worldview.

To describe the stage that correlates with Peck's Stage IV, I have chosen the word *Mystic*, despite certain connotations that may cloud our understanding. In some circles, the term *mystic* refers to people at much more profound levels of spiritual experience than we find in the stories I present. In others, it points to those dealing in paranormal activities and the occult. I use it here because it corresponds most closely with the traits we associate with this stage. Readers who object to the word *mystic* in this context are free to substitute the more pragmatic, (but equally effective, for our purposes) term *post-critical faith*.

We will discuss the Mystic level in more detail in later chapters, but for now I will simply list its characteristic traits below.

The next section introduces a few people who begin to embody post-critical faith. Their stance may at first surprise you, but as you read their stories, if you listen for the hints between their words, you may be able to discern ways in which the people in these stories each embody some of the Mystic-level traits. It is important to realize that no one person could possibly be one hundred percent Mystic or post-critical, just as no one person could ever be entirely in the Faithful stage. But these stories do illustrate, if not the Mystic level or post-critical faith itself, then at least the process of spiritual growth as some people have experienced it.

Chart 4: Mystic-stage traits (far right) compared to those at the Lawless, Faithful, and Rational stages

ISSUE	LAWLESS TRAITS	FAITHFUL TRAITS	RATIONAL TRAITS	MYSTIC TRAITS
RELIGIOUS ATTITUDE	Disinterested or superficial interest only	Needs definite answers Won't question directly	Skeptical Seeks truth over comfort	**Prefers the Mystery Seeks unity over truth**
INTERPRETIVE STYLE	Self-centered	Literal	Reason/Science-based	**Metaphorical**
LOCUS OF AUTHORITY	One's own will Unprincipled	Oracle authority	Conscience authority Principled	**Spirit Authority (Will of God/Order of the Universe)**
CIRCLE OF CONCERN	Self (Egocentric)	One's own group (Ethnocentric)	All humans/ Social justice (Worldcentric)	**All that exists, incl. animals, nature, etc. (Universal)**
IDENTITY	Selfish	Defined by group Divisive against outsiders	Individuated—but **not** selfish	**Seeks community with those at all levels**

RELIGIOUS COMMUNITY	May join for own needs	The only "right" one	Questioning/May reject	Chooses one (or more) from many acceptable possibilities
VALUES	Personal pleasure	Security/Certainty/Comfort	Truth/Integrity	Unity
VIEW OF "GOD"	Self	External, separate Being	Science/Reason/Truth	Universal principle Inner light/Love Goodness/ALL
OTHER	Undeveloped Manipulative, Insincere Chaotic lifestyle	Naïve (pre-critical) Fear-based	Critical Seeking Involved in social causes	2nd Naïveté (post-critical) Humility/Forgiveness Gratitude/Acceptance Compassion

Part Three

Who Is a Mystic?

Chapter 7

What Is a Mystic?

Soon after reading about Dr. Peck's Mystics, I asked myself: "Who are these Stage IV people?" I had spent eighteen years in Catholic schools mixing with people at all levels of the church and even taught in a Catholic high school for five years. Yet, when trying to find a Mystic among all the encounters I could remember, I was totally earnest in concluding, "I have never met one! They must be very rare!" If the Mystic level of faith was something to which I should aspire, I wondered, "Where are my role models?"

Now, after nearly twenty years of study and pondering these questions, I know that Mystics had been there all the time—lots of them. Unfortunately, their voices had always been overpowered by the roar of the more superficial forms of religion I had come to realize could not be valid. I had never met a Mystic because, to me, all religious people resided in the same category, a closed-and-locked file drawer in my mind labeled something like "needy, gullible people."

Despite having long since perused the contents of that drawer, I must admit that I still find it hard to distinguish among the Mystics and the Faithful within organized religion. I believe there are many shades of gray between these two groups, and probably no one person is fully in one camp or the other.

The literal believers in traditional religion are so vocal that they unknowingly obscure recognition of the Mystic group. Plus, it is possible that certain religious leaders aim to suppress spiritual growth to the Mystic level in their congregations. They preach the Faithful level of religion not because they have not been taught about—or cannot understand—the Mystic level, but rather because keeping people Faithful is better for the longevity of their institutions. If people didn't feel they needed a certain church and set of beliefs, they would be free to conduct a spiritual search on their own.

In contrast to the other stages (which I had already experienced myself), my understanding of Mystics was more theoretical than experiential. Never could I have imagined that an army of Mystics would come parading into my life wearing nametags! I don't claim that any one of their following stories presents a full-blown Mystic. But each one exemplifies at least one of the Mystic-level traits and enough of the person's life to show what they went through to develop it. Readers will note that these narratives are all longer and more complicated than the part 1 stories, with their clear-cut decisions about faith and ensuing dramatic life changes. The beliefs of a Mystic are not cut and dried, and nor are their stories, but they should provide a glimpse into the post-critical mindset.

The Mystics in the following stories may participate in organized religion or they may not. I don't believe any belong to the church into which they were born. In including mainly nontraditional believers in this book, I do not mean to discount the fact that what applies to them could just as well be said of post-critical participants within traditional religious institutions.

Chapter 8

Don't Fence Me In (Nilah)

Nilah was nearing eighty when we worked together on this story. Her long life has brought her through many turns, as you will see. If she experienced an explicit Rational stage, or critical distance, it was the breakthrough at the Mennonite Health Center. Because (perhaps only because) of her openness to growth, her life has turned out well. Imagine the life she would have had if at any point she had stubbornly dug in her heels, refusing to expand her worldview beyond the one she was born into.

As you read this story, notice how the traits of spiritual maturity come into play (see chart beginning on page 90): a metaphorical interpretation of scripture; acceptance of that which Nilah could not change; her willingness to change her beliefs over time according to new information; and, most of all, her deep humility. Among the Mystic-level stories, Nilah's is probably the one most closely associated with traditional beliefs.

—◦◦◦—

Early Fences

Even before I was old enough to understand what faith was, I knew about Jesus. I cannot remember a time when I was not aware of "the presence" within. I grew up during the Depression years in a very rural area in Indiana. We didn't have running water, indoor plumbing, or electricity until I was in junior high school. Our farm was pretty self-sufficient; if we didn't raise it, we didn't eat it.

Our church was an "Old Fashioned Shoutin' Methodist" one, complete with altar calls, testimony meetings, tent revivals, and baptism by immersion in the nearby river. In our family, church attendance was as regular as clockwork: Sunday school and worship on Sunday mornings, Sunday evening services, and Wednesday-night prayer meetings. We almost never missed any of these. In church, the men sat on one side, the women in the center, and the children on the other side. Fervent *hallelu-iahs* and *amens* would arise spontaneously from the pews whenever the congregation was moved by the preacher's message.

Despite my family's steadfast church-attendance policy, there was one controversial issue. Farming families such as ours depended heavily upon the success of our crops. With our crops we fed ourselves and our livestock; we sold the remaining grain to buy necessities. Every year during planting and harvesting season, Dad complained that going to church seriously cut into his crop-tending duties. Mom would say, "If we attend church, God will take care of the crops!" Dad would reply, "God expects us to use our heads in taking care of the crops whenever the weather is fit!" Dad finally settled the question once and for all when he declared, "I see it this way—I may as well be out in the field thinking about God as being in church thinking about my crops!" I have never forgotten the honesty and clarity of that thought. I was also stunned at my dad's original, freethinking, spiritual prioritizing. I believe that for Dad, his crops and God's abundance were one.

In church, the message from the pulpit often emphasized God's wrath. Much attention was paid to the pervasive sins of the world and the fast-approaching Day of Judgment. Anyone who didn't testify in church was assumed to be a nonbeliever. Thus, many otherwise good people, whose lives clearly bore what we called the fruits of the spirit—love, joy, peace, patience, kindness, goodness, faithfulness, gentleness, and self-control—were judged harshly if they failed to testify in church.

In the first two decades of my life, my interpretation of religion—had anyone bothered to ask me—would have been to list the Thou Shalt Nots:

- Thou shalt not lie.
- Thou shalt not cheat.
- Thou shalt not steal.
- Thou not shalt gossip, get angry, tell lies, dye your hair, polish your nails, dance, go to the movies, drink whiskey, or smoke.

There were a few Thou Shalts as well:

- Thou shalt attend church.
- Thou shalt obey authority.
- Thou shalt pray before meals.
- Thou shalt forgive those who mistreat you.

The religious message was clear: If we sinned—did not obey the Thou Shalt Nots and the Thou Shalts—we would go to Hell.

No one I knew ever even thought of questioning the Bible and its stories. Adam and Eve, the serpent, and the predictions about the end of the world were accepted as literal fact. After all, the Bible was the inspired word of God and he had dictated it, word by word, to his Chosen People. And no one in our community ever questioned our belief that we Methodists had the only correct interpretation.

Our neighbors were God-fearing, honest, hard-working people. Any family disaster or hardship in the community would be shared by one and all. My mother was strict but very loving. She emphasized the positive value of doing the right thing, as opposed to the sin involved in doing wrong. I think that is the key to my seeing God as loving rather wrathful. Mom always looked on the bright side, even when there wasn't one. Because I had no brothers, I grew up working the fields with Dad. He taught me the discipline of tackling whatever needed to be done, and that it is important not only to work hard but to take pride in whatever task is at hand.

Life in my early years was not easy. I never realized we were poor, because everyone we knew was in the same boat—and of course there were lots of good times. In my humble childhood home, I never felt unloved, unwanted, or rejected, and I was given all the tools necessary— love, direction, solid religious teachings—I would need to deal with any- thing life would ever throw my way.

At the same time, my early years brought a lot of suffering resulting from the influences of our church and the greater community—and the way I interpreted their message. As I see it now, for the most part the type of religion I encountered in church and my community served as a fence. Inside the fence were the things that were right to do and think. Outside it were the things that were wrong. The rules provided a *fence of fear* to keep us from sinning. The church gave us definite answers about exis- tence that precluded our needing to think much for ourselves. And the church barred us from anyone who believed differently. In retrospect, it seems a lazy kind of religion, since all one had to do was follow the rules.

The Breakthrough

After graduating high school, I got a job in town and soon met the man who would become my husband. My parents and his were extremely pleased with our choices, and I do believe that he and I sincerely felt we would be life-long, loving partners. We were married a few months after we met and soon thereafter joined the church. We started our family, which eventually grew to include five children, and reared them on practically the same Christian teachings by which we had both been reared. I did all the things a good mother does—or so I thought. I tended the kids, cooked, and cleaned while my husband worked hard to provide us a good living.

Yet I realize now that there must have been something missing in our children's upbringing, compared to the religious teachings by which I was reared. I was brought up to think of God as primarily a God of love and of Jesus as my friend. For our two oldest daughters, however, the message about God's wrath came through much more strongly. They found the religious rituals empty, restrictive, oppressive, and guilt-inducing. Today they resent the strict religious rules with which they grew up. Somehow we, as parents, didn't supplement the basic Christian rules with the strong message about God's love and acceptance that had pervaded my childhood home.

After about fifteen years of marriage, our home life and my relationship with my husband began to crumble. At first, I couldn't admit to myself, my husband, or anyone else that my marriage was less than I had hoped for. I was perplexed: How could our marriage have come to such a painful state? Were we not both Christian? Over time, I became depressed, and the chasms in our home life deepened.

Leaving me out of all discussions, my husband talked over my behavior with our minister. They had me admitted to a local Mennonite Health Center for psychiatric treatment. In what they called "semi-inpatient care," I was given intensive therapy during the day at the center. In the evenings and weekends, I stayed with local families who opened their homes and hearts to me and other center patients without compensation. The love I experienced from those families was as curative as any therapy at the center. In their homes, I was treated as a family member. I helped with chores and participated in family outings. I observed family interactions very different from what I experienced in my own home. I was especially surprised to note one family's ability to resume normal discourse quickly after a vigorous argument. Never before had I been exposed to free expression of opinion and easy acceptance of differences.

At the center and in the families' homes, I learned some important lessons. I learned it was okay to disagree. It was even safe to get angry and to admit it when you were hurt. Most shocking of all, I found it was okay to discuss and to question the teachings of the Bible! Many of these lessons were counter to my understanding of the teachings of the church. In fact, if the program had not been sponsored by a Christian church, I am pretty sure I would have rejected everything they tried to do for me. So certain was I of the rightness of my beliefs that I would have been suspicious of anyone from outside Christianity talking to me about how I should live my life or how I should think. (In addition to my depression, I suspect I was a bit of a self-righteous, overly pious Pharisee.)

In fact, one of the most stunning lessons I learned from these people involved a view of religion I had never encountered before. I asked why they didn't hold regular services in their chapel or talk to me about being saved. Their response: "Nilah, you are welcome to go into the chapel to pray or meditate anytime you want. We accept you, as we hope you accept us. It is our hope that you will see Christ's love manifest in the way we care for you." This was so different from the religion I had known all my life.

Dealing with anger was especially tough for me as an adult. As a child, I had my feelings hurt many times. When kids teased me at school, my anger would boil within me. But I had been taught that one must keep his thoughts and feelings to himself and that becoming angry was a sin, so I would just smile and act like their insults didn't bother me at all. I thought I was really being Christian, for the Gospel said, "[W]hoever shall smite you on your right cheek, turn to him the other also."[1] I never once thought about standing up for myself.

At the treatment center, one counselor guessed the truth about my anger problem and provoked me into a cure. He gave me an assignment to sand the paint off an old kitchen chair that was already in hopeless disrepair. He kept walking in and asking how I was doing. I repeatedly told myself I had to maintain my self-control, but I was getting angrier by the minute. Finally the breaking point arrived. I glared at him: "I am really, really mad at you for having me sand this chair. It's a piece of junk and a waste of time. You have pushed me too far!" I could not believe that I was the one speaking—I was out of control! The counselor smiled at me, gently took the chair and the sandpaper from my hand, and went on his way. I knew then what his lesson had been: we must learn to express our feelings *before* we get to the boiling point.

I grew up thinking my feelings, fears, and frustrations were no one else's business. Until I came to the treatment center, I don't think anyone in my life had ever asked me how I felt about anything. For this reason, I had never given it any thought myself. I knew about physical pain, but I knew nothing about emotional pain. At the center, I learned how hiding my feelings was yet another fence I had built and that others would accept my feelings and validate them, not because they were right or wrong, but because they were *mine*.

In this process, I learned that denying my real feelings and ignoring the insults of others was a form of martyrdom that undoubtedly had contributed to my depression. Learning not only the importance of sharing my feelings and ideas, but also the very act of thinking them through for myself, began a life-changing growth process for me. It gave me new self-respect and permission to love myself.

Also at the center, I realized that I must not look to my past teachings for all the answers I need in life. I learned that the religious questions or uncertainties I had squelched for years were not sacrilegious or a sign of weakness but were necessary for spiritual growth. I underwent a gigantic leap in consciousness. "Chaos precedes creativity!" I learned to take responsibility in deciding for myself how I should live my life, what I believed, and why. I grew in my own authenticity.

I had been admitted to the Mennonite Health Center because of a *breakdown*, but in the end, for me, it turned out to be a *breakthrough*.

Fencelessness

Through the experiences gained at the center, I began to feel like I was in the middle of a wide-open field. My belief-system fences had all been torn down. The responsibility of using personal discretion to govern my everyday decisions from that point forward, relegating the mental tapes of stale messages from the pulpit to permanent storage, was daunting. Yet, surprisingly, I was exhilarated, not afraid. For me, this was a panoramic change, an epiphany.

With my therapy largely a success, I returned home and resumed my homemaker role. I continued to read and pray—and to think for myself.

Despite the pain of having to face a broken marriage, I held fast to my newfound emotional stability.

I realized that my home church was not the place to rebuild my belief system. Their sermons had not changed, but I, of course, had. In place of traditional church membership, I joined a mothers' study club associated with the Mennonite Church. I found that most of the members were dedicated Christians with belief systems similar to the one I was developing for myself. Was that because they belonged to a different church, or (more likely) that my old "belief bondage" had stemmed from my own insecurities in my prior years?

As I worked to build a belief system that worked for me, I came to see that, every time I built another fence, I would eventually realize that I needed to tear down a few sections of it and enclose a larger area. (Conversely, I occasionally needed to pull the fence *in* a bit. In time, I not only became accustomed to making changes in my belief system; I began to welcome them. I came to realize the rewards of moving on—of seeking fresh, new grazing area for my thoughts.

Eventually, I realized that maintaining all those belief-system fences was a bit of a pain. Then came my breakthrough moment: I didn't need fences at all! Which reminds me of an old Cole Porter song only we old folks can remember: "Give me land, lots of land, under starry skies above—don't fence me in!"

Once I had done away with the fences, I was free to be myself and began to take the concept of personal responsibility to a new level. I worked at developing ways to understand the teachings of Jesus as they applied in my own life. I allowed that understanding to direct my path as I carried out my responsibilities to myself, my family, and others.

It has now been almost fifty years since I broke through the philosophical fences of my youth. My winding path has included many twists and turns: divorce, relocation, a new career, several job promotions and relocations, some illnesses, and finally retirement. Now I have more time to listen to tapes, watch videos, and read books and articles about spiritual issues. I like to keep an open mind and thrive on being exposed to new and challenging ideas. It does us no good to consider only those things with which we can nod in agreement while excluding those that challenge us.

Today, each of my children and I are all on seemingly diverse spiritual paths, each according to the dictates of our own hearts. These differences do not separate us in any way. Some are spiritual but not religious; some spiritual *and* religious. They have tried different religions over time. I found the service in the Buddhist Temple to which my son once took me to be beautiful and reverently filled with spirit. I was surprised to learn that at a Unitarian Universalist Church, people with very different beliefs could come together to learn how to live a more purposeful life. I found beauty in that.

A single comment from my son was especially meaningful. I had just mentioned that I was striving to become a better Christian. He countered with "Mom, I strive to become my Higher Self." To which I replied, "Hallelujah, Son, we are both on the same path!" Another time my daughter said, "Mom, don't be concerned about what a person professes, look at how they live." I have learned so much more from my children than they ever learned from me. In our case, in place of the old adage, "Children, listen to your elders" ours should be, "Mom, listen to your children."

Feeling that we are all on the same *general* path, I am comforted to note that all my children are dedicated to their family and are always willing to offer an empathetic ear to anyone in need. I am proud that all have chosen career paths of service. I not only love them; I admire them. As I grow older, they continue to inspire and amaze me. I recognize and respect each of them as they are. The religious diversity among us causes no separation; for me, spiritually, we are one.

Though I will always have further to go along the path of spiritual learning, at least I have knocked down most of those awful fences from my younger days.

My Mother's Influence

Until I sat down to write this story, I never realized the extent to which my mother was a defining influence on my spirituality. Yet now, as

I approach my eightieth year, more and more situations come to mind in which I see the pivotal role she played.

In our family in those days, everyone was divided up into two categories: religious and not religious. To all appearances, my mother was clearly in the former category. Yet Mom's personal depth, intellect, and complexity were far above her grade-school education. When she was about seventy-five, we learned a little surprise about her. My sister had accompanied her to the hospital lab for some medical testing. As the office nurse droned out her list of routine questions, my sister heard a definite "No" from my mother that should have been a "Yes." Thinking Mom had misunderstood, my sister said, "Mom, now listen to the lady. She just asked you if you are religious. Of course, your answer is 'Yes'!" Emphatically, Mom said, "I heard the question, and the answer is no. I'm not religious at all—but I feel like I'm deeply spiritual." That was the first time my sisters and I had heard anyone make that distinction. We didn't really understand it then—but Mom did.

I realize now that there was a depth to my mother's wisdom that surpassed the rules and beliefs of the church. As I grew older, from time to time Mom would point out evidence of the divine presence in everyday situations that most people would have missed. One incident from the period when I was moving out of my room in town (in preparation for getting married) demonstrates this. I had loaded all my belongings into my fiancé's car and was apparently driving along with my head in the clouds, for at one point I came to a fork in the gravel road and missed the turn. With an upcoming cement bridge abutment just ahead, I lost control of the car and slid off the side of the road. The car came to a stop just short of tipping over into the creek.

It was some time before I stopped shaking. There were no nearby houses, so I decided to wait until someone came along who could help me. After some time, no one had come by, so I started the engine, put the car in reverse, and floored the gas pedal. The car lunged backward forcefully, but at least I was back up on the road.

Driving with a little more caution, I finally arrived at my parents' home. Once inside, I began to tell Mom about my close call. But she stopped me and said, "Nilah, you don't need to tell me a thing. I was standing at the sink, washing dishes, and the thought came to me: 'Go pray for Nilah.' So I went into the bedroom, got down on my knees, and prayed for you. And I knew you would be all right." If only I could be as tuned in to the needs of my own children! That is my wish to this day.

When our eldest daughter was in her late teens, she went out west to live. She sent me a letter describing her enthusiasm for a very young (adolescent) guru who was in vogue at that time. Being the pious pharisee, and frightened about the blasphemous path my daughter was on, I sought my mom's advice. I think I was secretly hoping she would mirror my concerns. But she surprised me again with her unique perspective: "Nilah, I would not try to convince her to let go. Let her know that you believe in her and trust her judgment. Tell her you believe that by his fruits she will know if there is goodness in his teachings." Not at all what I had expected her to say, nor was it the course I had been planning to take. But, with doubt in my heart, I followed Mom's advice. Not long afterward, it became clear that the much-feared guru had faded from my daughter's radar.

As far as I could ever tell, my mother never felt fenced in by her religion. Mom always appeared to be doing the right thing—not because it was right or out of a sense of duty, but because it gave her joy. Living out the ideals she professed seemed to come naturally to Mom without any apparent effort. I don't recall her ever saying anything bad about neighbors or family. She took in my grandparents and never once complained. She cared for the sick. She went without and gave to others. I doubt that Mom's life or religion ever included any fences.

I realize now that my mother's example formed the underlying basis for my faith today. Though it took me a while to reach this level, as I have gotten older, I am more and more able to see the divine spirit, as she taught me to recognize it, manifest in my own life and that of my family. I know my mother would be supportive of the spiritual path I am on today.

I feel less and less at home in church and rarely attend anymore. I often find I am not much attuned with the sermons, and all the old hymns I loved have been replaced with modern music. If I do go, it is to enjoy the fellowship of family or friends. What I find missing in church is the potential vibrancy and reverence, the communal spirit that scripture promises wherever "two or three are gathered together in [his] name."[2]

At this point in my life there are three elements to my spirituality: faith, belief, and truth. For me, faith is something I feel, an intangible abiding presence, an inner connection to my own spirit—my soul. As an old hymn goes, my faith gives me "strength for today, hope for tomorrow." It is intuitive, sustaining, and constant. It is circular, with no beginning and no end. It is in fact the divinity within, the spiritual essence of my being that has been with me ever since I was a child.

In contrast to faith, belief is constantly evolving and dependent upon intellect, tradition, reason, individual interpretations of scripture, and personal experiences, which continue to occur over time.

The differences in belief among denominations, churches within a denomination, religious sects, cultures, nations, and generations are all just details. We worry too much about who believes what and too little about how our own beliefs shape our day-to-day lives.

With so much opportunity to do good all around, it makes no sense to spend my life just trying to save my soul to get into Heaven. I want to spend each day—right here, right now—doing my best with the unimaginably wonderful gift of the life I have been given.

Personal responsibility is an important value. I see it as my responsibility to accept myself, my family, and all others, without judgment. I want to listen to anyone who confides in me with an empathetic ear, offering fair and compassionate counsel if asked, as I would hope anyone would do with me. I want to be trustworthy, responsive, forgiving, attentive, and to keep my word—as I would have others do unto me. What it all boils down to is living by the Golden Rule.

Truth, the third element of my spirituality, is something much more personal and fluid, more subjective even than belief. What I say I believe at any given time is what I perceive to be truth based on the information, experiences, and spiritual guidance that have been revealed to me thus far. I take full responsibility for what I accept as truth.

On some issues, especially certain religious beliefs about which many people in church are so sure, my personal truth is that I simply do not know the answer. If we somehow discovered indisputable evidence that evolution is a fact, that Jesus was married, that people are reincarnated, and that scriptures contain good stories written by men with no divine inspiration, that would affect what I consider my truth—but it would have no effect on my faith. No amount of information or learning will ever shake my faith.

Regarding scripture, through my studies I have learned that the original texts have been modified and reworded, in some cases by spirit-directed and well-meaning translators, and in others by people with less noble intentions. I believe in the *sanctity* of the scriptural message but do not believe in its infallibility or literal truth. Moreover, I think the scriptures are too often used by pastors, priests, and even laymen to condemn good people who disagree with them—and, worse, to defend doctrine in such a manner as to prevent further discussion or study. Having said this, I find that the scriptures offer me solace, conviction, guidance, assurance, and inspiration in everyday situations, whenever I need such help.

I do believe Jesus was the greatest teacher who ever lived. I consider his basic precepts for fruitful living as true today as they were during his lifetime. I want to learn more about him. I believe that the divinity—the Christ Spirit—that was in him is also in me. I believe the admittedly immeasurable difference between his life and mine is the degree to which God consciousness came to fulfillment within him. Within me, that divinity is still a tiny seed just beginning to sprout. I believe there is a spiritual energy source for my life, a Power that enables me to reach for my Highest Self. I choose to call that energy source *God*. But as I heard someone explain it once, we are each a part of God as a wave is part of the ocean.

My prayer life is strong. When I pray, I feel the presence of a Holy Spirit within me. I am known by and commune with this Spirit. I believe in the effectiveness of prayer, though I do not pray for personal favors. Most importantly, I believe *prayer changes people*, in that it can relieve stresses that cause them problems. In the case of disease, I do not believe prayer can kill germs, but through relieving stresses it may enable the body to produce the antibodies to kill off bacteria. In the case of mental stress, prayer may reduce tension and may thereby allow a person to see a solution that they could not see before praying. In the case of hostility between two people, prayer may calm their spirits enabling them to come together in peace. To put this another way, I don't see prayer moving a boulder out of the road, but I do think it might help the one lifting the boulder to exert more strength.

As I approach my eightieth year, I trust this ongoing process of spiritual growth is the herald of wisdom and enlightenment, not the frailty of an aging mind. In this, the autumn of my life, I truly feel, as I did in my childhood, that I am blessed.

—⟁—

It is clear that this is a story of growth. In the course of her life, Nilah learned to trust herself over the dictates of authority and learned the importance of honestly expressing feelings instead of hiding them. Overall, her life story is one of steadily increasing personal authenticity.

Chapter 9

My Kind of Hell (David)

Watch for the importance of conscience in this story and in David's ability, as an adult, to stand in the shoes of his childhood victim, Peter. The ability to take the perspective of another person, or of a group other than one's own, is another trait of spiritual maturity. David credits what was probably a near-death experience[1] with his expanded conscience, which makes him very careful of how he treats people now.

The reader will also note David's strongly developed sense of personal responsibility, interestingly tied to his view of Hell. He does not need God or a church for the purpose of supplying rules by which to live or threatening punishment; his conscience and sense of personal responsibility is all he needs to keep him on the straight and narrow. He is self-regulating.

David's Rational stage began in third grade with his question to Sister Michael Frances and continued through the period of trying out different beliefs and for a time declaring himself an atheist. Parts of his story suggest that he still has a Rational mindset. But David's metaphorical sense of all beings as connected points him more toward the Mystic level, as does the fact that he has joined a church out of a desire to serve others and to participate in community, despite not holding exactly the same beliefs as the more traditional members.

Most indicative of a Mystic stance is the part at the end, where David makes it clear he doesn't need or want the certainty of definite beliefs. He prefers to keep questioning while remaining open to spirituality.

———◦◦◦———

Peter's shoes were brown, so we formed the Club for Kids with White Shoes, just so we could exclude him. But one day, as we played in the neighborhood, he sauntered up to us with a huge grin. I looked down, and there were Peter's brand new, gleaming white shoes. Did we welcome him with open arms? No. Instead, within minutes, our group was renamed the Club for Kids with Black Shoelaces. Once again, Peter was excluded.

Poor Peter was a good-natured kid who just wanted to be friends with the rest of us. There was absolutely no good reason why our neighborhood clique targeted him as a designated outcast. From the first days of kindergarten to high school graduation, he was our pariah. All his attempts to fit in, all his attempts to impress us, were cruelly dismissed as show-off behavior on his part. We were mean and unfair, for no particular reason.

Sometimes I initiated this bad behavior. Other times, I just went along with the group. It felt good to be one of them. Never once in those days did I stop to consider how our actions might make Peter feel. Never once did I stop to extend any kindness to him. Could I really have been so insensitive? I feel sick just writing about this now.

While I never did anything *really* bad as a kid, Peter was not the only one to whom I was unfair. How many times did I taunt a little kid at Boy Scouts for the simple reason that I was bigger and I could? How many times did I join in on the bullying of another kid at school just because others had targeted him? I never once held myself accountable for these actions or stepped into the victim's shoes to imagine how it felt to him.

Well, as luck would have it, I would one day find out. At a time when I least expected such a thing, it all flashed before me in a singular moment—every single instance in which I had ever mistreated someone, belittled another child in attempt to quell my own doubts about myself, or lied to someone to cover my own faults and mistakes. Seventeen years ago, I was treated to what amounted to a life review. It occurred in connection with a dream of sorts that came to me shortly after my terrible accident. All at once, behavior I had never bothered to analyze before, and that most suburban American white kids would consider a normal part of growing up, suddenly paralyzed me with a type of regret I can hardly describe in words.

For each recalled incident, I could suddenly see that there had been no excuse for my behavior. No, it was *not* okay to say I was just going along with the crowd. No, it was not okay to say that I was just a kid back then and didn't know what I was doing. I alone was personally responsible for my wrongdoing, and there were no excuses. My sorrow at those behaviors pierced the depths of my being. Since that life review I have seen my role in interacting with others in quite a different light.

Twenty-two years ago, when I was twenty-seven, while riding my bicycle in training for a triathlon, I was hit broadside by a large truck as I passed through an intersection. I remember everything from the accident except for the moment of impact. I even remember seeing the egg-crate grill and blue oval Ford logo moments before I was hit.

Lying there underneath the truck's chassis while waiting for medical help, I was surprised to note that although I could not breathe, there was no pain. I remained conscious the entire time but had suffered massive injuries. Upon my arrival at the emergency room, I was given a slightly better than zero chance of survival. It turned out that my left lung was completely torn from its attachments and the right lung was punctured. I also suffered a torn diaphragm and liver. They had never seen anyone survive injuries like mine.

As luck would have it, a visiting thoracic surgeon happened to be giving a seminar at the hospital that day. This particular surgeon had recently read a journal article about the successful repair of blood vessels that had sustained injuries similar to the lateral and transversal tears that my left lung had suffered. He bravely offered to try this new surgical technique to reconnect my lung. While it is very unusual that a visiting surgeon be permitted to operate, knowing it was my only hope the hospital authorities agreed.

To make a long story short, I spent more than three weeks in the critical care unit and six months in recovery. I went through three complete changes of blood supply, twenty-one pints. About a week into my CCU stay, my blood oxygen-saturation level had dropped below 40 percent. A normal blood oxygen level is more like 95 to 100 percent. Anything below 85 percent is cause for alarm. I was rushed into a second surgery, and my parents were told I would most likely not come out of it alive. The thoracic surgeon later told me he had no idea how I survived, since blood oxygen that low is incompatible with life. Perhaps it was because I was a very fit athlete with an efficient cardiovascular system, but who knows? Another surgeon later confided that they thought they had lost me a couple of times during the second surgery.

It took a couple of weeks before I was fully alert and aware of the seriousness of my condition. At this point I recalled a sort of dream, in which a Creator had appeared and told me that it was time to "come home." I told this Being that I was not ready, that I had too much to do. He saw that I was sincere and not just afraid to die, so my wish was granted—but if I went back, I was told, I would live a long life, and it would not always be easy.

You might ask how I knew to say it was the Creator to whom I was talking. There was no introduction ("Hi! I'm the Creator"); it was more like a feeling. And this Creator was not a distinct, real being. It was a part of everything, not a separate entity. Maybe it was more like I was talking to the earth, or the universe. In any case, it was definitely *not* an authority figure.

Since then, I have studied near-death experiences (NDE) reported by others, and I am not necessarily ready to say that my dream was one of them. Yet it was not a typical dream for me, because, as an artist and product designer, I am a very visual person. My dreams normally contain rich, clear, colorful imagery, but this one was nothing like that. Instead, there was nothing to see, no visual image at all. It was more like remembering a phone conversation from yesterday. I can remember what was said, and it feels real because I can play it back in my head—but no image is involved. So, while I do not think that my dream of the Creator was a normal dream, I also do not want to claim that it was an NDE. I am not sure *what* it was. In any case, it was the life review that occurred just after that dreamlike conversation that had the greater impact on me.

Years earlier, as a small boy, I had sat before the dark-robed nuns in our Catholic school listening in fear to painful tales about the horrible place in which a sinful person would spend eternity. The fires of Hell, they told us, would lap at our sides forever after death as punishment if we dared to commit a mortal sin—missed Mass on Sunday, stole something, or (Heaven forbid) got a divorce. But the threat of Hell never influenced my behavior in any way. I never connected my habit of taunting little kids in the neighborhood with sin.

Years after my accident, I learned about people who held quite a different definition of Hell. They described it as a separation from God, or from whatever view of the Divine they held. That concept doesn't resonate clearly for me, either.

No, for me Hell is none of these. My own personal view of Hell is that rush of memories I had during my life review. I cannot begin to explain the horrible pain of seeing all the injustices I had committed flash before me with crystal clarity. No justifications, no excuses, just the very raw recollection of my actions in the harsh light where no illusions could survive. I alone was responsible for each of these transgressions. Everything from my repeated unkindness to Peter (and, occasionally, other kids in the neighborhood) to every selfish lie I ever told: they all marched before me in a single, endless moment. To me that realization, that raw unfiltered view of my actions, was a true experience of Hell.

But unlike the Hell that was promised by the nuns, my Hell was not felt as a punishment. While I knew that the regretful feelings

115

I experienced were well deserved, the only *consequence* was the feelings themselves and my realization that there was no excuse for my actions. It was not even about guilt, just regret and sorrow. So my life review served as wake-up call, bringing me to a new type of honesty and a new sense of personal responsibility.

Just to be clear, I did not experience the feelings the other person had as a result of my actions. The victim's feelings would have been interpreted by his own life viewpoint. What I experienced was even more raw than that. I simply had to face my own actions without any spin on it. I knew I was accountable in a very simple way for every instance of mistreating others. I began to feel a moral obligation to make amends and have been trying to do so where possible. I did manage to apologize to Peter for my treatment of him all those years ago. While he said he accepted my words of apology, I know I can never fully make up for the pain I caused him.

For Peter's pain and that of anyone else I have ever wronged, my Hell will always be the memory of those actions. In addition to leading me to make amends for the past, my life review illuminated my future as well. The sense of personal responsibility I gained regarding interpersonal relations has colored all my interactions with others ever since.

My first clue that something was amiss about my religion came in the third grade of my Catholic elementary school. In religion class, I asked Sister Michael Frances, "If God knows everything, why did he test Adam and Eve knowing they would eat the apple and then punish them for it?" She replied, "There are some things we are not meant to know."

From then on, it was a slippery slope of ever-diminishing credibility for the Roman Catholic Church. By my teenage years, my parents would often allow me to drive myself to the late Mass on Sundays, as they preferred the early Mass. At these times I often betrayed their trust by skipping Mass in favor of a visit to a nearby nature preserve and walking the trails for an hour. I really enjoyed the solitude of being in nature and thinking about the beauty around me. When I got home, if Mom asked,

"How was the service?" my reply would be to say it was "like a breath of fresh air." I am not proud of this repeated lie, but I justified it by saying that I was worshipping God's Creation in my own way. To me, this was much more authentic than sitting in church, standing with the group, kneeling, sitting again, standing, etc., falling asleep during a particularly boring sermon, smelling that noxious incense, and drinking out of the same cup of magical blood as hundreds of others.

After college, I moved to California and met friends of every imaginable faith. I became interested for a time in New Age thought. I liked how it brought together all kinds of interesting philosophy, and it was fun to read and learn about. I will admit that a large part of the attraction was the "wow" factor—the spirit guides, crystal energies, channeling, etc. Some of it sounded a bit unreal, but I wanted it to be true. After a time, however, I began to realize that many of the people involved were either fraudulent or self-deluding. For example, there was a man who claimed to channel a spirit guide in the form of a Native American shaman and chief. Strangely, this guide spoke through the man with a "Hollywood" Indian accent, not like a real Native American. I was pretty sure a Native American spirit guide would not come through speaking like a character out of a bad western movie. Of course I realize that many New Age people are very down-to-earth, honest, and sincere. But in those days I had little inclination to approach this philosophy with my heart open to its particular insights into unity and our universal search for meaning. After a time, I decided it was all too flaky and unreal for an empiricist like me.

Next, I checked out Buddhism. Its philosophy of compassion and oneness rang true, but I found the idea of reincarnation simply bizarre. No matter how I looked at it, I couldn't imagine how a soul could be reincarnated.

In the late nineties, after my accident, I read James Rachels's book called *Created from Animals: The Moral Implications of Darwinism*. It laid out a thorough train of reasoning asserting that, if you believe in the theory of evolution, you must believe that animals deserve a degree of respect similar to that afforded humans and should be treated according to the same moral standard. This got me thinking about our role as human animals and illuminated a kind of cosmic architecture in which people and animals are part of the same whole.

I then came across an article, *A Moral Argument for Atheism*, by Raymond Bradley. His argument first defines morality, proceeds to show how the God of the Bible fails to pass the test, and concludes that the Christian God must not exist. I found that I could not reasonably argue with any of these points. And so, for a time, I found that the label *atheist* fit me.

But through the extensive reading I have done since—I especially enjoy reading science journals—together with what I learned through the experience of my accident, I have, over time, developed a more universal philosophy that includes and respects the interconnectedness of all beings.

Certain cosmologists and mathematicians liken our universe to a soap bubble. I take this analogy one step further to illustrate of the oneness of our existence. It is my understanding that everything we see as an object is made up of the same stuff at the most fundamental level: energy in the form of subatomic particles. The way the particles are organized gives the object unique characteristics. A human is made of the same kind of particles as everything else, so I do not view human beings as some kind of special creation.

I visualize the universe as a many-dimensional soap bubble. When I look at a soap bubble, I can see little swirls of colors moving about. To me, the swirls look like individual parts. However, they are not independent of one another. They are simply parts of the whole that reflect light differently, due to their particular makeup of soapy film. In the same way, people are simply parts of a whole. They appear different due to the particular makeup of their subatomic particles. If I touch one of the swirls on the soap bubble, everything on the bubble reacts, not just the swirl. Likewise, every action we make ripples throughout the universe, even though we are mostly unaware of the ripples or our connection.

We humans are not individual things living within, but separate from, a natural universe; we are each a collection of particles with certain characteristics that make us appear separate from the whole. If a soap bubble pops, everything that was part of it collapses into a single, tiny droplet. There are no more swirls of color, no more film, yet all the matter still exists. The soap bubble was created from this droplet. In that sense we can say that that droplet or bubble is the creator, the source of creation.

In my analogy, human beings, deer, rocks, etc., taken together all form the "film" in that soap bubble. The universe and its contents, including us, were formed, or created, from the "droplet," and in that sense we are the creator and so is the universe. Likewise, if the universe were to collapse, we humans would not be left behind, floating around in nothingness. We would collapse with it back to fundamental particles—to a tiny droplet of energy. Thus, as all the particles within the soap bubble (whether it is in droplet or soap bubble form) are interconnected and therefore part of the same whole, we are all interconnected and part of the same whole that is the universe.

This is what I tell children, and they seem to get it whether they are Judeo-Christian, Buddhist, atheist, or whatever else: Imagine that the Creator is the only thing that exists. He is lonely and wants to make something. What can he make it out of? There is nothing else there. No mud, or clay, or wood to carve. He has to use himself as the source of material and energy. So it is easy to see that everything in the universe is made from a part of the Creator. From here it is simple to visualize that the universe *is* the Creator and we are part of the Creator as well. To me, this is metaphorical. It is a way to convey the concept of oneness in the tradition of mythic storytelling. But to a religious person, it can be seen as literally true, as describing "the body of God."

As you can see, my views are something more than purely humanistic. Moreover, I do have a fuzzy concept of some all-encompassing Higher Power. But I believe that if there is a God of some sort out there, it is not an anthropomorphic being. My belief is that, if there is a Higher Power, it is beyond anything that we can possibly comprehend. I prefer to think of this Higher Power simply as Nature.

Some people would say that with a naturalistic point of view and without belief in a judgmental God, there is no reason to be good. Personally, I find the notion of a judgmental God who will decide whether you spend eternity in Hell or Heaven one of the most reprehensible inventions of organized religions. I have actually had someone tell me, "If there is no God, then I might as well go out and murder and rape anyone I want." I *hope* that person just said that to make a point!

Others have said, "I would be a very bad person if I did not believe in God." Well, for me nothing could be further from the truth. For me, not believing in an afterlife and a discrete Supreme Being only adds to a heightened sense of morality, by way of empathy. Without a belief in final judgment and eternal salvation, it becomes *my* responsibility to make life better, here, in the present moment, and to help people live better lives. If I want a friend to heal from an injury, I need to do what I can to help. Praying will have no effect at all. It is a call to action. I cannot say to myself, "It is God's will." If I want something to happen, I must act.

As a rational human being, I know that I feel pain, both emotional and physical. I am quite confident that people and nonhuman animals around me feel pain as well. I also feel love. Because I feel love, I do not want the people I love to feel pain. This is all very natural; no deity is required to inspire this behavior. Empathy also tells me that the people I care about all care about other people, many of whom I do not know. So, if their loved ones feel pain, some of it gets transferred to some of my loved ones, which I do not want. This is another sense in which we are all connected. If I am unfair or cause pain to any being, it is certain to affect others to the point that it affects someone I love, or even me. By extension, this applies to every living thing on this planet. This is my framework for compassion and morality: the reduction of pain and suffering for everyone. I also believe this applies to the inanimate natural world. While a rock does not feel pain, it is still a part of me and everything else. To carelessly damage a natural thing is to damage myself. We must give careful consideration before using natural resources of any kind. Remembering that all actions have a ripple effect (and definite consequences), this philosophy of compassion and love is all I need to assure my own moral behavior. With or without God, I would live my life the same way.

I want to make clear that I hold no animosity toward practitioners of any religion. Everyone has his or her own unique path to travel. I enjoy hearing stories of these paths and can learn a unique lesson from each one. It is not for me to judge anyone's beliefs, and I very much appreciate it when others treat me with the same respect. People should not force their religion on others through coercion or legislation. These days I have made a conscious choice to participate in organized religion, even though my beliefs differ somewhat from the bulk of the congregation.

When our kids were toddlers, my wife and I decided that we would like them to have a moral foundation upon which to build a personal philosophy and that it was worth joining a church for this purpose. I would have liked to join a Unitarian Church, but there were none within forty-five minutes of our rural, north-central location. A friend who was a United Methodist pastor told us about his church, and we found we agreed with many of its principles. We liked the democratic way the congregation chose many things about the direction the church would take. We visited that church for several months and decided we felt pretty comfortable there, so we joined.

The church feels much like a family. Just as in a family, we don't always agree with everyone's beliefs, but the ties that draw us together are strong. I enjoy the fellowship, opportunities for community service, and compassionate support. It feels very different from the Roman Catholic Church of my youth.

Unlike many people in my congregation, I view all sacred holy books as metaphorical—sort of like Aesop's Fables, but on a grander scale. I have been able to participate in this church at many levels, including teaching Sunday school, because I am never forced to go against my beliefs. Many Christians claim that the most important teaching is that Jesus is our Savior and he died for our sins. I do not accept that in a literal sense; in fact, I am not really sure Jesus actually ever lived. But I have always felt that Christianity holds a message far more important than its theology.

The message attributed to Jesus in the Gospels radically changed the way we think about compassion toward others, both friend and enemy.

When I listen to or read religious texts or listen to a sermon, I look for the moral of the story. I find excellent life lessons contained in the Gospels and take those lessons as their main message, as opposed to relying on the literal meanings. I am sure that is why a lot of these stories were included in the Bible in the first place.

In talking with my children and in teaching Sunday school, I always ask, "How can you apply this story in your life?" "Does it have a lesson you can use for yourself?" The lessons I try to point out revolve around the virtues of compassion and service. For example, after telling the story of Noah and the Ark, I asked them, "Do you really think this is a true story about all the species of animals in the world getting on a boat in the Middle East and a storm that lasted forty days? Or is it a story about doing what is right, even when people are trying to humiliate you and the task is very difficult?" I wonder if this approach may not trigger some interesting discussions at these kids' homes.

I've said that my life review was a form of Hell, but its greater impact was the way in which that experience has improved my life. They say that with every challenge we meet in life, there comes a hidden gift. Well, I guess you could say my accident was so terrible that it has brought me many, many gifts.

For one, it illuminated for me the importance of other people in my life. After three weeks on a respirator in the critical care unit, I was released to the general ward for a while. I could not speak, so every conversation was one-sided. Yet I don't think I was ever alone during my entire hospital stay. The kindness of friends and family was overwhelming. Of course, I had not asked for visitors and would not have thought I needed them, but just knowing they were there lifted my spirits and gave me hope.

One particular visitor has left a permanent imprint on my heart. On one of my last days in the hospital, a young lady, an acquaintance from work, came in to visit. She arrived alone and looked tired the whole time.

She kept me company for maybe twenty minutes and then stood up as if to leave, saying she would be right back. I watched her walk to the door and stop. Then she collapsed on the floor. The nurse on duty rushed over to help and insisted that she get checked out before leaving.

Later, back at the office, we discussed her visit. Through tears she explained that she had put off visiting me until the very end of my stay because she was very frightened of hospitals and blood. She was not sure she could handle being in the hospital, even as a visitor. But her strong desire to be there for me pushed her to summon the courage to come see me that day. She had stayed as long as she thought she could, then walked to the door and passed out.

That she would do that for me, knowing the pain it would cause her, was, for me, the ultimate gesture of kindness. Overcoming her deepest fear to give me the gift of a few minutes of her presence was a selfless act that affected me deeply in a way I will never forget. I realized then how important our friends and loved ones really are. It is because of her selflessness that I will never hesitate to pass on a kind word, never think twice about helping a stranger, never wait to visit a friend or neighbor in the hospital.

Before the accident, I cared about the people in my life but didn't feel that I needed them in any way. I was mostly self-sufficient. I felt I would be fine whether they were around or not. After my accident I felt not only that they were important in *my* life, but that I was important in *their* lives, too. So if I see that someone needs help, I have a strong desire to help that person in a way I didn't have before—not so much as an obligation but as something I very much want to do.

Another gift from my accident was a new appreciation of time. As a young adult, I was centered on my own goals; I put a lot of time and energy into my sports training, for example. Rather than being focused on what I could do to help people, I was more concerned about where I was going. Since the accident I see things differently: at our birth, we are given a certain bagful of time, and we have no idea how much is in it. That bag might be empty tomorrow, or there might be enough in it to last a hundred and twenty years. But each moment is irretrievable. Any moment wasted on selfish behavior is gone forever. I now view every moment as an opportunity to accomplish something for the good of others. It can be as simple as smiling or saying something pleasant to the checkout lady at the grocery store. I view each good deed as a thank-you card for however much remains in my bag of time.

Another gift of my accident and life review is that now I view everyone as loving, kind, and of exceptional value—unless they prove otherwise. This perspective enlightens and elevates my posture toward my fellow humans almost to reverence. Not only do I treat others better myself, but when I see selfish or misguided behavior in others, I have a kinder reaction to them. I understand that their negative behavior is a response to some kind of emotional pain on their part. That doesn't excuse poor behavior; each person should still be held accountable for his or her actions. But these days it is easier for me to consider others' point of view, ponder what caused them to act that way, and, in many cases, forgive them.

A fourth gift from my accident is that possessions and material success have become far less important to me. Sure, I have a few possessions that I cherish for sentimental or symbolic reasons, such as my wedding ring. But I do not buy into the American cultural philosophy of accumulating all you can and keeping up with the Joneses.

A fifth result, which could be seen as a gift, is that this experience returned me to who I was when I was little. When I was a kid—between, say, three and six years old—it seemed I loved everybody and everybody loved me. I was happy all the time. But, as I think happens with most of us, during my school years my peers and various situations changed me. I think my NDE (if we want to call it that) restored the core person I had been at the beginning. I can do things for the mere joy of doing them; I like to be around people; I have a sense of being a better, happier person.

Regarding my supposedly supernatural experiences following my accident—the dream of a conversation with a Creator and the life review that followed—I am fully aware that it all could have simply been a hallucination in my oxygen-deprived brain. In fact, I am willing to admit that as the more probable explanation.

But what really matters to me is not the explanation but rather the effect that experience had on me. My life, behavior, actions, thoughts, and motivations have all improved since my accident. Since gaining an appreciation of the interconnectedness of all things, I am more poised to help others and living a fuller, more complete life. I am convinced that the lessons I learned are, for me, the Truth. Whether this Truth came through a conversation with the Creator or a hallucination is irrelevant. I don't go around preaching about it and telling people I've met God. What I do tell people is that they are important and valuable to me—and loved. What is important about the experience is that it ultimately led to my realization of the interconnectedness of our existence. I try always to act accordingly and hope to spread the essence of what I have learned through the example of my interactions with others.

So what does that make me? Am I spiritual? Am I secular? Am I a Methodist? Am I an atheist? I find it difficult and counter-productive to label myself. My moral framework is decidedly secular in nature, as I act from my own principles rather than love of God or the hope of eternal reward. The Hell I experienced in my life review has revised my behavior toward my fellow humans, all beings, and even all objects. It has also led my beliefs to evolve over time.

By now, despite my largely secular moral framework, I would say I am more spiritual than your average humanist, more reverent about my purposes here on earth. My realization of the oneness of every-thing—all beings, all of nature, all objects, all moral considerations—begins to raise my appreciation of our existence to a level I am now comfortable calling sacred.

———ᴖᴖ———

In contrast to Nilah, David has a much stronger underlying Rational basis to his spiritual stance. But though he talks an outwardly Rational line, most of the points he makes come out sounding more Mystic. He is a good exam-ple of how individuals are too complicated ever to fall completely into one category or another. The children in David's Sunday school class are lucky: with his suggestions that they look for meaning beyond the literal words in the scripture stories, many of them may soar right past the need for a critical distancing from their religion. The lack of any need to reject the literal may allow them as adults to mature more gently into a post-critical stance.

The question of whether near-death experiences are real or "hallucination[s] in an oxygen-deprived brain" is apparently still controversial in the medical arena. But available literature shows surprising consistency in the reports of people who have had them. Most consistent seem to be results similar to those David reports (all the while denying his experience was necessarily an NDE). NDEs often include a life review, similar to David's, in which life events parade before the person's consciousness, sometimes forcing her or him to realize the effects their behavior has had on people.

I especially like the way David is able to list the "gifts" that arose from his terrible accident. In and of itself, the ability to see something like that as a gift is an example of the Mystic's way of accepting the greater purpose behind everything. But David goes further, claiming that the effects of the accident have improved the way he interacts with others—to the point that he sees every moment as an opportunity to give something of himself to others. David's third illumination from the accident, the one that allows him to see selfish or misguided behavior in others as a reaction to some kind of emotional pain, is a good example of the expanding perspective typical in spiritual growth. He has become able to take others' perspective and see—and feel—the world as they do.

The decreased importance of possessions and material success David describes is also typical in spiritual growth. Look for more about this in part 4 in the discussion about Caroline Myss, who relates the chakra system to the spiritual stages. Myss places possessions and material success at the "below the waist" chakra level, one people must rise above if they are to become spiritually mature.

The fifth gift David describes is that he has discovered joy in life, similar to that experienced by a little child who has not yet bought into all the superficial goals of our material world.

Chapter 10

My Path (Charles)

Charles is a midcareer New York scientist who displayed several traits of spiritual maturity from a very young age. His refusal to attend Sunday school when the class violated his view of reality gives evidence that, even then, his personal truth was stronger than the dictates of religious authority. It also shows him assuming a measure of personal responsibility for his beliefs. Whether arising from a Rational mindset or a Mystic one, an action so extraordinary for someone that age illustrates how the six-year-old Charles was able to see past the Faithful-level myths of the religious authorities—something many adults never do.

Charles's outright rejection of the Christian doctrine that only those who believe will go to Heaven sounds like the inclusiveness and universality of the Mystic, even at the age of six. And the inherent inclination to follow his own path that dates way back to his younger years indicates he may have been driven by a Spirit Authority from very early in life. Certainly the metaphorical view of God that Charles now holds suggests a Mystic stance.

CHAPTER 10

Early Leanings

"This does *not* make any sense. It is *just not* this way!" I heard these words in my six-year-old head so clearly and forcefully that I might as well have shouted them aloud. What had triggered this strong and sudden feeling was a Sunday school assignment to color a picture of a robed and bearded Jesus holding hands with my family and me. The following Sunday, when my mom dropped me off at the church education building, I waited inside the door until she was out of sight, then I spent the class time in the park across the street. I simply could not participate in that class any longer. And I do not recall ever going back. This is the first instance of what would later turn out to be a life-long penchant for adhering to my own truth.

Growing up in a small town in the Midwest, I had a contented childhood in a caring environment. Both my parents were educators. My father, who died unexpectedly when I was twelve, had never shown any interest in organized religion. My mother at one time had felt a calling to become a Roman Catholic nun and went so far as to enter a convent. But she later decided this was not the right path for her, and beyond enrolling me in that Catholic Sunday school, she was not involved in organized religion either during my childhood.

After my father died, my mother, brother, and I made a few attempts at attending church. The most memorable of the services we tried took place at a kind of hip Catholic ministry associated with the university where my mother taught. Despite the folk music and priests who did everything they could to avoid sounding traditional, even this service failed to captivate me. I was not hostile to religion, but I never connected with its meaning or purpose. I do remember, as a teenager, discussing with my mother whether I was an atheist or an agnostic. Because of my curiosity, and because I did not want to say I necessarily had the final answer, the agnostic label seemed the safer, more preferable tag.

Although religion never figured much into my life during my youth, I always took matters of ethics and truth seriously. For example, in order to represent my school at a statewide mock-government meeting sponsored by the American Legion, I had to sign a form stating that I believed in God. As I greatly wanted to participate, I did sign the form, albeit with some hesitation. But once I arrived at the meeting, guilt for my untruthfulness set in. One new acquaintance said he wasn't sure he believed in God either, yet he had had no qualms about signing a statement that his faith was certain. Making that false declaration was just not a big deal for him. In contrast, for me it was a very big deal. Rationally, I knew that I would never get caught for this dishonesty and no external harm would come of it. But I had made a false statement, and intuitively I knew that I had absolutely been "caught" by something or someone at a much higher level—an entity of some sort that was aware of everything. In no way, however, did I connect this entity with the God of the church.

The issue of truthfulness, and the consequences of being untruthful, kept coming up for me. I played sports in high school, and at one point we all had to pledge that we would not use drugs or drink. Once I signed my name to that agreement, it seemed like that was it—I had made a deal, and I intended to keep it. When my friends and I went off to parties, I would bring a carton of milk with me. If anyone asked me what I was doing, I would say, "You guys are all in sports. We said we wouldn't drink!" Needless to say, this set me apart from the group in a way, but fitting in with the guys was not all that important to me. What was important was the sanctity of the promise I had made, though I never considered it an agreement with God or any other being. Maybe it was just a contract with myself. But there was something binding about that agreement not to drink that seemed extremely important to me. I simply could not break a promise I had made in my heart.

When it came time to choose a college, I had nearly been set to attend a distant powerhouse university. But at the last minute, I went with my instinctual feeling that, given my temperament and personality, a Catholic liberal arts college nearer to home would be a better choice. This was a most fortunate decision, as I ended up very happy in the community atmosphere of my college. Since I found science ridiculously easy, I chose that track for my career.

Meanwhile, I found classes in the humanities much more difficult. But, coming from a family where everyone else was much more literary than I was, I was attracted to the school's many elective humanities offerings. Looking back, the most life-influential course I took was a yearlong seminar on issues of modernity and faith. At the time, almost nothing of the course's content stuck with me. However, the course's lasting benefit was the great library of books we were required to purchase. These books introduced me to contemporary philosophical issues and opened questions that would lurk at the back of my mind to be reconsidered many years later.

The Search

After college, I largely abandoned all extracurricular reading for the next twenty years as I established myself in my personal life and in my career. I completed graduate school and post-doctoral training, a very intensive program in biochemistry and biomedical research techniques. The early stages of my career demanded intense work and focus on things scientific. Marriage and family demanded even more of my attention.

During these years, I really had no energy available for spiritual searching. Yet I noted many occasions where my natural response to a given situation seemed much more ethical and moral than that of most other people. More than once I heard the same sort of remark from various religious friends: "Charles, you are about the most 'Christian' person I know!" Yet there I was, a lifelong skeptic—at least as far as Christianity was concerned—who had not set foot in a church for several decades.

Some years ago, several events coincided that triggered in me a renewed focus on spiritual concerns. On September 11, 2001, I was working in New York. While the whole nation and much of the world reeled from news of the events that day, those of us actually in the city at the time found ourselves shaken to our core. A few months later, my mother died after a very long bout with cancer. This would be an intense experience for just about anyone, but for me, following so closely on the heels of the 9/11 tragedy, it sparked an inward-looking crisis. Also, shortly afterward I noted that systems I had implemented in my research work were allowing me to be much more organized; for the first time in years, I had extra energy left after my workday.

Knowing I was open-minded, over the years friends of mine who were serious students of religion recommended that I read and think about certain things. While I had never previously had time for such pursuits, I now began to pick up books on consciousness and decision-making, the psychologies of temperament and of human development, the meaning and origins of organized religion, and mythology. I would read a bit, spend some time contemplating, read some more, and contemplate some more. I let my studies follow their own course.

In all these studies, what was I pursuing? I was trying to learn exactly who I am. There are two things about me that I have always found puzzling. For one, I have always been careful not to go against my own truth. I have never been interested in the idea of religious salvation, nor have I ever felt the need to avoid eternal damnation by following the rules of a church, even when I was young. But something else kept me from attending that Sunday school where they made us color pictures of a strangely dressed man from another time and place holding hands with my family and me; and something else kept me from drinking with the guys in high school once I had promised not to. Why did I insist on strict adherence to the truth, while others around me did not seem to mind these little discrepancies?

The second puzzling thing was that I always felt the need to treat everyone with equal respect. Whether traditionally religious or not, people I knew never seemed concerned with the fact that they saw their own religion, political party, or country as more important or more right than others. I, on the other hand, tended to think of us all as part of one big world community, brothers and sisters connected in our humanity, regardless of race, color, creed, or political party. What was it that made me different?

In trying to answer these questions for myself, I have spent approximately the last six years in intense study. I have been taken to places of which I had only the smallest inkling before. I have studied Eastern religions and philosophy, perused overviews of Western intellectualism, and recently read some serious literature.

The Findings

What have I found in all these studies? For one thing, I have come to appreciate the wider world of spirituality beyond the limits of the Christian churches. In the homogenous, small-town environment of my youth, I was never exposed to other faiths while growing up. Once I became an adult, the demands of the modern technical world consumed my energies and kept me focused on the immediate realities of the here and now. So I spent the first forty years of my life sheltered from awareness of the contents of other religions. Recently, just by following my own instincts as to what to read next, I have developed a far better perspective. I have come to understand the much broader contexts in which humans can approach belief, faith, ethics, and personal integrity beyond the limiting precepts of popular organized religion.

Most importantly, I understand now that I myself have the most profound faith! My faith is that there is something unknowable all around us; call it God if you wish. But I see it more as just trying to follow what is right for me and not going against the order of the universe. For example, when I chose the less prestigious, nearby college over the distant powerhouse university, I was simply following my instincts about what represented the better path for me. No superficial motivations such as prestige or pride stood in the way of that decision.

In refusing to violate my high school pledge not to drink, I was obeying some innate, silent command from within to maintain strict fidelity to my path. Even as early as age six, in playing hooky from Sunday school when the depiction of Jesus with my family felt dishonest, I was obeying a personal imperative that barred me from compromising my own truth. Though I had no words with which to express this, all these actions were attempts on my part to follow a path of personal integrity laid out for me by some unknown order of the universe.

Though I am quite certain there is no deity standing in judgment of my actions and no punishment involved, straying from this path is my idea of sin. Rather than fear of eternal punishment or damnation, I have always been afraid of *acting against what is firmly within me.* When in my youth friends would speak of their guilt over sex or other behaviors, I could not relate to them, because I always seemed to have an internal standard of what was right or wrong for me. Signing that form in high school saying I believed in God was wrong for me and provoked a sense of guilt, because I knew that such a false statement violated my own path and went against the order of the universe. As I see it, the day I signed that form, I committed a sin.

Now that I can articulate this, I will say that, throughout my life, my decisions have stemmed from an effort to see and follow this path and not stray from it. Thanks to this philosophy, in a lot of the big decisions I've made in life—like deciding whom to marry—I was able to act in total confidence, because it all seemed so right. Today, my wife and I act together on all the bigger decisions, such as when we decided to adopt our daughter. There has never been much second-guessing or arguing. When you can act with confidence, so many things just seem to work out. At least, they have for us.

I can truly say that I am very happy with my life so far; so many things have worked out unbelievably well. I find my professional work— as a manager of research projects at a large, complex medical institution—very rewarding. I have a great family, with two kids who are both happy and doing well in school. I have provided them with a beautiful home in a nice neighborhood in a wonderful town.

My faith entails the idea that we are all connected in a huge, all-encompassing system—all part of one big entity. Many of my choices come from the idea that a person can be part of this all-encompassing system simply by respecting everything that is going on. I want to be part of the system by not upsetting the order. I want to know my place in the system and be gentle within it. Just noting the things that exist and accepting what is around me: that is the reality of my faith.

From all my readings, I have come to understand that the philosophy I have always unknowingly followed fits closely with the ideas of Taoism. Taoism is a very natural kind of religion. The word *Tao* means "the path" or "the way." Some people call this path God. Following the path can be equated, therefore, with seeking to align oneself with God's will—which is what I have spent my whole life trying to do.

While the image of the bearded guy in the sky was always too limiting for me to accept as my God, I acknowledge the infinite essence denoted by "the path," or "the way." This concept is beyond all the anthropomorphic images, creeds, scriptures, and dogma, beyond even good and evil, as Nietzsche said.

Further Musings

In my recent period of spiritual study one question kept coming up: "Why worship?" I used to think the word *worship* referred to a feeling of being afraid of God or participating in seemingly meaningless rituals with a group of God-fearing people in church—or praying for some sort of divine intervention. That is what it means for some people.

But now I see that, just as the word *God* can mean many things to different people, the same is true of the word *worship*. While doing my spiritual reading and contemplation, I have often noted an awesome feeling of blissful connectedness and purpose. The time I spend contemplating or focusing my thoughts on the greatness of what I really believe in is, for me, a form of worship. Now I am more comfortable using the word *worship* to describe my own experience when I contemplate the overarching unity of our existence, the Ultimate. Appreciating the beauty in the unknown mystery: this is my path, my God, my form of worship.

Another form of worship for me is being thankful for being con-nected. My thanks are not directed at any particular being, but sometimes I simply feel very happy and connected. As far back as my twenties, I can recall times—particularly outside, especially at night, if the air was cool and I was perfectly comfortable—when I would get a feeling of fitting in perfectly, as if I was made to be on this planet, a part of everything that comprises this universe. My jaw would fall open and I would think: "My God, what a feeling!" I would feel so blessed and so thankful to be part of everything. Today I have this feeling more frequently. Sometimes when I look up at the sky, I feel that wave of happiness, and I give thanks.

More recently, another strong feeling repeatedly comes over me, this one having more to do with the human world than with nature. The first episode occurred after we had just moved to the town where we now live, so I did not really know anyone. I took my son to his first big Cub Scout meeting in the school gym, and there were probably between fifty and a hundred families there. Kids were all running around screaming. As I stepped into the room, I didn't recognize anyone right away, but I was overcome with the warmest connected feeling. I must have been smiling like a fool. I felt so happy—like I really belonged there, as a part of what-ever was happening. It was a nice, comfortable feeling that everything fit together very well. This may sound a bit mundane, but to me it was anything but ordinary.

My faith is also the foundation of my worldview and my approach to others in the human race. I believe every single person should be treated rightly, whether in one-on-one interactions or in institutional situations. I do not ever want to see one person or one group, not even mine, favored over another. That would be unjust. If you believe in justice, you would want everybody to be given equal respect, equal opportunities, and equal application of the rules.

This idea ties in loosely with my view about organized religion. Even as a young child, when I first heard the Christian doctrine that only those who believe will go to Heaven, I rejected it outright. I knew for sure that the God whom Jesus is supposed to represent would not have left out all the people in China and elsewhere who did not have an equal chance to hear his story and believe in him. I have since learned to describe my position with regard to other beings in the world as *universal*.

My wife and I are working hard to be sure we have a comfortable lifestyle, can fund our kids' college educations, are secure in retirement, and have the ability to travel. That said, we strive to balance our financial objectives with some of the more meaningful goals in life, such as rearing our kids to be happy, satisfied, productive, principled members of society.

In terms of spiritual goals, these days I have been contemplating the word *centering*. I am beginning to get an important understanding about this. About a year after I began my reading and spiritual quest, I had a strong vision—a kind of a waking dream—about centering. At the time we were staying at the ersatz pyramid hotel in Las Vegas, the Luxor. The building is built in the shape of a huge black pyramid, and at night a beacon shines out from its top. At 42.3 billion candlepower, the "Luxor Sky Beam" is the strongest beam of light in the world. On a clear night, this beacon is visible up to 250 miles away to an airplane at cruising altitude; it is clearly visible from outer space.

Not surprisingly, the building partly inspired my vision. I saw a pyramid in my dream and wanted to be centered at its base, because from there I could reach up to the very highest part. I felt that if I were centering myself in my faith and reached up into the sky—like at the height of the pyramid—I could best interact with other people in the world. That is how I would have the greatest impact on others and be most fulfilled. Perhaps my impact on the world would be like that very bright Luxor Sky Beam. Try as I might to read more into the dream than this, at this point I feel it just had to do with centering. I think its most valuable message was simply that it is important to be centered as a person, centered in one's humanity in order to maximize the chance to have more impactful and honest relationships.

So this is a summary of my God and my faith. I completely love my God in the abstract way that I choose to conceptualize this entity. For me, love and appreciation of this God *is* my faith. I feel this philosophy—or faith—has led me through a life that is exactly appropriate for me. I feel truly fortunate to have naturally come by a personal spirituality so strong and so meaningful without the need for supernatural deities or religious doctrine and without going to church.

———

Did Charles go through the stages? Though he showed certain Mystic traits from childhood, I would bet that if someone had asked him about his religious stance when he was in his twenties or thirties, he would have described it as agnostic or atheist. Had someone made him study all those philosophical texts at age twenty-five, I doubt he would have come to the same conclusion about his faith being similar to Taoism, or even that he had any faith at all. When a person is ready to realize something, the opportunity tends to come along.

This is the third story in which a spiritual breakthrough was triggered in part by the events of 9/11. With full respect for the deep personal and national tragedies wrought thereby, do we dare contemplate the possibility that one of the most horrific events in our nation's history could have triggered spiritual growth in many—the direct opposite effect from what its perpetrators most likely intended?

Chapter 11

Lotus Opening (Jean)

Jean is a lovely, poised, graceful middle-aged lady from the Midwest who never minds being out in the forefront of a controversy. Watch for her Rational or critical-distance stage around age eight. Even at that young age, she rejected the incongruity of the "loving" God who would nonetheless "send us off to burn in Hell." Despite an upbringing that did not encourage her to feel valued as a woman, it is apparent from this story that no one discouraged Jean from free thought.

As far back as her young adulthood, when she felt called upon to fight the environmental disaster in her town, we can find an example where Jean followed a Spirit Authority (however she might define that). Hers is also a fine example of the social action typical of either the Rational or Mystic stage.

———◈◈◈———

Seeds Are Planted

From as early as I can remember, my father insisted that my sisters and I accompany him to church every Sunday. After sharing the first part of the service in the big church with the adults, we children would be herded off to our separate Sunday-school program.

I found much of our Presbyterian religion perplexing, especially the fearful parts. Week after week, the minister would preach about this God who "loved" us but nonetheless would send us off to rot and burn in Hell. As early as eight years old, I recall thinking to myself "What? That makes no sense!" At school in those days I had a classmate, a very intellectual guy for our age, who had his own strong, anti-religious views. His opinions led me to think, "Well, at least there is someone else who finds this religious stuff unbelievable!" In a way, his skepticism gave me permission to reject formal religion as well.

It would be years before I understood the implications of this, but another fact from my childhood was that my father would bombard my two sisters and me with a constant message: "Everybody knows that women are stupid."

Roots Are Developed

In college in the late sixties, I was involved in all sorts of marches and activities geared toward changing the world and encouraging healthier living. As part of the newly emerging environmental movement, I spent some time on an organic farming commune. Living and working together with numerous friends in a large cooperative community, I formed strong social ties.

I cherished the deep connections and profound sense of community I got from campus life, from the various groups in which I participated, and from the overall culture of my generation in those days. I drew tremendous strength from the collective effort of so many of us working together toward the common goal of changing the world for the better. There were many levels to the movement I was a part of, but in general it was based on the idea that we needed to live more authentically and make more conscious choices, with respect for a newly dawning awareness that we all are connected.

Aspects of Eastern religions began to filter into our awareness, fueling a rejection of our Western notion of God. An atheistic attitude began to permeate not only my thinking but also that of many people I knew—seemingly, our whole generation. Buddhism, especially Zen, appealed to me. Gurdjieff and Ouspensky, who spoke to the oneness of everything in the universe, deeply influenced me as well.

During these years I also participated in a women's consciousness-raising group. About ten of us would meet about once a month and share details about our lives. From listening to other people's stories, I began to see that my experiences were similar to those of everybody else. The ups and downs of life, my fears about supporting myself, my desire to be happy and loved—all seemed to fit in with the general scheme of everyone else's life.

After college I moved to Carmel, California, and worked with a dress designer. Later, for a while in New York, I designed and sold my own line of clothing. During these years, all my relationships were one-on-one; I missed the feeling of an integrated community, being part of a group of people with common interests living and working together. I began to feel separate and alone. I wondered where I would ever find another group of people with whom I could have such deep spiritual connections.

In the mid-eighties, because my parents were aging and needed my help, I moved back to the Midwest where I had grown up. At the same time, my younger sister, Sharon, was expecting a baby. She and I were best friends, and I wanted her child to grow up knowing his Aunt Jean.

About that time, my hometown was building a large, mass-burn incinerator—right next to my father's business property. An incinerator is supposed to dispose of trash by burning it, thus eliminating the need to haul it away. However, it creates tremendous amounts of smog and air pollution, and there are more environmentally appropriate alternatives. While I questioned the merits of this project, I wasn't planning to take any specific action to oppose it, but my environmental activist friends were saying, "Jean, you aren't going to let them build that, are you?" My reaction was, "Well, I am just one person. What can I do—lay on the road so a truck runs over me? That's not very effective!"

I had majored in recreational therapy out of a desire to help people help themselves. But over time I came to recognize environmental concerns as my deeper calling. I saw that our culture had adopted a style of living that was destructive to the planet. I felt an urgent desire to protect our environment in whatever way I could.

It may have been only coincidence that this environmental atrocity was in the planning stages just as I arrived back in town and that it was to be located right next to my father's business. But this synchronicity called me to a greater cause. I felt the call to awaken our community to awareness about what an environmental disaster that mass-burn incinerator represented. I became what is called a NIMBY—Not In My Back Yard—and found myself involved in the environmental politics in our town. And fighting that incinerator became, for me, a spiritual experience.

My strategy involved working through my neighborhood association, which happened to be the most powerful and active association in the community. I used their monthly publication to announce the formation of a group I was starting in order to create a community recycling program. Sixteen people came to the fore, and over a two-year period we organized a citywide curbside recycling pick-up program. Although the incinerator was eventually built, our efforts sparked a new level of environmental consciousness throughout our city.

My environmental work brought additional benefits into my life. At the first meeting of my recycling group, I was amazed and delighted to see my house filled with strangers, all united in a common cause. In time I found myself once again engaged with a group of like-minded people, similar to the one I had so enjoyed in college. The sense of community we were able to create was awesome—yet another spiritual experience for me.

Because I had organized the curbside recycling program, I was asked to participate on several different boards and became involved with the Earth Day organization. Then the governor invited me to sit on the Recycling and Energy Development Board. This was actually a paid position, for which I was qualified because I had become known as a solid-waste expert.

As my environmental work continued over the years, I began to wonder, "How did we get to this place on the planet? Why is the human race killing itself with such disrespect for the environment?" Soon after these questions arose, there came a single day in which three different people gave me a total of seven books. All of them had to do with the environment—and spirituality. "That's interesting," I thought. "That's definitely a sign."

Reading those books and other extensive materials, and after much thought, I came to a realization: Most people living in the city keep the windows shut in their houses to hold in the heat or air conditioning. Then they get into their cars through an attached garage and drive to work, keeping the car windows closed. They park underneath the building where they work and take the elevator up to an office where they couldn't open the windows even if they wanted to. People don't realize their connectedness to the environment, don't recognize that they are part of nature, because they don't experience it! They don't realize that nature is alive with the same spirit that makes them alive.

Another factor in this lack of awareness about our connectedness was the change in the way cities were structured after the Second World War. In the old days, cities were designed so that every so many blocks there would be an intersection with some kind of business at each of the four corners—stores and restaurants to which people could walk from home and be in community with their neighbors. But after the Second World War, shopping malls came into existence—and sprawling suburbs with no sidewalks. As people flocked to accept the supposed improvements afforded by these modern lifestyle changes, community-style neighborhoods fell apart. In trying to stimulate the economy, we did away with the factors that allowed people to live in community. As a result, people could no longer feel a connection to their neighbors, the community, or nature.

Along with the attempt to make things faster and cheaper came the idea of planned obsolescence. Products were made for one-time use only. Plastic bottles, utensils, and many other common items were designed to be discarded with no thought of recycling or reuse. No one understood the long-term consequences this would have on our landfills—or that we were rapidly moving toward depleting the earth's resources.

Studying these factors allowed me to understand why our society would build such an atrocity as an unneeded mass-burn incinerator. At the same time, it crystallized my resolve to do whatever I could to save the environment. This mission became a spiritual discipline and motivated me to deepen my own connection to nature.

First Shoot Breaks through the Fertile Soil

Soon after I returned home, my sister had her baby. Sharon and I were so close that we would talk on the phone several times a day and get together at least three or four times a week. Wherever we went Evan, her son, came with us. She and I had a great time with him. It was so much fun being the auntie! I remember saying one time to Sharon: "You know, it's kind of like we're both his mother." This statement angered her. "No way! He's mine! I am the mother!" she responded. At the time I had no idea of the literal truth my chance statement had portended.

In 1993, everything changed. Sharon was diagnosed with cancer. Then my father died of old age, and about four months later, my mother also passed away. At that point I took over the management of my father's business property and, together with my siblings, became an owner. Two weeks later, my sister Sharon died of cancer after a one-year battle. Evan, my nephew, was seven at the time, and with my sister's death he became an orphan. When Evan was an infant, Sharon had married a man who wasn't Evan's biological father, so her widower was only Evan's stepfather. For various reasons, Sharon's husband was not well suited to rearing a child. Yet Evan was my flesh and blood; there was no question in my mind that he was my responsibility.

Though Evan lived at his stepfather's house for another two years after Sharon died, I was the one who picked him up from school, arranged his sports activities, volunteered at his school, bought his school clothes, helped him with his homework, fed him dinner, tucked him in bed, and read him a story—all this while having to run my father's business.

One thing that really saved me during this whole experience was a couple in their seventies who were living with me at the time: Moon and Mary. I had met Moon years before through mutual friends. When an unusual type of cancer required that he come to the city for special treatments, I invited him and his wife to stay with me rather than make that several-hours-long drive all the time. Eventually, they moved in with me altogether and stayed for two years. The kindness I extended to them wound up being a total blessing to me. They were there when my parents and sister died, and their support was an incredible gift. They were my angels, my best friends, my anchor. They heard my feelings, concerns, fears, and sadness about all my losses in that intense time. A kindly pair of surrogate parents, they dispensed sage advice and lent me strength through my trials.

With the sudden loss of his mother and grandparents, I felt my nephew, Evan, had had more than his share of abandonment. As the only family constant in his life, I made it my mission to give him all the stability I could. My house was just a few blocks from where he had lived with my sister and his stepfather. So even when he came to live with me I was able to keep him in the same school, in the same neighborhood, with the same friends. My main priority was to do everything I could to help him adjust to the drastic changes in his life.

Arranging my life to meet Evan's needs put the plans I had for myself on hold. I had always seen myself spending the rest of my life on one or the other coast after my parents had passed on. Once Evan came to live with me, such a move was out of the question.

A major part of my social life in those days revolved around activities at Evan's school. I made friends with the other mothers; I went to teas and luncheons and joined book clubs with them. But though I made lots of daytime friends, I found that, as a single woman, I was never included in any evening activities.

With the lack of a thriving social life in the city, on the weekends I found myself wanting to spend more and more time at my log cabin, which sits in the wooded hills about an hour and a half south of the city. Scattered about the hills are quaint log cabins and old farmhouses. Deer are everywhere. It's a simple lifestyle, rustic but very rich, an oasis for renewal where nature thrives. It was also only about twenty minutes from my college town, so there were many friends I could visit. Whenever Evan spent the weekend with his stepdad, I would go to my wooded retreat in the country.

But over time, even this attempt to replenish myself in the grace of nature and friends at my country cabin fell through. As Evan reached his teenage years, he needed more supervision on the weekends than he was getting from his stepfather. I had to give up the nature renewal I got from my country visits and was cut off from the friends and community feeling that so deeply nourished me.

A Bud Is Formed

One day while visiting my chiropractor, I mentioned my feelings of isolation and told her I needed to find a circle of women. She immediately handed me a flier about a feminine spirituality workshop—eight sessions set to take place over a period of a year. There was a single requirement: one had to start with the first session—which, as coincidence would have it, was scheduled for that very weekend.

Though I was a little skeptical at first, the group turned out to be perfect for me and triggered a big turning point in my life. It consisted of two women facilitating the workshop and eight participants. The program centered around three major activities: sharing meaningful facets of our lives; nature-based rituals designed to grow awareness about our connection to nature; and lessons about women's history, especially in terms of spirituality. Each of these facets improved my life in a major way.

In the first two-day session, each woman was given about two hours to share her spiritual history. At session's end we all knew each other's "herstory." At each subsequent gathering, the personal sharing would take off from where we had left off, so there was continuity as each woman's story unfolded over time.

While initially it was not crucial to me that the group consisted of all women, I soon noticed that, as an all-women group, we could be more open with each other and reveal things differently from how we might have if the group had included men. Listening to these women's stories month after month was very helpful to me mentally, emotionally, and spiritually, and I gained perspective about issues in my own life. All our stories seemed to boil down to a common theme: we all have the same fears of being hurt and the same hope of being loved. My story was basically the same as anyone else's story—a search for meaningful human connection.

The sharing in those circles gave me the perspective to overcome the gender-inferiority feelings from my youth. My father had often proclaimed, "Women have no brains for business," along with "Everybody knows that women are stupid." Participation in this group allowed me to develop the personal confidence to realize that I was just as good, smart, and capable as anyone else. I had just as much right as anyone to feel whole. It let me realize that we all have some personal flaws, and that, despite any limitations, I should approach the world in the expectation that I will be accepted as I am, imperfections and all.

In those days, I was under a lot of stress. I had been called to take over the leadership of the family. I was rearing Evan and managing my father's business. And I was madly in love! But alas, the boyfriend was an alcoholic, so this was both a joy and a torture at the same time. Sharing with these women helped me to forgive my boyfriend for the pain I suffered in that relationship. (Al-Anon helped too, as did a year of tears and two very dear male friends who allowed me to vent my sorrows with them.)

I came to see that boyfriend as someone who carried a lot of pain from a torturous childhood. Picking up the bottle may have eased his pain for the short term, but only made his life worse in the long run.

What allowed me to break up with him for the final time was that I realized I could help him more by leaving him. I had concluded that if there were anything I could do to help him, it would be by my example. In not allowing myself to be further drawn into the drama of his drinking, I was choosing a more whole life for myself. I was drawing the lines I needed to keep my life intact, however much pain it caused me. Even if it meant I would be more alone, I was choosing a life of health, wholeness, and happiness. I hoped this would light a path for him toward greater wholeness as well. It was in sharing my sorrows with the women in the group that I came to this conclusion. This was one of the most important decisions of my life.

The ritual portion of each women's spirituality session began with all of us lining up in crone order, eldest first, as we filed into the area where our ritual would take place. Our two leaders would anoint each woman with water and cleanse her with the smoke of burning sage as she went in. Each woman would say the words, "I enter this circle in perfect love and perfect trust." In the center of the room was a table decorated as an altar, depicting symbols for the particular season of the year we were celebrating.

Our ceremony would revolve around the four directions: east, south, west, and north. These represented the elements of air, fire, water and earth, respectively. And each of those directions and elements would correspond to aspects of ourselves, which we would honor as well. The east/wind represented the mind, intellect, reason, sciences, travel, and youth. The south/sun represented strength, passion, transformation, will, sex, and energy. The west/water corresponded to emotions, intuition, daring, wisdom, clarity, and healing. The north/earth corresponded to stability, order, grounding, silence, birth, death, beginnings, endings, and fertility. We would then sit, and each woman would in turn light a candle on the altar and say her name.

At this point the circle was officially "closed," and our two leaders would begin the readings and exercises. The substance of the closed circle would vary with the theme of the season we were honoring. Each gathering was creatively unique; we found multiple ways to express gratitude for our lives and honor the Creative Energy that is the Spirit of All.

There usually would be a thought-provoking reading from the amazing library the two leaders kept. I remember one reading from Judith Duerk's *Circle of Stones* that led me to ponder what it would have been like for me if, when I had had my first period, my mother and grandmother had taken me to buy my first bra, we had met my dad for lunch, and he gifted me a piece of jewelry. How different from our hush-hush culture where such life passages are barely mentioned, let alone celebrated.

Many of our ritual exercises were done outdoors. We might go sit by a creek, meditate on the creek, and write a poem about it. Sometimes we would do a meditative walk in a nearby labyrinth, a circular, winding footpath used to quiet the mind and enhance contemplation via "walking meditation."

We always ended our session by identifying what we wanted either to let go of or to manifest in our lives. We might throw roses into a pond with our thoughts of what we wanted to let go of; to manifest, we might plant seeds with manifestation wishes or write our wishes on ribbons and tie them in the trees for the wind to deliver to the universe. The leaders were gradually working us up to the realization that *we are nature*, and that how nature works is how *we* work. Nature is a source from which we can draw, and it is the same force that we are.

Sharing such ritual experiences in this community of women was just about the perfect thing to fill the need I had been feeling for greater connection, meaning, and community. But of even greater impact was the third element: the *history* I learned about women!

For the Healing History lessons, part of each session would be spent with our two leaders reading to us or showing videos about history. However, this was not "your father's history lesson." We started with *Women and Spirituality*, a series of three videos. The first one, *Goddess Remembered*, examined goddess-worshipping religions from before the time of Christ. The second, *The Burning Times*, told about the witch persecutions that swept through Europe only a few hundred years ago. The third, *Full*

Circle, focused on the ancestral roots that connect us to each other and to all living things.

This information amazed me. From my upbringing and from lessons in school, I had gotten the impression that male dominance—where men would beat women over their heads with clubs and drag them to their caves by their hair—had been prevalent in society from the earliest times. Instead, in this group, I learned that human history is tens of thousands of years old. In ancient times, the divine essence of the universe was considered to be a feminine energy. As the entity through which life came into being, the female had been regarded as sacred for tens of thousands of years, so women actually had a rich history. And it is only in the last sixty years or so that this material has become more widely known.

The group leaders taught us about the work of Marija Gimbutas, an anthropologist known for her research into the Neolithic and Bronze Age cultures of "Old Europe," a term she herself introduced. Her works, published between 1946 and 1991, introduced a new perspective that largely differed from the previously male-dominated schools of anthropology and mythological interpretation.

Gimbutas, our group leaders told us, was the first person to shed light on the role of the female divine in prehistoric times. She unearthed female figurines, most of which had round bellies and very large breasts. Where previously archaeologists had assumed these to be sexual objects, Gimbutas saw them as sacred objects. She pointed out that these were goddess images reflecting the spiritual importance of the feminine in these societies.

After Gimbutas, our workshop covered a number of other writers who have described women's role in history as other than one of submission. The works we read included *The Chalice and the Blade,* by Riane Eisler; *When the Women Were Drummers,* by Layne Redmond; and *When God Was a Woman,* by Merlin Stone.

We learned that in the development of agriculture, the wandering-tribe lifestyle gave way to the first small towns. These societies were egalitarian: Men and women worked cooperatively in partnership. There was no such thing as male dominance. The largely peaceful communities they lived in didn't even have walls around them for protection.

While neither gender was dominant, these societies were matrilineal. Before the institution of marriage, it was not so evident which child came from which man, but it was always clear who the mother was. For this reason, parentage and possessions were passed down from generation to generation through the mother's side.

Over time, these peaceful communities were subjected to invasions by cultures that are called Indo-Europeans. These male-dominated tribes would descend upon these villages to rape and pillage. Because these Indo-Europeans came from Nordic climates around the time of the ice age, it is thought that the extremely harsh weather to which they were accustomed influenced the type of spiritual entity these people envisioned. Theirs was a fiery war god, and male. For hundreds of years, these Indo-Europeans plundered the peaceful societies of old Europe.

These Indo-Europeans gradually devastated the matristic cultures and destroyed their matrilineal inheritance patterns through the use of fear and force. Eventually laws and social institutions were set up, marriage among them. This ensured that women could only have sex with one man, and therefore men could know for sure who their children were. In this way the parentage could be passed down through the male line, and the wealth could remain in male control as well. Gradually the matrilineal societies yielded to patriarchal ones, and the feminine goddess concept was supplanted by the male warrior god.

In the women's spirituality group, we were also taught about how, three hundred years after Jesus died, the Bible was changed. Apparently, before the Roman emperor Constantine, there were many more books in what was then considered to be the Bible. Some were redundant and poorly written, but perhaps more open-ended, or less definitive in the type of spirituality they described. In the hope of making the scripture more accessible to a general audience, Constantine called together the Council of Nicea, where, together with the leaders of the church, he eliminated at least twenty books from the Bible. Another twenty-five or so were edited, condensed, and simplified.

Constantine and his priests effectively designed what they wanted people to believe about the Christian religion. Unfortunately, the eliminated parts were the ones that spoke of the ways we humans are connected to the world around us (which we know from scholars who are now reading the Dead Sea Scrolls, in which some of the original documents can still be found in their original form.) Hence a link between our Western civilization and the wisdom of ancient times was broken, leaving us largely unaware in our culture of ways the ancient civilizations had portrayed divine Spirit. They saw the Divine not as something separate but as something that dwells within each of us and connects us to the whole Universe. In contrast, thanks to Constantine, the religious worldview handed down to us through Christianity is one of fear, exclusiveness, rules about behavior, and threats of punishment.

In summary, through the history portion of the women's spirituality workshop, we learned that in ancient times the feminine principle, the goddess (and not the usual patriarchal male god) was humankind's earliest notion of the spiritual entity responsible for our existence. And we learned that these ancient notions of spirituality most likely encouraged each person to develop a personal relationship with the Divine, as opposed to having it mitigated by a church authority such as a priest. That worldview contained a wisdom, a beauty, and an inclusiveness that I prefer to incorporate now as my own.

The Lotus Unfurls

Being taught that women were once considered sacred enabled me to begin to feel my power and had a huge and healing impact on me. My collection of replicas of the little sacred female goddess figures now brings me confidence and joy. The knowledge about the goddesses, and learning about the matrilineal societies of the past, erased some of the ill effects of the patriarchal society into which I was born.

What are the effects of growing up with your own father telling you, "Everybody knows that women are stupid?" I knew I wasn't stupid but felt that, as Dad had said it, it must be that everybody else thought women were stupid, too. That profoundly affected the way that I related to men: I thought they all would be like my father and assume that, as a woman, I was stupid. I never had the self-confidence to open up to men enough to share who I was, what I had to say, or what I thought about things. I felt powerless. I kept the lotus inside me, my true essence, tightly wrapped up.

From the knowledge I gained in the group, I began to see that, just like everyone else, I have imperfections—but that has nothing to do with my being a woman. Now I can forgive myself for my flaws. I am no longer afraid of men. I no longer withhold my comments for fear they won't be respected. I have even been able to forgive my father for the worldview he imposed on me, for his assertion that "women are stupid" was simply something he himself had been taught to believe.

The feminine spirituality program helped me feel better as a woman and empowered my sense of the essence of who I really am: I am nature. What makes the tree alive is the same thing that makes me alive—Creative Energy, Divinity, the Power of the Universe, the Power of the Goddess' womb—God. I am nature that came from the earth, which came from the Creative Energy of the Universe. Everything is of the same Source; everything is linked. Whatever happens to one affects everything else. So every thing, person, animal, thought, word, deed has immense power over what happens to all of creation. The more I learned about my relation to the earth and to nature, the more grounded I felt. For the first time in my life I was walking on really solid ground. I realized that I am part of the web of all there is!

From that sense of groundedness, I moved on to develop a sense of balance. In the past, if someone criticized or made fun of me, I would want to melt into my chair and retreat in humiliation. Now I feel I can handle anything someone might throw at me. If I don't agree with someone, I have the guts to say so. And if someone says something rude to me, rather than become unnerved, I can maintain my equilibrium. Over time, this groundedness and balance has expanded into a feeling of contentment. No matter what challenges life might bring, I now know I can deal with them.

Lotus in Full Bloom

As a result of the feminine spirituality group, I experienced these different levels of empowering wisdom. Over time, out of the feelings of groundedness, balance, and contentment there arose another sensation, much more intense than the others. It is as if a lotus had unfurled inside of me.

In the past, I had kept my sense of my true self, what I now call my "lotus," tightly bound in a kind of psychic twine. Through the insights, growth, and spiritual experiences in the women's workshop, I eventually unwrapped this restricting twine, and an all-encompassing feeling of peace blossomed within me.

With my lotus blooming, wide and beautiful as can be, I no longer live in fear of someone hurting me. I allow the lotus to be fully open, come what may. Who I am is not my body—not my fingernails or the shape of my legs. My body is the package, the vehicle that carries around my essence.

When two people first fall in love, the feeling is very intense. After they have been together for a time, the feeling becomes subtler. My intense feeling of peace, my fully-blossomed-lotus feeling, is like that. At first I was very aware of its presence swirling in the middle of my gut. Now it has become a subtle sensation that I know and trust is always within me. Occasionally it might get rattled; I can sometimes actually feel it shake, letting me know when I am in a situation in which I need to be mindful and to protect myself—an unloving situation that I need to move away from.

This feeling of the blossomed lotus, the awareness of peace at the center of my being, is a most precious treasure. I might explain what happened by saying that I was able to merge my physical awareness with my sense of myself as a spiritual being. The creative energy that makes me who I am is the same energy that makes up everything in the universe. My being able to open up to this sense is what the blossomed lotus really is. It is this essence of peace, the true essence of myself. It is me loving all there is, and all there is loving me back in a weaving called the Universe.

Only after the year-long feminine spirituality workshop ended did I wonder critically about its origins. Did its rituals characterize a pagan spirituality? Were they Wiccan? I see now why our instructors left these associations unsaid. There are many misconceived notions surrounding pagan/Wiccan spirituality that could deter people from the learning offered in the workshops. I myself would definitely have hesitated to sign up for that program had I known it involved Wiccan rituals.

Now that I know and understand the true basis of Wicca, I can actually call myself a Wiccan. It's not that we Wiccans actually believe there is a god or a goddess that requires worship. I don't really worship anything. The basis of my spirituality is simply that I honor the energy from nature of which I am a part.

Now that my nephew, Evan, has grown up and is spreading his own wings in the world, I have gone to live full-time in my beloved country retreat. I live a very rustic lifestyle in my log cabin, immersed in the nature of thick-forested hills.

I am in community with a group of women who get together throughout the year to celebrate the eight Wiccan holy days. Each woman shares in hosting and leading the rituals. But the Summer Solstice is always celebrated as an annual retreat at my cabin for a week at the end of June, when Nature is in full summer peak bloom. We dance and sing, share stories and revel together in the womblike comfort of Mother Earth—the holiest temple there is.

I continue to broaden my conscious awareness of the spiritual essence of all there is through various spiritual practices: meditation, yoga, and walks in nature. I read books by spiritual leaders, old and new. I go to presentations and interpret dream messages.

I aim at being good to myself: to my mind, my body, and my spirit. I seek to be better able to help others have a happy, peaceful life, to light the way for them by my example. I also seek to help Mother Earth, in her trauma, to survive in beauty and health as the nurturing presence on which all life depends.

In my town I have become known as a ceremonialist. People will have me come to bless their studio or do a ritual for an event in their life. I feel lucky to have come to claim my inner power. My further studies have led to a master's degree in wisdom spirituality through Wisdom University. I have trained as a spiritual director and am currently in training to become an eco-spiritual mentor. I see all of this work as an ongoing attempt to raise consciousness regarding the bigger picture of reality.

Despite my childhood brainwashing about the presumed inabilities of women, today I successfully manage the business property my father had cautiously left in the hands of a man from outside our family. That man lived only a short time longer than my dad, and I was the only one who could take over—just one more example of how I have been able to transcend the supposed limitations my society would have imposed on me for being female.

There are many women like me, reared in a patriarchal environment and brought up to feel insecure about themselves because they were born the "wrong" sex. Lucky as I am to have surmounted all that, I have shared my story in the hope that it might help some of those women (and any men who might find it relevant). My goal is to help others come to know the precious, sacred essence of love that they are.

The end result of my spiritual experiences is an understanding that all religions are focused on Love. And Love is really what the cosmos is. And the cosmos is God! All that is, is the Cosmos of Love. We and everything in the Cosmos are part of the ALL. God, not so much as a being, but as the universal concept of Love, now forms the basis of my philosophy and my faith. A large part of what I have realized as I have gotten older is that the ALL is pretty damned awesome!

—⌘—

Despite Jean's atypical choice of tradition, many aspects of her path point to a probable current Mystic stance. Her whole life story seems to be one of continually seeking ever more community—certainly not because she is afraid of being alone, nor because any such group would help support her identity, but rather just for the opportunity to participate with others in celebrating life.

Note Jean's interpreting the event that, in a single day, three people handed her seven books dealing with the environment and spirituality as "a sign" of a personal direction she should take. Though some in more superficial spiritual circles can take this concept to ridiculous levels, being able accurately to read such signs as personal messages is a trait of spiritual maturity.

One of Jean's clearest Mystic traits is her deep connection to nature; another is the way her circle of concern has broadened to include the environment.

Her strong sense of personal responsibility is evidenced in her willingness to rearrange her life around the needs of the nephew who fell into her care and in the way she framed her decision to leave her alcoholic boyfriend as using her example for his benefit.

Note her ability to take the perspective of the people who harmed her and allow that perspective to lead her to forgiveness. She "came to see the [alcoholic] boyfriend as someone who carried a lot of pain from a torturous childhood" and said of her father that the cruel dictates about women with which he filled her childhood years was just "something he himself had been taught to believe." Through that ability to take the perspective of the other person, Jean was able to forgive both the boyfriend and her father.

Of course, her wording about the Oneness of creation and the single message from all religions is also typical of the Mystic stance.

Chapter 12

The Higher Power . . . and I (Catherine)

Catherine is an exuberant Baby Boomer-aged lady with strong positive energy that belies her chaotic past. I could not help but wonder how a person with her frightening story could hide so much pain behind the bright cheerful face she presents to the world. But in working with her on this story, I have come to realize that the answer really lies in her spiritual focus. Despite amazing odds and unimaginable insults from those closest to her and from life in general, Catherine's spirituality leads her to look forward to each day, exuding energy and happiness. Her main position toward life is one of gratitude—just for the joy of being alive, just for the opportunity to be going to work, for the simplest things life has to offer.

While Catherine's story fails to describe an explicit distancing from religious belief on Rational grounds, watch how her current Mystic traits are displayed in almost catalog form in this story: forgiveness, gratitude, a unitive worldview, and a willingness to submit to the will of the God of her understanding.

—◦◦◦—

Forced Powers

Dad and the Russian Church: these are the two powers I recall most forcefully from my 1950s childhood. Dad was a strong man who controlled his family with an iron hand. Though we lived in a small town in Pennsylvania, our Russian identity was very important to Dad, as was participation in the Russian Orthodox Church. He had arranged our family's entire social life around that church. My siblings and I were reared in the Russian Church, learned the Russian language, belonged to a Russian club, and sang Russian hymns in the choir. Even the prayers we said were in Russian.

Despite extensive Russian lessons and Dad's insistence on close church participation, I never really understood all those Russian prayers—and certainly never expected any effect from them. I never really understood the church precepts, either. From an early age, I felt that the church brought only empty ritual into my life—that, and the threat of an angry, punishing God, spying on my every move. At the same time, our house was quite chaotic in those days, with lots of yelling. My brother had fallen in with a wild crowd and was constantly in trouble, drinking, missing school, and even going to jail. My parents had so much going on with him that I felt mostly ignored. Though I tried hard to please my dad by getting all A's in school, he hardly even saw me. Between the chaos in the house and the fear of sin instilled in me by the church, I lived in constant fear of doing something wrong. I spent most of my childhood alone in my room, where I could easily escape into the words of a story, any story—I would sometimes read the same one over and over again. Books were my escape into a warmer, softer world.

Losing Power

When I married, I moved to a part of Wisconsin with no Russian churches. I suffered continual criticism from my father about my lack of church attendance. He could not understand that there was a place with no Russian churches and would have been horrified if I sought out a church of a different denomination. Even for me, my Russian identity was so engrained that a church of another denomination was unthinkable. So I ceased to participate in any type of worship services.

Once that happened, and without the support of a church community to bind me to religion, any faith I might have had slipped away over the years. Eventually I rejected God and religion altogether. I had two children by then, and my husband traveled a lot with his job. With no family in the area, I had no one around to help out. With neither God nor man around to lean on, I isolated myself and became used to handling things on my own. This made me strong, really strong.

And a good thing it was that I became so strong, because life had some surprises in store. When my adorable baby boy, James, was about one year old, he fell gravely ill. We feel it was the DPT shots that caused the problem. He was very sick for a long time. That illness left him with serious permanent developmental delays we are still dealing with, thirty-three years later. During all this time of unimaginable stress, my husband reacted by escaping even more and was almost never home. This put a huge strain on our marriage and was extremely painful for me. My baby's illness only increased my isolation; still, I did not reach out to anyone for help. Eventually, my marriage broke up, leaving me even more alone. Even though I was a single parent rearing two children by myself, one with serious disabilities, I received no physical, financial, or moral support from my family.

Unfortunately, during this incredibly difficult time I never thought to call on the one thing that could have made my life more tolerable. It had been a huge part of my upbringing as a child, but as an adult I could not see it. It was free, and there for the choosing, but I never chose it. In the darkness of those days, I could not see the hand God held out to me. In my troubles, I never once thought to reach out and take that hand. After all, what type of God would have allowed my baby to be so sick? Instead, I chose to deal with all the problems on my plate entirely on my own.

Before long, I met Jack, a handsome man at work with dancing, bright blue eyes and a marvelous sense of humor. For three years I tried to ignore him, because I had a firm policy of not dating coworkers. Besides, he was a bit wild and a drinker as well—not my kind of guy. But he pursued me persistently, and we began to hang out together. Over time we became close, and at some point I realized that he was just in my life. I found his wild demeanor scary and exciting, but did not connect any of it with alcoholism. I just thought that guys who liked beer, liked their beer.

The day I met Jack's mother, I got my first warning. "Catherine," she said, "Jack is an alcoholic. If you are going to be involved with him, you must get yourself to Al-Anon. And he should *not* be drinking around your children." I was devastated. I really liked this guy. But behind my denial, I knew that he was irresponsible. He just wanted to play and drink and was certainly not husband material. I went to Al-Anon, but I did not get what they were trying to tell me. During a spell when it seemed Jack had quit drinking, I went ahead and married him—naively thinking everything would be fine.

I could not have been more wrong. Our marriage deteriorated rapidly into a hell I can barely describe. I called the police night after night. James, my younger son with the disabilities, was terrified. Jeremy, my older son, left our home. Sometimes Jack and I would have awful fights. I was hurting so bad inside myself. What I didn't know then, but would later find out, was that some of my hurts had nothing to do with my husband, but instead went back to my own childhood. Though Jack was the alcoholic, my own internal pain rose up from the depths of some of my childhood experiences and spilled out onto him, thus compounding our problems many times over. At one point, when it seemed things had hit a bottom, I somehow found the strength to insist Jack either get help with his alcoholism or get out.

Finding Power

By the time I demanded that Jack get help, I must have been ready to allow a small crack in my psychic armor. Through this crack, it seems the entity most people call God was able to slip me some of his grace. I thought Jack was the only one who needed help, but, though I could not yet see where it was coming from, a divine finger from above pointed *me* in a direction that would forever change *my* life.

Jack agreed to visit a local substance-abuse rehabilitation center. Here we learned that the whole family would require treatment, because alcoholism affects everyone it touches. For my part, I would go, once again, to Al-Anon. This time I heard what they were saying and, from that moment, my life began to change.

Al-Anon has been offering hope and help to families and friends of alcoholics for more than fifty years. In that wonderful program, I saw the wounds of folks who had suffered great tragedy in their lives and yet had a peacefulness about them. Something good was definitely going on there; the program was generating tremendous hope. I too had suffered tragedy, and I wanted some of that healing.

I learned so much from the weekly meetings. I was assigned a terrific sponsor who really reached out to help me. She always attended my group meetings with me. In this small and intimate group, with my sponsor by my side I found I could be more comfortable sharing. The love and understanding I felt from these people would bring tears to my eyes. I loved these meetings and never missed a chance to attend.

Over time, I came to realize that what I had always considered to be normal Russian behavior on the part of my father had actually been alcoholism, something I had no inkling of before. I had always pictured a drunk as someone who lay on the road and didn't work. Well, my dad never missed a day of work, but he was a binge drinker. And oh, how our family had suffered for it! I had always hated my brother for stealing all the attention when we were growing up, but I never understood why. Once Al-Anon helped me learn it was all about the alcohol, I found some degree of compassion for him.

Slowly, I gained the strength to face the hurts alcoholism had caused way back in my childhood and to see how it had colored my life ever since. I learned that behavior I had ignored in my first husband had also been due to alcoholism. And I learned that in my relationship with my alcoholic second husband, I was a codependent. It was not Jack who had introduced me to alcoholism; my entire life had been determined by my family's association with the disease.

Once I learned all this, it felt like a weight had been lifted. Previously I had thought that everything that had gone wrong was my fault. Now the Al-Anon people were telling me I had been born into this problem and they would be showing me a way to escape its ugly grasp. I had thought I had begun attending these meetings to help Jack: I thought they were going to tell me how to get him to stop drinking. But I learned that it doesn't work like that. Instead, *I* was the one who had to change. Al-Anon taught me that as long as a person is a codependent, living with alcoholism in their family, he or she is not growing. I found out those meetings were to help me get well, to learn how to stop being a codependent. To get well, I would have to detach from the disease. Of course, this meant I had to detach somewhat from my husband. It was a loving program, but I learned that you have to take care of yourself first.

And for me, it worked. I gradually came to accept that I was powerless over the dreadful illness that had so plagued both my original and my adult families. Before long I learned how to surrender to the effects it had on my life and began looking for ways in which what I had learned could help me grow. I came to love the peace of the recovery program.

The people at Al-Anon helped in other ways as well. They helped me go back to school. Then they helped me get a business suit so I could get a professional job. Suddenly, I had a life of my own and special people who supported me and helped me along my path. After a while, I didn't even care if my husband was drinking or not. I was getting my life together, because there were people at Al-Anon who loved and accepted me. I continued with the program because it was helping *me*.

Soon enough, I started getting well. Then the big miracle of the program happened. When the spouse of an alcoholic person finally starts getting her or his own life together, the drinker sees that if they don't clean up, they are going to lose that person. They start to think, "Hey!

I better make some changes." That is the miracle of the Al-Anon program. So when Jack saw me learning to put my life in order without him, he began to take the AA program more seriously and was able to stop drinking. Then we would go to meetings together, and that was just fabulous. We were able to begin to become a family.

But the greatest thing I learned at Al-Anon was news of the Higher Power. If I wanted my life to get better, the members had told me at the beginning, I would have to turn my life and will over to my Higher Power. Once I learned to recognize the voice of this Higher Power, I felt surrounded by a genuine caring. Because of my Russian background, the most natural thing for me to call this Higher Power is "God." But, unlike the cold, distant, unyielding God of the Russian Church, this Higher Power was more loving and less demanding. I felt for the first time in my life that this Higher Power, my God, loved me and wanted the best for me. It was sweet; it gave me hope. Call it whatever you like, but the work of this Higher Power was magical, and it was here to help me!

My Power

Those things happened over twenty years ago. I guess I was never destined for an easy life because, to this day, I seem to have more challenges thrown my way than the average person. Without the Al-Anon program and the Higher Power, I would have been headed for a very negative existence. Instead, in looking back, I can see that I have Al-Anon to thank for helping my life course totally change direction. The people at Al-Anon showed me how to get my outer day-to-day life in order, and the Higher Power they introduced me to brought strength to my inner being. This got my life on a more even keel. Now I feel I have the skills and spiritual backing to deal with just about any trouble that might arise.

Now, rather than spend my life fending off one hardship after the next, I find I can put more energy into focusing on my spiritual walk. The more I surrender to the Higher Power, the more I find I can grow.

The more I grow, the more I can bask in joy. Thus, I want to remain ever open to further progress on my spiritual journey. I begin each day with a spiritual reading, in an effort to continually refine and deepen my spiritual beliefs. I look for further growth wherever I can find it.

So my affiliation with the Higher Power has brought a type of personal power to my existence—not a way of controlling things, but rather a means of finding the grace in whatever challenges life throws at me. I have my reliance on the Higher Power, the God of my understanding, to thank for giving me a spiritual stance I love, for the perspective I have gained in trying to approach my family in a loving way, for the understanding I have about some of the life circumstances that have brought me to this point.

Gifts from the Higher Power

For about twenty years I had worked at a huge law firm, eventually managing their database program. It was a negative and viciously competitive environment, full of big egos interested only in money. There was no hint of human compassion in that office, let alone any notion of a spiritual purpose for the company. Every day I would ask myself, "Why am I here?"

When the firm broke up, I planned to take a year off. I wanted to do some gardening and reading and just relax. I began to pray for the type of job I would want when it was time to go back to work. Every night I would pray and write in my journal, "I want a really special job. I want a part-time job, close to home. I want a job that will allow me to be a part of the community and contribute to its betterment. Most of all, I want a positive environment—the opposite of the law firm." That is all I put out there.

Since I had been in the law firm for so long, I thought I should get some practice interviewing for a job, just for the experience. So I began sending out my resume even though I didn't really want a job yet. Occasionally I would go for what I had intended as a practice interview, but, possibly because I was so relaxed in it, by the time I got home I usually found a phone message offering me the job.

One night as I was leaving the community center after exercise class, I picked up a copy of our weekly county newspaper. There was a tiny ad at the bottom of the last page that somehow caught my eye: "General office assistant with computer skills needed for small Christian school." The area code and exchange matched mine, so I knew it was nearby. I faxed my resume the next day, and within a minute they called me. It turned out the school was within walking distance of my house. When I arrived for my interview, I could immediately feel the positive atmosphere. They were especially impressed with my experience with the Customer Relationship Management (CRM) database system I had managed at the law firm. They were about to implement a similar system and really needed my help. I tried hard to find something wrong with this job, but there was nothing. It was exactly what I had been looking for: close to home, part time, positive atmosphere, and the job description matched my skills exactly. And what better way to contribute to a community than working in the school? This was almost too good to be true. So I never got my desired full year off. I accepted the position and have been there ever since.

I am especially pleased with my job, because my initial impression about the positive environment turned out to be accurate. I can feel the Christian influence there every day: they do good things for each other; they love helping each other, and they pray daily for others.

The Church and Me

It may seem that I don't necessarily follow the same beliefs as the people I work with; they tend to hold a more literal view of God, seeing him as a human-like being in the sky. On the surface, it would seem that a Christian school would serve purposes different from mine. Yet I choose to be with these people each day, because I believe they are really doing what we are here for: helping children learn and allowing them to grow in faith. What they do in service to their God—an entirely separate Being who demands certain behaviors from them—I would do in service to goodness and to humanity, in service to the will of the Higher Power. In my case, my good works—the reason I dedicate my time to this job—are fueled by my belief that we are all connected. All people and the God, or Power, that created them are all part of the same entity.

I no longer attend the Russian church, at least not regularly. I do tend to trek back east every year at Easter to visit the old Russian church of my childhood, a place that represents my heritage. I go there mainly to honor my father and mother, who have long since passed. I can feel their spirit in that church when I go.

But I don't believe that I must be in church to feel God. While I believe there is a Creator of the Universe greater and more powerful than we are, I am quite sure it is not the punishing, judgmental God of the church of my youth. This Higher Power wants the best for me. While I don't know exactly what this Power is or what it looks like, I love feeling confident in its goodness. At Al-Anon they tend to refer to "the God of my under-standing." I like this phrase, because none of us really understands what God is. *God* is just a word we use to talk about this Higher Power, who could be anything, a concept totally beyond our comprehension.

Prayer

My job is an excellent example of the way prayer has worked in my life. I prayed for just the right job, and I got it, though not at all on the time frame or in the way I had planned. Today prayer, for me, is nothing like it was growing up, when it meant nothing to me. In my childhood, prayers were repetitive, ritualized, and all in Russian. The congregation had no choice about them, and I did not understand them. In fact, I think I mainly associated prayers with punishment, as they were often assigned in confession as penance for our sins.

One of the best things I learned at Al-Anon was a very different way to pray. It was there that I learned the most meaningful prayer of my life, the Serenity Prayer: "God grant me the serenity to accept the things

I cannot change, the courage to change the things I can, and the wisdom to know the difference." At the worst point in my marriage, when my husband was sometimes a raving maniac due to his substance abuse, the Serenity Prayer was what let me get to sleep at night. I would say it over and over again, and it would bring me peace. Through the Serenity Prayer I learned that I must accept whatever comes into my life as the will of God. This marked the beginning of a deeper type of prayer for me.

Now I love prayer, but not the ritualized prayer of my youth, nor prayers that ask for special favors from God. Rather, my prayer is very personal to me. I pray every day just because I love communicating with the Higher Power I call God. If I have an issue, I pray about it. I accept that whichever way things turn out, it will be in accordance with the will of the God of my understanding. So in my prayer, I am not trying to accomplish anything; I am not asking for any particular outcome or to control things. I now know that I can only be an instrument either for good or for evil. If I were to try to control things through my prayer, that would be a form of evil.

Acceptance

Ever since I learned the Serenity Prayer, accepting the will of God has been a huge theme for me—not only in my prayers but also in my daily life. I had to work hard to learn that acceptance is a form of goodness. Now, just knowing that the outcome is really not in my hands brings me peace. What happens is in the hands of the Higher Power, whom I trust. Where I used to be controlling and anxious, today I can say I am neither.

Just as I had to learn to accept the life circumstances imposed on me by my family's alcoholism, my son's permanent disability gave me yet another opportunity to learn acceptance. I have come to believe that he was given to me to help me learn this lesson in my life. Now I would not have him any other way, and I hope there is something he is learning from this experience as well. Through my studies, I have come to believe that each and every thing that happens to us is an opportunity to learn.

Growth

My studies and meditations have led me to the belief that humankind is immortal. What we are doing here on earth is learning lessons. Every experience that happens to us is for our personal growth. If we do not learn everything we are supposed to learn in one lifetime, we may come back many lifetimes until we finally get it.

I believe we are all connected and we are here to help each other. It's easy to talk about love, charity, and faith, but we must actually act on those values; we must *do* things that reinforce them if they are to enable us to grow.

The more we grow, the more Godlike we become. I believe each lifetime brings us closer than the last one—provided we are open to learning the lessons we were sent here to learn. I feel I have come very far; but when I compare myself with spiritual leaders like Gandhi, Mother Teresa, the Dali Lama, or Jesus, I know I still have a lot of growing to do. I need to work more on forgiveness.

Forgiveness

Having come to believe that people are placed in our path to help us grow spiritually, I feel I should be willing to forgive those closest to me who have heaped untold difficulties into my life—or, at least, I should work at developing this kind of forgiveness. Seeing how an unhappy experience has helped me grow can make it easier to forgive the person who caused it. The best example of this is my father.

One night not long after he died, I had a dream in which my father came into my room and sat on a chair with a sad but peaceful face. When he was alive he had been very controlling. I would never have dared tell him what I was feeling or thinking. He had never even acknowledged that he was an alcoholic and would never have listened had I tried to tell him about all the wrongs he had done our family with his alcoholism. Yet that evening, in my dream, I did tell him. In fact, I yelled at him. I yelled and yelled and he just let me vent. I told him all the things I should have been able to say when he was alive but could not because he was so mean. His drinking had affected my entire life.

Once I had that opportunity to vent to my heart's content, I felt my heart soften toward my dad. I could see how his alcoholism had shaped all the subsequent experiences that had helped me grow. After that I completely forgave him and never felt anger toward him again. I found he no longer had any control over me. In fact, in place of being angry, I began to notice traits I had inherited from him that I could be proud of: perseverance, a fierce determination, and tenacity. Another example is that he was very organized and kept careful notes about everything. I too am organized. This helped me tremendously when I was rearing two children alone and now helps me keep tasks on track in my job. These days, I hold only positive feelings toward my dad; I am grateful for the gifts I inherited from him and for the lessons his life has taught me.

Thinking back over the rest of my life, I realize I have been wronged by many of the people who were closest to me. Approaching people who are still in my life with forgiveness is an ongoing challenge. When things were at their worst with my husband Jack, I was forced to throw him out of the house, and I stayed mad at him for two years. Now I am not mad at him anymore. While we are not sure where we are headed with our relationship, I think I have at least managed to forgive him. I love him and want to move beyond the grudges. I just want to be able to say, "Okay such-and-such happened. Let's move on." I am working on my capacity to forgive all the time; it may be that forgiveness is something I will always need to work on.

Gratitude

I love the saying, "There, but for the Grace of God, go I." When some unexpected good thing happens, the first thing I do is thank God—or the universe—for honoring me this way. Even when there is a hardship, I try to find a position of gratitude from which to approach it.

Not long ago I had a most unfortunate encounter with an exercise belt and had to be rushed to the emergency room. It was very early in the morning, and the thing hit me right smack in the eye. I quickly clasped a towel to my face as the blood poured out—I thought—from my eye. As anyone would, I panicked and became hysterical. But that lasted only a few moments. Then suddenly I heard a voice softly say: "You are going to be okay." Right then, despite the blood still flowing, a feeling of deep peace enveloped me. I knew that even if I lost my eye, I would be okay. When the paramedics arrived and gently removed the towel from my face, I could see! It was blurry, but I had vision in both eyes. I became so grateful that at that moment, nothing else mattered. I have never experienced such a heightened state of gratitude in my life. I floated off to the emergency room and received twenty-two stitches to my face.

But the story doesn't end there; it gets much better. For many years, I have been estranged from my adult son, Jeremy. In the past, I had tried to do everything possible to change this, but it was his choice and I was forced to honor it. Over time I had grown to accept his decision and focused all my mothering efforts on James, my younger, disabled son. To my surprise, one day shortly after my accident, there arrived a lovely bouquet of flowers and a beautiful note. Jeremy had heard about my accident and wrote to tell me how devastated he was. Well, I am so thankful! He and his family are now back in my life. This brings me such joy; I am over the moon through it. I mist up just thinking about it. And just imagine: it all happened because of my freak accident. And so I continue to remain grateful for everything that happens in my life and am always excited to find out what will happen next.

Values, Purpose, and Love

Everything I care about involves my connections to people and the God of my understanding. Possessions and material success are unimportant to me. Recently in fact, I have been on a quest: I have been giving away many of my possessions. I want to live more simply. The more stuff you have, the more responsibility you have. If you purge your house of all the unnecessary stuff, you clean up your life. The Christians I work with talk about the riches gained from filling one's heart with love, faith, and hope—practicing charity and dispensing kindness. Even though their beliefs are not the same as mine, I have to agree that following the values the Christians preach helps one live a better life and works to create harmony and balance in one's life. The happiest people I know are the ones who aren't in a race for the next new gadget, new car, or largest house. In fact, I've noticed that folks who are most intent on pursuing material wealth and possessions are never satisfied and seem always to want more. By contrast, the Christians I work with find peace in the "goodness" values. And so do I.

Despite all the hardships I have had, I see every day as a wonderful gift. This morning as I drove to work I said a prayer: "I am so grateful just to be alive on this beautiful day and to be going to work." From where I sit now, I am thankful for every experience I have had. I can see almost all my life's hardships as gifts from a loving Power who wanted me to grow. If I had not had such trying circumstances—my family's alcoholism, my son's disability—all directed by the Higher Power, I would not be the person I am today. I truly believe that, whether good or bad, nothing happens without a purpose. What we do about it is the key to who we become.

Though I am very fortunate to have overcome most of the devastating effects of growing up in an alcoholic family, I cannot say it was easy—especially with respect to my marriage. I have had to throw my husband out of the house several times. We have sought counseling together. We have grown. Through all of this Jack and I know we love each other and are still very close. Most marriages like ours do not make it, and ours is complicated and uncertain. We marvel at the fact that we are still married. Officially, we are legally separated, but these days he is living in my house, and we continue to be great friends. I don't know where we are going, but for now, today, he is home and we are together as a family, and that's all I care about.

I have had to work very hard to learn some of life's major lessons. I am not in control; I am a pawn. Knowing this has allowed me to become stronger, more patient, more empathic, more loving. I also feel more responsible for my actions and have become more accepting of others. Most importantly, I have learned about forgiveness . . . and love. Love transcends our lives and is the key to our existence. Love is all there is.

—◦◦◦—

Catherine's first step toward spiritual maturity was to allow Al-Anon to help her rise above adversity. She could just as well have chosen not to accept that challenge and instead retreated in an effort of self-protection. We can pretty much guess how her life would have wound up had she preferred the victim role.

Nilah, David, and Jean also had to deal with serious life adversity. Like Catherine, each of them rose to the challenge and chose a transformative response to the hardships with which life presented them. The opposite approach would have been a defensive, self-protective one that would have left them seeking comfort and security, protection from the rocks in the road. We can begin to see how choosing the more vigorous, more flexible, and more challenging response can lead to a Mystic stance, where retreating in fear would lead a person to dig his heels ever more firmly into the Faithful level.

Further along the path these days, Catherine does a large amount of reading on spiritual topics. Certainly this has given her clues as to what constitutes spiritual maturity, and she has been able to push herself to progress from there. But isn't that how any of us grows? It seems growth can only happen when we rub up against ideas and thoughts that challenge our ordinary view of things.

However counter-intuitive it may have seemed when she first read about it, Catherine was open to the notion that forgiveness and gratitude toward those who had wronged her would be the more spiritual position, so she is working her way into it. She could just as well have settled into resentment, but as she says, "What we do about [the challenges thrown our way] is the key to who we become." Though it is obviously not an easy path, Catherine has chosen the positive way, the spiritual way. Her story clearly shows how exposure to spiritual-growth concepts and openness to the messages they offer has allowed her to become a very different person from what we could have predicted, given the life circumstances into which she was born.

Chapter 13

Learning to Fly (Inés)

Inés's richly spiritual story is probably our clearest example of progression through the stages. Although always deeply spiritual, her early literal beliefs from childhood were followed by a Rational period of questioning and rejection of literal religious belief during her college and young adult years.

Her reintroduction to a type of spirituality she could be comfortable with came at the same time she was being prodded to expand her circle of concern to include the diverse races and lifestyles represented in her church. Note the calling to a higher level of personal responsibility as her newfound faith took hold. Note how she describes the thrilling but frightening call to explore a spirituality devoid of pre-set creeds. The power of her early religious and cultural influences probably would not have left her inclined toward a faith community as unstructured as Unitarianism had she not had support and encouragement from that community.

—◦◦◦—

I begin this reflection on my spiritual journey with an overwhelming sense of love and gratitude. Life has given me so much richness, mentally, physically, and above all spiritually. I especially want to thank the many treasured masters, both living and departed from this earth, whose guidance paved the way for me to partake of the exquisite elixir of maddening love for the Divine.

A Fledgling Spirituality

My mother was one of those masters whose guidance fostered and eventually inspired my current faith. She would often say to me: "My darling little daughter, what man on earth can imitate, much less create, one of these diminutive flowers? Who could produce a majestic mountain or a rainbow? Only God with his merciful generosity could have given us all of these wonders to enjoy." Other times she would say: "If you lift even a tiny rock, you will see a myriad of life growing under it." She was an excellent example of a highly spiritual person, but I would have a long way to go before finding my own personal spirituality—that is, a spiritual path that allowed me to be true to myself.

I was born nearly seventy years ago in Colombia and lost my father when I was three years old. Wanting to give me the best education possible, my mother scrimped and saved to send me to a Catholic boarding school, though it meant we would be separated for a large part of the year. At the school I learned a lot about prayer, meditation, and the lives of Jesus, Mary, and Joseph as well as of the martyrs and saints. Their spirituality moved me to try to imitate their lives.

Like so many other young women educated by the nuns, I decided at one point in high school that I wanted to enter the convent. The Mother Superior rejected me, however, on the grounds that I was too vivacious. Besides, I was the only child of a poor mother who needed me to support her in her old age. With this decree, my vision of my ordination day, with me dressed in white as the bride of Christ, was dashed. I would never have the chance to join that select group of his chosen lovers. While I was very sad, an inner voice told me I was chosen to follow a different path—and that I would be happy and fulfilled there.

There were some points among the religious teachings of the nuns and priests that I rejected from an early age. One emphasis was on avoiding sin for fear of eternal punishment. One day when I was around eleven, after listening to yet another scathing sermon about how we should fear God and fear Hell, I was removing the scarf from my head when suddenly I heard a voice clearly speaking straight from my heart: "If I want to go to Heaven, it is through love, and not fear, of God."

My Catholic upbringing left me with a few negative effects that were reinforced by my culture. One message from the church was that life here on earth would consist mainly of suffering. Somehow, we were told, this suffering would ensure our reward in Heaven after death. At the same time, Latino culture conveyed a related message that enjoyment of good things would, sooner or later, be paid for with pain and tears. I remember repeatedly singing a popular song that said: "For every minute of peace and of pleasure, there are twenty of pain." Between that negative message from Catholicism and the influence of Latino culture, I grew up fearful of having any happy moment, lest I should suffer twenty times over or risk my chances of eternal reward.

Another negative effect of the church teachings, also reinforced by my culture, was the idea that women existed only to obey and serve men. Despite our poverty, and thanks to my mother's unwavering determination, I had plenty of opportunity for education and travel to other countries, via scholarships, exchange programs, and even job prospects. The latter is how I wound up spending most of my adult life in the United States. But the disempowerment of women that pervaded my culture managed to color my early life choices. I was angry about the injustices and the privileges men had over women in general. The result was an undesirable philosophy that would prove difficult to change.

Grounded

Always fascinated by the night stars and other celestial bodies, I chose to study mathematics and physics in college. I had intended to become an astronomer, though life circumstances would direct me into a different profession.

In college I began pondering some of the illogical things the church said we must believe. For example, how could Jesus have been the son of God and born of a human virgin? The given explanation was that these are mysteries we should simply accept. If I expressed doubt—or, worse yet, disbelief—I would go to Hell. How foolish I felt when I learned that all the emperors of ancient Rome were also said to be born of virgins. Feeling betrayed and disgusted by the Catholic teachings, I renounced them altogether, thus beginning a period in which I remained detached from all things religious.

Throughout my childhood, I had accepted a paramount teaching that was drilled into my brain: the Catholic Church is the only true religion, outside of which there is no salvation. The disgust I felt, beginning in college, for the version of religion I had been taught as a child would only increase in later years, when I realized that this simple assumption had prevented me from realizing the beauty and wholeness of other world religions.

So alienated was I from all forms of religion by 1971 that I did a very rude thing at a banquet in Tucson, Arizona, in honor of a professor I knew. During a delightful conversation, a gentleman on my left, a certain Dr. Yoshino, surprised me with the question: "By any chance are you a Unitarian Universalist?" I had never heard these words before, but I so resented the idea of being labeled or put into a religious box that I became uncomfortable and felt my defenses rising. "No," I said, "What is that?" My poor dinner companion tried to compose a gracious explanation, but the only words I took in were "liberal religion." The heat shot up my spine as I realized that this genial conversation had led us into a discussion of religion. I blurted out, "Does this religion have anything to do with Hell, or—or—or Jesus?" Kindly and almost apologetically, he said: "Well, yes, and . . . not really. Its roots are Judeo-Christian, but now . . ."

I cut him off: "I really don't want to hear anything that has to do with religion. Thanks!" I then swerved abruptly to my right, ending our conversation. Although there was no excuse for my behavior, my angry reaction told me something important: I was carrying a load of anger toward the Catholic Church. Beneath my calm demeanor, I was still boiling from the religious misrepresentations I had had drilled into me in my youth, still hurt by the distortions of reality so deeply practiced by the Church.

Taking Wing

Six years later I was introduced to Unitarian Universalism once again, this time in Milwaukee. By then I had married and divorced and was the single mother of three young children. I still did not want to hear anything about religion or churches. But a very insistent friend had been pushing me for months to visit her church. One Sunday, bored and needing to get out of the house, I thought, "What do I have to lose by checking out Sophia's church?" So I gathered up the children and carted them off to the Brookville Unitarian Universalist Congregation. As luck would have it, the Reverend Robert Latham had chosen that very day to preach about quantum leaps as a metaphor for spiritual life. Surely this brand of religion was different from what I had known before. Having chosen a topic that linked two of my earliest pursuits— my scientific interests and the spirituality my mother had inspired in me—Reverend Latham had me hooked before I even heard the end of this first sermon. After that, I found myself in his church every Sunday, almost against my will.

It was not only the sermons that attracted me to this church. The warmth and acceptance that my children and I found in that congregation allowed us to freely explore our spiritual leanings and gain inspiration from the concepts espoused by this group. I joined in all sorts of workshops and retreats. I felt liberated and came alive mentally and spiritually. Most importantly, in that church, I learned to value myself as a woman. One by one the spiritual wounds I was carrying in my soul began to heal. Little by little, my enthusiasm for helping others and for relating to the Divine came back.

Over time, I learned that the Unitarian Universalist religion espouses seven major principles:

- the inherent worth and dignity of every person;
- justice, equity, and compassion in human relations;
- acceptance of one another and encouragement of spiritual growth in our congregations;
- a free and responsible search for truth and meaning;
- the right of conscience and the use of the democratic process within our congregations and in society at large;
- the goal of world community with peace, liberty, and justice for all; and
- respect for the interdependent web of all existence of which we are a part.

A free and responsible search for truth and meaning—while the other principles were important to me, these words stood out. How different this principle was from the rigid, mind-numbing religious dogma of my upbringing! For Unitarian Universalists, all religions have some worthy message; all sacred books can be a source of knowledge, and examples of all kinds of prophetic men and women can offer lessons to the seeker. In this faith, we are encouraged to try different theories, philosophies, and paths of knowledge. Furthermore, we are encouraged to discard without guilt the ideas that do not fit us anymore. Here I, a woman brought up to defer to others' authority, was being asked to think and feel for myself. Here, no truth would be handed to me intact by self-assured male authority figures. Here, I alone would be responsible for finding, and moreover, constantly reevaluating, my own truth, a truth found within my own soul.

Along with this free and responsible search for truth and meaning came the opportunity for free religious expression. I used to be envious of men who said they did not believe in all the stories told by the priests and who thought that those who were afraid of Hell were sissies. Even at a young age, I did not believe in Hell myself; that is why I secretly admired their nerve, although I was too intimidated to say anything. I hated not being able to read books on the "forbidden" lists kept by the Vatican. I also resented not being able to become a priest—or even do something as menial as handling the censer[1]—because I was a woman. Now I had been given the precious gift of thinking for myself, of reading anything I wanted, of expressing my truths the way I saw fit, and even of enjoying the freedom to change my mind once I found a truth that better fit my values and aspirations.

Free of the constraints that had originally caused me to cast aside what I understood of my birth religion, I was delighted to explore my spiritual nature instead of running away from it. I felt like an eagle perched atop the highest mountain, set loose to try my wings. I could see a vast, free terrain extending before me. My heart pounded with excitement at the new skies to explore.

But alas, my stunted religious wings refused to open. I feared the lack of restrictions this new theology brought with it. Navigating these skies on my own terrified me. Would I plummet straight to the ground, or be carried off in the wind to unknown scary places? My spirit had been bound for too long. Like many people who convert from dogmatic and patriarchal religions to Unitarian Universalism, I experienced the paradox of being at once bound and free. I was not yet ready to fly.

The vastness of expression and thought now open to me amazed me, but owning that freedom brought astounding ethical and moral responsibilities. Unitarian Universalism provided no theological safety net for my spiritual adventures. The ecstasy of freedom was tempered by the fear of falling hard. What if I did something really wrong? There was no priest to absolve me. Whom could I blame for my problems and the problems of the world? This faith was calling me to a new definition of personal responsibility.

Furthermore, in order to fit into this new religion I needed to eliminate a few personal prejudices of my own. While I had easily found it liberating to denounce the supreme male authority figure of the Catholic

Church—the Pope—it was a stretch at first for me to accept the other extreme I found prevalent in the Unitarian Church—women ministers! In my congregation were people who held all sorts of different allegiances and beliefs. I was not so excited to share my spiritual journey with those who saw the human being, rather than God, as the center of their moral and ethical reality. Even worse, I learned there were some pagans in our midst. There were some gay people and transsexuals as well. As a member of this church, I would be expected to honor each of these paths. Could I rise to the challenge of this total acceptance and open-mindedness?

At first this was difficult for me. Fortunately, I was not forced to do it alone. My congregation offered constant support and understanding. Inspired by the example of my fellow church members, most of whom held a very inclusive worldview, I managed to overcome my prejudices. And thanks to the practice of this life-enhancing faith, I have accepted and now cherish the freedom and responsibility that accompany the gift of free religious expression. I have come to understand that no matter what ideas or doctrines I encounter, I can choose them as mine or let them go without guilt or anxiety.

Now I rejoice in my path and cherish the empowering, liberated feeling it brings me. I now feel comfortable saying I have dealt with most of my original prejudices and am usually able to keep my judging mind at bay. I treasure the ability to experience spirituality freely, without the constraints of repressive dogma.

Quivering in Mid-Air

Once I overcame my initial uncertainties, I became a Unitarian Universalist in 1978, feeling spiritually renewed and liberated. Over time I learned that I could laugh heartily and enjoy life without fear of having to pay for it later with suffering. Also, I was finally able to internalize that I, as a woman, was as valuable as any man. I came to accept sitting side-by-side in church with people of all different lifestyles and beliefs.

Little by little, my enthusiasm for helping others came back. And to my delight, the joys of this new faith allowed me to find my way back toward the deeply felt spiritual inclinations of my childhood. I was finally free to navigate the skies of my early longings toward the Divine. In fact, I believed the Divine was beginning to communicate with me directly—something I would have never thought possible.

The first time this happened, I had attended only a few services at the Unitarian Universalist Church. On one particular Sunday, the minister asked us to join hands and slowly start chanting "Om." It was my first experience with this practice. To my surprise, between the resonance of the chant (from within my body and outside of it) and the feeling of belonging once again to a spiritual community, I found myself transported to another place: For a second or two, I felt lifted from the earth. My body seemed to disappear into an amorphous blob of soft pink and blue cotton clouds. In that momentary state of utter nothingness, I had a very clear and complete realization. I totally understood one thing: that we are all one. In that instant, I knew that the whole universe is a seamless tapestry of people, animals, vegetables, rocks, and more—all sustained and nurtured by the Great Mystery. In the midst of this knowing, a voice said clearly: "For a moment like this, it was worth having been born." The power of that essential awareness, bestowed upon my soul that glorious morning, ended for the most part my feelings of isolation. No longer was I alienated from the world. I knew I was one with the universe and with all its sentient beings and that I would forever after know for certain that I am not alone. But this new worldview brought me another surprise realization. I began to feel a growing sense of my own personal responsibility. Permeating my thoughts and actions was the notion that I must use whatever gifts I have to contribute to the welfare of all.

In another amazing instance, Spirit spoke to me again on the last day of a transformational retreat. The farewell ceremony consisted of everyone standing in a circle, holding hands, eyes closed. The leader asked each person to compose an affirmation that would sum up the wisdom acquired during our time together. At first I resisted, for the last thing

I wanted to do in that moment was to think, share, and be judged. When my turn came up however, these words sprang from my mouth: "My power is in my joy, and my joy is in my power." I couldn't believe what I had just heard myself say! Where did this message come from? These words—a far cry from the dire predictions about paying for any current joy with sorrow in the future—were a tremendously liberating gift for me. Ever since that day, *joy* and *power* have become part of my vocabulary and form the very fabric of my existence.

In yet another encounter with the Divine, I was letting go of tensions at the beginning of a meditation, just entering into a peaceful state, when, without warning or consciousness on my part, I felt a hand touch my right shoulder. When I turned to see who it was, a full-length image of Jesus stood before me and said gently, "I love you." To this day I don't know what to make of this experience. Was it real? I had neither been thinking of Jesus, nor was I even friendly with him in those days.

Recalling this incident reminds me of another transcendent experience. Just after my mother died, I unexpectedly saw a beautiful, diaphanous figure, dressed in a flowing gown, ascending slowly toward the sky. As she rose, my mother's spirit form turned her head toward me and smiled. I do not know if this was a vision in the true sense. I only know I remember every detail of the scene. That memory brings peace, love, and gratitude to my heart to this day. I thank both my mother and the Divine for giving me such powerful assurance that her soul was at peace and, as always, still loved me.

Full Flight

In 1990 I attended a weeklong church district leadership school. Midweek, during the worship service, I had message from the Divine—a voice from within calling me to a new kind of existence. I can still hear the distinct words: "If worship services can move people the way we have been moved this week, I want to do this for the rest of my life." What was this? Was I to embark on a new journey?

At first I was afraid that this call might be real. It would mean I had to give up my good job, leave my home, and move far away—in short, pursue a whole new life. If the call was real, I would be compelled to rise to new levels of trust on several planes. First, I must trust that the voice I heard calling me was truly from the Divine and not just some trick of my brain. Secondly, I must trust that my own personal resources would carry me through the staggering demands of the call. Some days I felt ready to give up my current comforts in service of the divine Will. Other days, feeling the weight and consequences of my call, I would see that this plan was madness and lacked any reasonable assurance of success. Filled with doubt, I did not know which way to turn.

But, bit by bit, I came to terms with the mad urge to abandon everything and leap forward into an uncertain future. Aided by the generous gift of time and counsel of Reverend Bob Reed, I applied to and was accepted at the Starr King School for the Ministry in Berkeley, California.

In seminary, a colleague defined me as a woman "with the mind of a scholar and the heart of a mystic." My studies appealed to both these aspects of my personality and served to deepen my respect for this faith I had come upon seemingly by chance.

My scholarly side warmed to the knowledge of the Unitarian Universalist history, which provides many excellent examples of personal and spiritual development. William Ellery Channing (1780–1842) has been called "the prophet, preacher, and hero of New England Unitarianism." Channing rejected the Calvinist teachings about divine election and human depravity he had heard in his youth. Over his life he evolved to a position of faith in a God who would bestow his love on all people. Channing also came to trust that all people have an innate moral sense by which they perceive and can choose goodness.

In the second half of the nineteenth century, the Transcendentalists—Unitarian mystics like Ralph Waldo Emerson, Theodore Parker, Louisa May Alcott, Margaret Fuller, and many others—stressed that each one of us could connect directly with the Divine, and therefore there was no need for intermediaries between God and humans. Emerson, in his masterful essay "The Over-Soul," says that sin is to let our faith be dictated by others, since "faith that stands on authority is not faith. The reliance on authority measures the decline of religion, the withdrawal of the soul."[2]

My studies and work within Unitarian Universalism have also led to development of my mystical side. Saint Thérèse of Lisieux has been a particular inspiration. Once I was able to open my eyes to the ways of this saint, I took delight in her beautiful and courageous "Little Way," finding joy in completing the little tasks of life, beautiful and courageous. Routine and sometimes uninspiring tasks such as cleaning, cooking, going to the gym, or doing the laundry give us an opportunity. We can learn to find joy in them, in doing them out of a sense of gratitude to the Spirit of Life and because we want to contribute to the betterment of our fellow humans. Living day by day with this sense of humility and gratitude regarding menial tasks actually takes more mettle than doing something spectacular once in a while or being the hero on rare occasion. I have been trying to live this way in my daily life, sacrificing or going a little further than I normally would in small ways that nobody would notice —when traveling, for example, I use the paper towel I dried my hands with to clean the area surrounding the sink, so the next person does not have to use a wet, dirty area.

In effort to further deepen my understanding of mystical faith, I reread Saint Teresa of Avila's *The Interior Castle*. I find that I have grown spiritually since I first read this masterpiece in my youth. I can now appreciate the difficulties a woman of intelligence must have had writing in the sixteenth century. I can see that despite—or perhaps because of— her incredible intelligence and elevated level of spiritual development, Saint Teresa needed (and had been able) to craft her language carefully to keep it acceptable to the patriarchal forces that dominated her society. Reading Teresa this time, I did not let the passages implying that women were less intelligent, less capable, and less advanced than men interfere with my appreciation of the text's depth. This time, my own soul was in a place where I could receive the gifts Teresa was trying to share, and I was grateful for her dedication and passion.[3] These days I feel Saint Teresa of Avila calls to me to educate and inspire, even if only in a small way, those to whom I have the privilege to minister as they grow into more harmony with the Divine.

Poor old Dr. Yoshino! Would he not be surprised to learn that that religion-hating feminist he sat next to at a banquet in 1971 has become a Unitarian Universalist minister? I wish I could tell him more about it. I would tell him that mine is a religion with neither a creed nor an authority figure to show the way to Heaven—or to scare people with the flames of Hell. It is a religion that encourages us to listen to the Divine *within us* and to create our own theology based on our direct experience of the sacred. My religion gives no assurance of an afterlife but encourages its members to live every moment in *this* life to the fullest, according to the highest ideals of humanity. It encourages people to live in the questions, rather than be comfortable with easy answers. It supports us as we evolve according to newfound truths. Mine is not a religion for the faint of heart.

Looking back at my Unitarian Universalist journey, I can honestly say that in trying to live by its lofty principles I have been challenged, confronted, and stretched to my limits.

My personal challenge was to allow my life experiences to take me from a childhood religion of complete orthodoxy (as I understood it) through a period of complete disavowal of all things religious, and from there to grow, with the help of a very supportive faith community, into a faith in which my relationship with the Divine forms the center of my life. For me, worship is not a separate activity reserved for church or special occasions; nor is it tied up in images of a judgmental deity. Instead, my form of worship involves every minute of my life, a constant dwelling in reverent and grateful connection with the Holy, though my understanding of that may vary over time. Now I am graced to be able to practice worship from the depths of my own heart.

Through my Unitarian Universalist community, I have been confronted with the value of learning to respect other peoples' right to their own ideas and values no matter how they may differ from mine. Learning to accept—or, better yet, appreciate—the company of those I used to despise because they were different from me infuses my life with a great sense of dignity and companionship. Inspired by my growing compassion for those who differ from me, I now am confronted with the importance of social activism. Whenever possible, I march for causes that support freedom and justice for all—promoting world peace, combating world hunger, and advocating for women's rights. I also sometimes represent my church in Gay Pride parades. And I contribute regularly to causes such as Mothers Against Drunk Driving (MADD), gun control, the Nature Conservancy, and the like.

My faith journey has led me to stretch myself in two ways. As I moved from a culture where women were oppressed to a faith community where every individual is valued, I have had to develop an ever-stronger sense of who I am. No longer defined by the cultural stereotypes of my heritage, I have had to evolve toward more authentic ways to express myself. As this sense became stronger for me, so too I wanted it for others. I want to help others be free of oppression. One of my life missions is to advance "counter-oppressive education" in our denomination and anywhere else I might have any influence. I preach awareness, vigilance, and compassion to get to the roots and eradicate the effects of oppressive cultural and institutional environments. I speak about this from the pulpit, in workshops and retreats, and at every appropriate exchange with congregants and the public. Like worship, education for me is a way of living. I believe that one of the best ways to educate those around us on how to treat others is by modeling through our own example. I hope people will recognize my efforts in this arena enough that when I die, my epitaph will read: "In her presence, I could be myself."

The other way my faith journey has caused me to stretch is that I have widened my idea of the community to which I belong. In my life I have had to live in many kinds of cultural and physical environments and relate to many different kinds of people. The variety of human experiences I have had have helped me develop a sense of universality, an appreciation of the commonalities in our human condition. This understanding has led to a sense of belonging to the world, rather than to a specific country or class. More than a good Columbian, a good American, or a good Unitarian Universalist, I seek to be a good citizen of the world—a good human being.

Through all the ups and downs in my spiritual life, what shines through now is a deep, unshakeable love and surrender to the Divine, which forms a permanent subtext of all my thoughts, words, and actions. I try to live each day as an act of thanks for the gift of life and for the myriad other gifts that come my way in the form of love, family, friendships, health, nature, books, and all that I value and enjoy. Since my early days, when I was taught to fear a judging, punishing God, I have grown to where I now love, respect, and exist in grateful communion with what I call the Awesome Mystery, my Father/Mother. All I want to do with my life is to help create sacred spaces for healing and to help people grow into more harmony with the Divine.

—⚬⚬⚬—

Inés describes what is called an episode of unitive consciousness. When, in a group chanting "Om," she suddenly realized that "the whole universe is a seamless tapestry of people, animals, vegetables, rocks, and more—all sustained and nurtured by the Great Mystery"—she knew that we all are one. Episodes of unitive consciousness, in which the person's individual identity dissolves temporarily into the universe, are thought either to lead to, or to be signs of, spiritual growth. But for an unprepared person who doesn't understand such episodes, or doesn't have the strength to accept them, they can also cause hardship. In extreme cases, a person reporting these episodes may be ostracized by society and treated for mental illness. But Inés interpreted her unitive episode, as well as her other mystical experiences, as a source of joy, which is probably the way it is supposed to be.

This story is not meant as an endorsement of the Unitarian Universalist Church, per se. It serves only to point out how congregations with "looser"

191

religious interpretations may be more prone to lead members beyond the ethnocentrism and triumphalism of the Faithful stage.

Once Inés became ready to reengage spirituality at a post-critical level, she could likely have worked her way into any faith community, or even back into the Catholic Church. I suspect, however, that the challenges in re-approaching a traditional religion would have been greater. In encountering Unitarianism, it is not that Inés found the "right" church with the right answers, but rather that she found a church (one of many possibilities) that is right for her.

To provide an example of something is to show what other things of the same kind are like; when we do so, we are more or less claiming that our example is what things of that class should be like. In contrast, a sample claims only to provide a small taste of something, to give an idea of what the rest might be like. Whereas an example implies "ought to," a sample is more random. In light of this distinction, let me say that, while each story in part 3 has provided a sample of a Mystic, it has not been meant to be an example. In part 4, we will consider what various theorists can contribute to our understanding.

Part Four

Toward an Understanding of Post-critical Faith

Chapter 14

Again, What Is a Mystic?

So again, what is a Mystic? Spiritual development theory states that the Mystic stage is what happens when a person at the critical, or Rational, level keeps questioning, remains open to further growth, and keeps seeking deeper truth. A Mystic displays "post-critical" faith. The stories you have just read purport to be about this level of faith. Of course, no one person resides completely in any one of these stages. In no way do I mean to imply that we can judge anyone's level of faith on the basis of a simple story. Surely the phenomenon of Mystic-level faith is far too complex ever to be exemplified in one person or by any given story.

The word *mystic* carries with it many connotations that could cause confusion or objection among some readers. I like the description offered by Andrew Newberg, Eugene D'Aquili, and Vince Rause in their book *Why God Won't Go Away*. They write that mystical experience is "nothing more or less than an uplifting sense of genuine spiritual union with something larger than the self."[1] The Mystic, then, is one who experiences faith in this way. To belabor this point, it is not the presence or absence of transcendent experiences that characterize the Mystic. Such experiences may come into play here, but they do not define the Mystic.

We can rely on the advice of early twentieth-century spiritual theologian Adolphe Tanquerey regarding mystical experiences. He said that we must look at the effects of such experiences to determine their validity. In the case of the true mystic (as opposed to what Tanquerey called "hysterical persons" having arguably unhealthy visions), "there is a steady mental growth, an increase of the love of God, and a devoted service to the neighbor."[2] Tanquerey added that when true mystics "have the opportunity of engaging in some public enterprise, they give evidence of common sense, of an open and strong mind, of a determined will, and success crowns their efforts."[3] Tanquerey hints at a distinction that will become more important as we delve deeper. To those unaware of the distinctions, Mystic-level faith can sound a lot like those "hysterical persons" having unhealthy visions. In fact, a large part of society lumps all people claiming contact with metaphysical entities or reporting non-local experiences into a group whose members we might call "flakes" or suspect of having poor reality-testing skills. Indeed, within the general spirituality camp, there are many who profess expertise but who may not be authentic examples of spiritual maturity. As opposed to those who have progressed through the stages in a genuine manner, some, but by no means all, "New Agers" and others who claim access to the metaphysical come by their nontraditional spirituality through the facile tactics of their own ego.

In the clearest examples, Mystic-level faith will embody certain favorable traits by which we can recognize it. (Some of these traits may not sound healthy at the outset, but I suggest the very ability to understand just how such traits could be advantageous is what marks the movement to the post-critical, post-conventional, or Mystic level of spirituality.) Let's examine these traits in turn.

Doubt versus Certainty

A crucial trait distinguishing Mystics is their approach to doubt. A Faithful individual needs simple, immutable answers about the reason for her existence and about what happens after death. The Faithful and Rational stages are both very confident stages. The former is confident in tradition, the latter confident in the self—and in the findings of science. At these levels, certainty, especially religious certainty, holds the person's world together.

Both the Faithful- and Rational-stage person needs certainty about being "right." This need causes him to view everyone who believes differently as "wrong." The Rational person may feel superior to those at the pre-critical level and think them foolish for their naïveté. He may write brilliant manifestos against religion and the existence of God, like our New Atheist authors Richard Dawkins, Sam Harris, and Christopher Hitchens.

At the Mystic level, though, something new takes hold. The need for certainty is replaced by an ability to live in the questions. Rather than grasp at ready-made answers handed down by others, as the Faithful do, and rather than insist that those answers are false, as the Rational do, the Mystic rejects self-satisfied certainty on matters about which we can have no definitive answers. Mystics are people who have known doubt, have faced it without fear, and have grown as a direct result of that courage.

Having worked through her own doubts at different levels, the post-critical person tends to become comfortable with the idea that some things are unknowable and that exact answers are simply not to be had in this lifetime. Rather than maintain, as the Faithful person does, that the answers are found in this or that ancient book, and rather than insist, as the Rational person does, they will one day come to us through science and human reason, the Mystic accepts that the universe and her own existence within it contain mysteries she will never understand.

Whereas at prior levels, the unknown was something to be either feared and avoided or reasoned out of existence, at the Mystic level the unknown begins to look enticing. Because the Mystic can live in the questions and treasures the opportunity to continue the search, he is comfortable with, and actually finds beauty in, the fact that the answers about our existence will never come to him; the mystery itself is exciting.

Note how Inés's story showed a continual process of readjustment to newly encountered truths as she struggled to incorporate each new one into her understanding. Had she dug in her heels against the first message that conflicted with her childhood religion, instead of this marvelous example of post-critical faith she would have nothing to teach us but the traditional beliefs of a parochial Faithful. Remaining open to further truths, as Inés and Nilah did, is what is meant by *not needing certainty*.

Some Mystics will speak of certainty, but they mean it more in a sense of certitude, which is different. They are certain "there is something out there," some sort of divine Presence, even though they can't prove it and have very little idea of what that presence might be like. *Certitude* means something more like trust. Whereas the "certainty" grasped at by the other levels arises out of *fear* of the unknown, the Mystic is more likely to trust that whatever is out there, it is benevolent.

Contrary to what some religious leaders would have us believe, willingness to face doubt is a sign of personal courage. It is necessary to growth and a crucial step in forming a creative, mature personal faith. Religious certainty, on the other hand, closes us off from the possibility of growth, because it assures that we will not look further than our current beliefs. Worse, it makes us judgmental of others who hold different beliefs than we do.

In *The Individual and His Religion*, psychologist Gordon Allport (whose work the next chapter explores more fully) adds much to our understanding of the role doubt—or the type of questioning that occurs at the Rational level—plays in spiritual development. "Doubt," he wrote, "is an unstable or hesitant reaction, produced by collision of evidence with prior belief, or of one belief with another."[4] He added that "it is frequently in the pre-puberty period that [these] fatal collisions occur, when pennies have not fallen from heaven in response to a self-centered prayer."[5] Pointing out how an *effective* handling of doubt causes a person to grow, he wrote, "Mature belief . . . grows painfully out of the alternating doubts and affirmations that characterize productive thinking."[6] Allport also emphasized how doubt is crucial to reaching spiritual maturity: "Unless the individual doubts, he cannot use his full intelligence, and unless he uses his full intelligence, he cannot develop a mature [religious] sentiment."[7]

Universal (Unitive) versus Ethnocentric Worldview

A major defining characteristic of post-critical faith can be explained through a concept that was most clearly elucidated by contemporary philosopher Ken Wilber. In relation to Wilber's work, we can say that a person in the Lawless stage, who has not yet sincerely accepted any religion or any other limits on his own personal will, holds an *egocentric* worldview. His actions and decisions are directed toward attainment of his own immediate ends, without much concern for how this might harm others or even himself.

The Faithful or traditionally religious person goes beyond the self to identify mainly with his own group. He focuses his views and decisions around the opinions and needs of that group, which is certainly a more mature perspective than one centered around the self. To describe the worldview of the Faithful, we can use the term *ethnocentric*, which implies that the person sees her own group as being more deserving than others. So this stance still excludes a lot of people. Faithful-level people may gloat over their own salvation or the rightness of their own belief system or political views. This stance, now seen as a matter of course in our society, actually shows a surprisingly scornful indifference to, and lack of compassion for, the well-being of those outside the group. The only concern for those outsiders is the extent to which they can be brought into the fold, or "saved." The Faithful have a *triumphalist* message, in which those outside the group cannot be accepted on their own merit: "We have the right answer and, if you join us, you will be saved like us."

At the Rational level, a person's worldview is broadened to include all humans, including the poor, the uneducated, and the needy. The Rational person is often quite interested in social action. She would gladly extend a hand to help unfortunates *without* the need to convert them— not because an external God expects it, but out of an internal sense of moral obligation. So we can say that the Rational person is *worldcentric*.

At the Mystic level, a person maintains all the inclusiveness of the worldcentric perspective but goes beyond it in several important ways.

For one, the Mystic person has done away with the need to be right. Secondly, the Mystic begins to include input from that which cannot be seen and cannot be measured, so his worldview is *universal,* encompassing everyone and everything, including the spirit world. Thirdly, the Mystic is *unitive.* He does not need to have others justify his position by agreeing with him; he also does not like to hear of distinctions that might separate him from others. (For that reason, some Mystics may balk initially at the spiritual-stage categories described in this book!) The Mystic has transcended the walls of his own culture, his own faith tradition, even his political party; to the Mystic, everyone and everything in the cosmos deserves the same attention, respect, and concern. The overriding trait of the post-critical person is his all-inclusive, universal worldview. This inclusiveness is the main thing the Mystic has to teach us. (Please see chart 4 on page 90 for a comparison of the Mystic's worldview with that of the other stages.)

Unity versus Divisiveness

Because everyone and everything is included in her worldview, unity is a very important value for the post-critical person. Mystics at the extreme end may even say they are "one" with the whole universe—all people, animals, plant life, and even inanimate objects like rocks. Some Mystics may have had a transcendent experience that showed how we all are one. Inés, whom we met in chapter 13, described what is called an episode of unitive consciousness the first time she stood in a circle at the Unitarian Universalist Church and joined hands with the others chanting "Om." But whether informed by personal unitive experiences like Inés or not, the Mystic sees more connection between herself and others.

More moderate Mystics might simply say that no one's concerns should be excluded from consideration. Human rights, proper treatment of animals, and concerns for protecting the environment all fall into the domain of what the Mystic might consider important—and can be seen as a logical extension of Mystics' frequently cited experience of oneness: we all are one because we all are connected. A simple action on the part of one person can have a ripple effect that spreads to many others—much like David's soap bubble analogy (in chapter 9). What is done to harm one person harms all; at the same time, what is done to benefit one person benefits all.

Conversely, at the "lower" levels, life is seen as a zero-sum game where "If you win, I lose." This mentality fosters competition, profit to the exclusion of the general good, and health-care policies that benefit huge corporations and their stockholders over the needs of the patients they were established to serve.

The unitive stance looks for "win/win" opportunities. The Mystic will pursue such opportunities exactly because he realizes that, given our interconnectedness, if anyone loses, we *all* lose. How could anyone deny that we all are one in that sense?

Metaphorical versus Literal Interpretation

Another trait of the Mystic or the spiritually mature person is that she tends to interpret scripture metaphorically rather than literally. This probably occurs in degrees rather than being an all-or-nothing phenomenon. Some may take certain parts of their religion literally and other parts metaphorically.

True Mystics feel no need to proselytize, because they realize that all religions contain elements of the truth, no matter which view of the Divine they propound. Secure in her own spirituality, the Mystic has no need for those at different levels to share in her beliefs. David gives us an example of this in chapter 9. He participates actively in a church, motivated not by agreement with its literal teachings but by his own metaphorical interpretation of them. He even teaches Sunday school and has found a way to use Bible stories to teach useful lessons without getting caught up in the theology—or worrying whether the stories represent literal truth.

Tolerance of Paradox

The post-critical person tolerates, accepts, and even welcomes paradox in life in a way that those at other stages cannot. He believes that the answers he seeks are to be found in science—and also sees that there are mysteries we will never understand. Perhaps the big bang theory is valid; but maybe there is an Ultimate Reality after all. The Mystic will tend to see all religions as having a certain validity. Yet, at the same time, he may claim the atheists are right, too!

Spirit Authority versus Oracle Authority

In a further effort to understand spiritual maturity, we can compare the locus of authority of the four groups. For the Lawless individual, authority resides only in the tyranny of his own will. This stage is tyrannical because a person whose will is not submitted to either the principles of a religion *or* his own disciplined conscience will be sure to produce chaos in his own life (and in that of anyone with whom he interacts). Thus the locus of authority for the Lawless individual is his immature self, ruled by his own ego, undisciplined by conscience.

For the Faithful person, the rules of religion provide a welcome escape from the chaos of the prior stage and from the tyranny of her own will. A class I took in college called this rule-based type of authority "oracular." The preacher or the Bible stands as an oracle, giving authority to the precepts of the religion. So the locus of authority for the Faithful person is in the oracle of her religion.

At the Rational level, a person no longer needs the safety of an oracle authority because he has learned to rely on his own conscience. He is ruled by a "conscience authority." For the Rational person, this authority is more valid than the rules of the church. When the pre-stated rules do not apply to a given situation, the person with a well-developed conscience can reason out a valid answer on a case-by-case basis.

It was this type of situation that psychologist Lawrence Kohlberg (whose work is discussed at greater length in the next chapter) was trying to explore with his examination of theoretical "moral dilemmas." The best known is the case of Heinz, a man whose wife was dying from a rare disease. A certain pharmacist in his town had discovered a drug that supposedly would cure Heinz's wife, but it was too expensive. Heinz tried to borrow money to pay for the drug and begged the pharmacist to sell it to him for less, but all to no avail. The dilemma here is, "Should Heinz break the law and steal the drug, or should he resist the urge to break the law—which, of course, would result in his wife's death?"

The purely Faithful mentality can only decree that Heinz must allow his wife to die, because it is wrong to break the law. Peck used the phrase *the letter of the law* for people at this stage.[8] They would follow the law to the letter even in cases where it might not make sense.

By contrast, someone with a fully developed conscience authority will stop to consider how best to follow *the spirit of the law*, even when that means breaking the *letter* of the law. In the Heinz dilemma, the conscience authority will see conflicting concepts of "good" (saving a life may be more important than not stealing), will carefully consider both sides of the issue, and might decide in favor of breaking the law to save the woman. There is no clearly right answer to this dilemma, but it does demonstrate ways in which the rules of society may be inadequate in complex situations—and where the conscience authority may need to come forth.

Kohlberg called this ability to see conflicting concepts as both being right *post-conventional reasoning*.[9] A person at the post-conventional level understands that the point is to follow the spirit of the law—and that the letter of the law can sometimes be overruled by circumstance.

Thus, for the Rational person, the locus of authority is once again within herself. But unlike the Lawless individual, who is a victim of his own ego, the Rational person can generally rely on a valid conscience for her decisions. Many religious leaders seem to ignore this area, preaching that without a church, a person will fall into the moral ruin of the

Lawless state. But this is only partially correct. The person on the verge between Lawless and Faithful will likely fall backward into moral ruin without a church. But the person about to grow from Faithful to Rational is likely to grow stronger in accepting personal responsibility for his actions and in recognizing that his own conscience can provide a valid barometer for discerning right from wrong.

The Mystic still benefits from the self-governance and conscience authority that served so reliably in the prior Rational stage, but he builds on that occasionally to transcend reason in deciding on a particular course of action. Besides his conscience, he may now be guided in certain situations by a "Spirit Authority." Perhaps the Mystic hears the voice of Spirit urging him to quit his job and go serve the poor. This would not sound like a rational decision, but may be the correct thing for him if that is what the Spirit Authority tells him to do. Though his actions may seem to fly in the face of reason, he will be faithful to a message that comes from within.

A clear example of following a Spirit Authority from our stories is Charles (chapter 10), who chose the local Catholic college over the distant powerhouse university because his intuition told him he would be more comfortable there. Charles also "knew" he had done wrong when he falsely signed a form about his belief in God.

This self-governance is another way we can distinguish the true Mystic from the the New Age wannabe. Without evidence of being able to self-govern, no matter how much a person might talk about unity and transcendence, he may be just parroting what he has learned about that level from someone else. Spiritual maturity requires hard work, not mirroring. It is not imitative but developed from within.

Acceptance versus Despair

Where a person in the other stages would feel put out by all the personal disappointments life can bring, a Mystic sees meaning even in the tragedies of life. A Mystic accepts everything as part of a greater plan that extends beyond the particularities of his own life.

In her story, Catherine (chapter 12) shared details of two situations most people would consider major life tragedies: an alcoholic family background and a disabled child. Through significant struggle, Catherine not only accepts these two situations as givens in her life but also finds a way to frame them as opportunities for her own growth. Rather than resent her difficulties, she treasures the gifts they have brought into her life.

Forgiveness versus Blame

Understanding that those who have hurt him or done wrong did so out of their own weakness allows the Mystic to forgive even the worst evils.

Catherine models this concept well. She could easily have chosen blame and hatred—by far the easier and more natural human response—toward her alcoholic dad and two alcoholic husbands. Instead, she says she is working toward forgiveness, a monumental and probably lifelong task in her case. Though she says she still struggles to forgive, the mere fact that she can see forgiveness as a goal is evidence of her Mystic-level values at work.

Gratitude versus Wanting More

At the Mystic level, a person has come to recognize what are seemingly evils in life as part of a unity that does have coherence at some level, so he is grateful even for the trials that come his way. David (chapter 9) gives us an excellent example: as a youth he suffered a tragic accident in which he nearly lost his life, but he then used the experience to construct a positive, effective, and responsible life path. He is even able to list five life gifts that arose out of that accident. All those gifts—the gratitude for the presence of others in his life, the desire to use his time toward improving the lives of others, the choice to see others as being of exceptional value unless they prove otherwise, the decreased interest in material possessions, and the ability to return to his basic all-loving nature—are characteristic of the Mystic. So David appreciates how the accident served as a springboard for his own spiritual growth.

Community versus Solitude

The Mystic-level person is communal. He feels community with other people, animals, and nature—all part of the same greater unity of being of which he himself is a part.

Having gotten an early taste of community involvement in college, Jean (chapter 11) has continually sought new forms of community as the demands of her life change. Similarly, Catherine (chapter 12) chose her job in a church school because she wanted to contribute to her community. So the Mystic of the spiritual-development ladder is not a secluded hermit on a mountaintop. Rather, she is one who can put up with the vicissitudes of interacting with unsolvable situations, inconsistent people, and the frustrations of a largely imperfect world. Aware that she will never improve everything she would like to, the Mystic contents herself with doing what good she, as one imperfect person, can do.

Humility versus Ego

This is probably the hardest feature to describe. The word *humble* has a partially negative connotation in our culture; it implies a person or thing somehow fails to rise to the standard met by everyone else. But the humility of the Mystic does not fall behind accepted standards; rather, it transcends them.

The Mystic has learned that the self brings with it a tyranny—a need to win out over others, a need for lots of "stuff." These needs are ego-driven. In transcending his own ego, the Mystic escapes this tyranny of the self. He is less concerned with his own needs and more with the needs of others and the fate of humanity as a whole. He finds freedom in not needing to compete or win out over others. He does not need the status of lots of stuff to fuel the voracious appetite of his ego. Along with the humility of seeing that he is just a small part of an interconnected whole comes a freedom to just be—and perhaps more importantly—to just let others be. No longer is there the need to convert others to his religion, political preferences, or point of view. To the extent that the Mystic has transcended his own needs, he can be of more benefit to others.

Doing Good in This World versus the Need for Salvation

In general, the Mystic is not particularly concerned with saving his own soul. He would rather look around at a world full of opportunity for doing good in whatever ways are possible and apply his best efforts there. The Mystic trusts that the best use he can make of his life is to allow the Spirit Authority to direct him toward action in this world, making it better where he can and accepting its limits where he can't. Whatever might happen in an afterlife, if there is one, does not concern the Mystic nearly as much as making a difference in this life does.

In summary, the pre-critical religious person engages in religion to serve his own needs (for salvation, security, comfort, and structure) and needs easy-to-follow, authoritarian rules and black-and-white answers about our existence. The post-critical or Mystic-level person engages in spirituality or a faith community to serve others and to better approach the Mystery of Spirit, however he or she might understand that.

Chapter 15

Who Says?

Including M. Scott Peck and James Fowler, at least twelve notables have described a path of spiritual growth more or less corresponding to the stages presented in this book. Though they all use different terminology and different numbers of stages, if we take a bird's-eye view of these theorists' works, a general pattern can be seen. In this chapter, I will attempt to show correlations among the works of the eight theorists listed below. A few others will be worked into the ensuing discussion and later chapters.

James Fowler

James Fowler (1940–present), a minister in the United Methodist Church, was a professor of theology and human development at Emory University until he retired in 2005. In 1981, he published his seminal work, *Stages of Faith: The Psychology of Human Development and the Quest for Meaning*. Fowler's book was derived from his research project, for which 359 people were interviewed and their faith stances rated and categorized. From this data Fowler first proposed his six stages of faith development.

Fowler's use of the word *faith* refers to something broader and more universal than religion. He explains how our culture now takes religious *belief* to mean agreement that one particular view of the transcendent is valid—to the exclusion of views held by those outside that religion. For Fowler, *faith* has a much deeper meaning than *belief*: "If faith is reduced to belief in creedal statements and doctrinal formulations," he wrote, "then sensitive and responsible persons are likely to judge that they must live 'without faith.' But if faith is understood as trust in another and loyalty to a transcendent center of values and power, then the issue of faith—and the possibility of religious faith—becomes lively and open again."[1] For Fowler, faith refers to something generic to all people, "similar everywhere, despite the remarkable variety of forms and contents of religious practice and belief."[2]

Saint Teresa of Avila

Late in her life, sixteenth-century Spanish mystic Teresa of Avila (1515–1582) wrote *The Interior Castle,* a classic of Christian mystical literature. The "castle" represents a person's soul. Within the castle are seven sets of "rooms," or "Mansions," which represent seven stages through which a person traverses in the journey toward deeper spirituality. We can thank Mary Jo Meadow, a retired professor of psychology and religious studies from Minneapolis, for first pointing out the correlation between Teresa's "Mansions" and Fowler's stages.[3]

Adolphe Tanquerey

Adolphe Tanquerey (1854–1932) was a Catholic priest in the French Sulpician order who taught at St. Mary's Seminary in Baltimore, Maryland. In his book *The Spiritual Life: A Treatise on Ascetical and Mystical Theology*, he described three spiritual "ways." He admits that he chose the word "to conform to traditional usage . . . [but in fact] it is not a question here of three parallel or divergent ways, but rather of three different *stages*, of three marked degrees, which souls . . . traverse in the spiritual life."[4] Tanquerey himself pointed out how his "ways" correspond with Saint Teresa's Mansions.

Caroline Myss

Medical intuitive and bestselling author Caroline Myss (1952–) compared progress through the Mansions and the spiritual-development journey with moving up the chakras. As she described it while speaking at a seminar in 2009, "Your chakras are to your energy system as [Teresa's] Mansions are to your soul."[5]

Gordon Allport

Gordon Allport (1897–1967), though best known as a psychologist, is considered important in religious circles for his 1950 book *The Individual and his Religion*.

Walter Clark

Walter Clark (1902–1994) was a dean at Hartford Seminary in the 1950s and a professor of the psychology of religion at Andover Newton Theological School in Massachusetts in the 1960s.

Fritz K. Oser

Oser (1937–) is a retired professor of education and educational psychology at the University of Fribourg, Switzerland. Along with colleague Paul Gmünder, he delineated five stages of what they called (in their book of the same name) "Religious Judgement."

Ken Wilber

Ken Wilber (1949–) is a contemporary American philosopher and author of many books, the most directly relevant to our topic of which is *Integral Spirituality: A Startling New Role for Religion in the Modern and Postmodern World*. His stages are a measure of development in both culture and consciousness and therefore also in spirituality. In this work he calls his stages "Altitudes," refers to them by color names, and shows how they compare with other developmental theories. Wilber correlates his stages with Fowler's, so they also correlate well with ours.

Now let's take another look at the spiritual-development stages, this time in chronological order, pointing out how these theorists add to our understanding.

The Lawless Stage

The Lawless stage represents a mindset all children supposedly pass through in the course of normal development. When it persists in an adult, it represents an aberration, almost a pathological state. It is useful to our discussion mainly because understanding the chaos of the Lawless mindset allows us to see what the Faithful are so fearful of falling back into. Fowler's first three stages correspond more or less to Piaget's stages of normal child development and therefore only hint at how this would play out in an adult. Peck gave us the clearest understanding of the Lawless stage in an adult, naming it Chaotic/Antisocial and ascribing to it the traits of pretense, manipulation, self-service, and unprincipled behavior. Wilber's first three color levels (Infrared,[6] Magenta, and Red) also span the Lawless stage at an immature adult level. In short, these levels are egocentric, unprincipled, and to varying degrees not very aware of the world outside the person's own being. At Wilber's Red level, power over others begins to take on importance and a might-makes-right approach prevails.

The Faithful Stage

The Faithful level earns far more attention from theorists. Though Fowler's first three stages pertain to child development, his second and third stages often persist into adulthood; his Mythic-Literal and Synthetic-Conventional stages make up our Faithful level.

In the Mythic-Literal stage, concrete operational thinking is typical and the person expands his perspective from the egocentrism of the prior stage to an ethnocentrism centered around the values and opinions of his religious and/or social group. Stories used to transmit such information are adhered to in a concrete, somewhat inflexible manner; as Fowler puts it, "meaning is both carried and trapped in the narrative."[7] Beliefs, especially religious beliefs, are interpreted literally. Moral rules are absolute and unresponsive to varying circumstances. "The actors in their cosmic stories"—Fowler's code word for God—"are anthropomorphic."[8] For example, in the Christian tradition, God is viewed as an actual being, a sort of bearded, judgmental Superman.

There is an over-reliance on a system of exact reciprocity. "If I accept Jesus Christ as my Lord and Savior," the Faithful person's thinking goes, "I will be saved." This can result in an "overcontrolling, stilted perfectionism or 'works righteousness.'"[9] Or the opposite: if the person is subjected to lack of approval from perceived authority figures, she can wind up feeling that she is a bad person, a worthless sinner. While Mythic-Literal faith is most appropriate to school-aged children, "we sometimes find the structures dominant in adolescents and in adults."[10]

In Fowler's Synthetic-Conventional stage, Piaget's final cognitive level, formal-operational thought, begins to appear. The person becomes able to reason hypothetically and consider perspectives other than his own. Because he can now think more conceptually, his worldview is no longer so concrete. But Synthetic-Conventional is a conformist stage in which, because the person has not yet developed a sure grasp on his own identity, the expectations and judgments of his accepted authority figures take precedence over his own. Similarly, his faith group "must provide a basis for identity and outlook."[11] He is still somewhat ethnocentric. Because he has not subjected his faith to intense critical reflection, his "beliefs and values are deeply felt [but] tacitly held,"[12] meaning he has not directly examined or thought about the reasons why he holds these beliefs. Like Piaget's formal-operational level, Fowler's Synthetic-Conventional faith stage typically develops some time during adolescence, and some individuals never progress beyond it.

Saint Teresa of Avila's first two sets of Mansions[13] also help us better understand the Faithful level. In the first Mansions, people are still largely under the control of a lot of what Teresa called "reptiles," that is, the pull of the material world—possessions, honor, or business affairs that engender occasions of sin outside the "castle." They are also mostly unaware of their own failings. In Teresa's second Mansions, people have gained enough self-knowledge to realize that conventional or conformist religiosity is not what they want, but they have not yet made the leap beyond it. According to Meadow, being in the second Mansions is like being caught between Fowler's Synthetic-Conventional and his Individuative-Reflective Stage, between our Faithful and our Rational level.

Tanquerey lumped both Teresa's first and second Mansions into his more general term, the Purgative Way, which also relates to spiritual beginners.[14] Here the concern is avoiding sin. The person is motivated by the fear of Hell and the hope of salvation.

Relating Saint Teresa's Mansions to the chakra system, Myss asserts that at the level of the first chakra we deal with tribal issues, physical survival, gaining basic groundedness, and suffering the results of early life humiliations. Myss calls the challenge at the second chakra level "stuffology"; we must grow beyond the search for physical power, sexual power, and material goods if we are to progress spiritually.

Fritz Oser's second stage correlates well with the Faithful level, though his first stage also contains hints of it. He called his Stage 1, "Orientation of Religious Heteronomy" or Deus ex Machina.[15] God is seen as intervening in the affairs of mankind, and people are perceived as having no part in determining outcomes. In his Stage 2, *Do Ut Des* (Give so that you may receive), the Ultimate is viewed as external and omnipotent, capable of punishing and rewarding. But there is thought to be a reciprocal relationship with the Absolute, meaning that the Absolute can be influenced by a person's good behavior, prayer, etc. ("If I pray hard enough, I will get what I want.")

Ken Wilber's fourth level, Amber,[16] is a conventional and conformist stage. The person at Amber has expanded her level of concern beyond herself and now includes her group—indeed, favors her group above all others. Wilber tells us the person at the Amber altitude exists at Piaget's Concrete Operational level. She tends toward fundamentalism and an excess of patriotism. Her beliefs are concrete and literal. Law and order are maintained through guilt and threat of punishment. This mindset is essentially equivalent to our Faithful and Fowler's Synthetic-Conventional level.

The Rational Stage

Noting a fair amount of agreement among the theorists as to what constitutes the Faithful level, let us now look at what they had to say about the Rational level.

If a person at the Synthetic-Conventional, or Faithful, level runs into serious contradictions among some of his authority sources, he may be forced to assess a given situation for himself. This pushes him to venture outside the comforts of conformity where trusted authority sources do all the hard work for him—which is exactly what happened to each person in our part 1 stories. If the person is ready to move forward, he will likely wind up in Fowler's fourth stage, Individuative-Reflective faith—our Rational level—where there is "a relocation of authority within the self."[17] Fowler calls this the "emergence of executive ego."[18] This does not mean the person becomes selfish, but that he assumes responsibility for his beliefs, as opposed to having them handed down by others. He becomes his own authority and finds there a reliable source of judgment. Another essential feature of this stage is a "critical distancing from one's previous assumptive value system."[19] As you might assume, Fowler most likely did not intend here to delineate a stage wherein the person fully detaches from his religion, as did those in our Rational-level stories. Leaving one's church behind is a possible, but not essential, feature of this level. But the Individuative-Reflective level is a demythologizing stage, in which the symbols previously taken literally (e.g., God as an actual being) are recognized as symbols; they no longer exactly represent a literal reality. For some, this translates into religious disbelief—as in our part 1 stories.

Ideally, a person would transition to the Individuative-Reflective stage in his twenties. For a young person, the social and personal upheaval of having to redefine himself and subject himself to disapproval from significant others is real but typically manageable. When the transition occurs later, in one's thirties or forties, the struggles are often much more severe. Note the differences in the relative ease with which Jim (chapter 3) made the transition as a college student versus the extreme life disruption experienced by an older Abu Ali (chapter 2).

In the Individuative-Reflective stage, a person may put excessive confidence in his own powers of reasoning. This can make him critical and dismissive of those in the previous stages.

Saint Teresa's third Mansions correlate with our Rational level and Fowler's Individuative-Reflective stage. While others have spoken of this stage as one in which reason takes predominance over spiritual concerns, Teresa, with her more religious focus, turned this concept around, saying the goal in the third Mansions (if one desires to progress to the next level) is learning not to trust one's reason too much. Teresa spoke in the language of her time, saying that in the third Mansions people are at risk of forgetting to fear God. Thus, to progress beyond the third Mansions, a person has to lessen the importance he attaches to his own reason and begin to think in more spiritual terms. Another task in these Mansions is to learn that we must not try to convert others to our beliefs.

Tanquerey equated his second way, the "Illuminative Way," with Teresa's third Mansions. Here, having learned to avoid most of the temptations to lower forms of sin, the emphasis now becomes more positive. The soul begins to concentrate more on the practice of the moral virtues—prudence, justice, fortitude, and temperance—as well as what Tanquerey called the theological virtues—faith, hope, and charity. In this stage the person must have gained enough self-control to lead a well-regulated life (like our Rationals, who are self-governing) and must have profound convictions on all the great truths (i.e. ones he worked out himself, like our Rationals, not ones that were handed to him by others, like our Faithfuls.)

According to Myss, the third chakra level calls us to face the challenge between the forces of reason and those of the mystical life. The first, second, and third chakras are all located below the waist on the human body. According to Myss, concerns regarding the first three chakras—what she calls "below-the-waist" issues—are typical of an immature spirituality. Here our heart is controlled by the limited focus of these lower level concerns, and the word *self* goes with *selfish*.

Oser and Gmünder called their third stage "Orientation of Ego Autonomy." Here a person tends to push the Ultimate out of the world.[20] People are autonomous, responsible for the world and for their own lives. Here they formulate ego-identity and distance themselves from parental and educational forces. They will frequently reject religious and ecclesiastical authority.

At Ken Wilber's fifth level, Orange, the person begins to move away from primary identification with her tribe and begins to seek her own truth. As this happens, her worldview expands to include everyone, and she becomes "worldcentric." Orange is rational and conscientious and has reached Piaget's formal operational level. It most appropriately occurs between late high school and early adulthood—however, some people, of course, never reach this level at all.

The Rational (Plus) Stage

Oser and Gmünder's fourth stage, "Orientation of Mediated Autonomy," may be a transitional stage on the way to our Mystic. Here the earthly is seen as the "likeness" of the Divine, or the Ultimate appears symbolically in nature, culture, and human capacities for love. Social activism may take the place of religious practices. The Ultimate is mediated via immanence; that is, the person begins to see God in the self, others, and/or nature. Images of God exist, if at all, as symbols only. Despite not exactly believing in a separate

God, these people, realizing that much of life is not under their control, will surrender to the "will" of an Ultimate—similar to our Mystic.

The Mystic Stage

While some theorists describe the lower levels in more detail, others focus on the later stages. Allport and Clark chose merely to distinguish mature faith from the immature variety. They were friends, so it is not surprising that their concepts are similar. Allowing, as always, for discrepancies due to individual interpretations, we can see how their descriptions lead us toward the Mystic disposition.

Allport argued that a mature religious stance is well differentiated, explaining that it must be the outgrowth of many successive discriminations and much critical reflection. It is not accepted with uncritical abandon, as in the born-again experience. Similarly, it is not reduced to simple, definitive answers and easy criteria for salvation ("Believe and you will be saved!"). A corresponding criterion from Clark's list is that mature religion must be free from magic.

Both Allport and Clark determined that a mature religious sentiment must be dynamic in nature and not based on fear, self-interest, or creature comforts. In mature faith, the person has become a master over lower-level needs.

Allport and Clark both specified that mature faith must produce consistent moral results. Clark took it one step further, saying that these moral results must be consistent with the aims of a wholesome society and must strengthen the individual's sense of community.

Allport said a mature religious sentiment must be integral, meaning that it must integrate modern scientific thought (such as evolution) into its explanations about the world without letting that progress inhibit rightly considered prayer and worship.

Lastly, Clark argued that the supreme test of a mature religion is that it must be creative, must contain elements specific to that individual, and must not be a mere repetition of the religion of others.

As a person becomes ready to transition into Allport and Clark's mature religion (our Mystic stage), she finds out that reason and science are not the final word. Fowler provides an eloquent description: "[T]he person ready for transition finds him- or herself attending to what may feel like anarchic and disturbing inner voices."[21] She begins to realize that there may be some truth in the religious myths, stories, and symbols. More gray areas appear in distinctions that previously seemed black and white.

When Fowler's fifth stage, or Conjunctive Faith, begins to take over, the person opens up to unconscious factors, the "voices of one's deeper self."[22] Reality is seen as more multileveled; the person no longer needs the certainty so important in the earlier stages. Paradox is welcomed and appreciated. Rather than the clear-cut "either/or" distinctions of the previous stage, the person begins to allow that in life's complex arenas a "both/and" understanding is more comprehensive. (The scientist can be right about evolution, *and* the Bible can tell us something valid about our existence.) The person at Fowler's fifth stage knows there is no single correct answer and appreciates that understanding the Big Picture requires input from all possible sources—from science and reason as well as from other religions. He may begin to reengage with some form of spirituality. Though he may celebrate this spirituality as part of a community, he recognizes that whatever group he may join holds but a partial view of Transcendent Reality. (He also realizes that he will most likely never be able to attain a perfect and complete view of it.)

This stage exemplifies a "commitment to justice [that] is freed from the confines of tribe, class, religious community or nation."[23] The person develops a universal (as opposed to ethnocentric) worldview and may begin to feel the need to work in service of it. According to Fowler, Conjunctive Faith is unusual before midlife.

However, in Conjunctive Faith, a person may be trapped between her unitive vision and the divisive world she is forced to experience in reality. Out of concern for her own safety, or through a passive withdrawal, she may find herself unable to act. If she manages to transcend these concerns and move forward in promoting her unitive vision, then she has most likely moved on to Fowler's uppermost stage, Universalizing Faith.

In Universalizing Faith, the conflicts are reconciled. The person adopts a universal, totally inclusive worldview. He or she may be prone to bold actions that promote that worldview, despite risk to his or her own personal being. Religious symbols have become transparent, and the person understands they all refer to the same universal Reality. In this sixth stage, the person is willing to become an activist for unity. Citing examples such as Rev. Martin Luther King, Jr. and Mahatma Gandhi, Fowler says such people create "zones of liberation and [send] shock waves to rattle the cages that we allow to constrict human futurity."[24] They embody a superhuman level of trust in the power of an Ultimate Reality and a "trans-narcissistic love."[25] This means that their love expands to include the whole universe, transcending the limits and barriers that normally exist between people. It also refers to a type of love that transcends the person's own ego. This all-encompassing love accounts for the readiness on the part of such people to "spend and be spent"[26] in making their view of the Transcendent Reality come alive for others.

Such people are often seen as subversive by those at more conformist levels and are likely to be more honored and appreciated after death. People at this level are very few. I was unable to find any for inclusion in this book.

Essentially equivalent to our Mystic stage, Tanquerey said his third way, the Unitive Way, is characterized by a "need of simplifying all, of reducing all to unity. . . . [A]ll things converge toward intimate union with God through charity."[27] This wording hints at the way these upper spiritual levels express themselves, that is, *through charity* toward people we find here on earth, in *this life.*

Saint Teresa's fourth through seventh Mansions represent further distinctions within our Mystic stage. In the fourth Mansions, the soul has generally risen above the level where the "reptiles" of sin can tempt it; it is self-governing. The person stops striving and allows grace to take over. In the fifth Mansions, the ego is diminished, and the importance of self and petty worries is reduced. One no longer feels the need to control events. Together with the fifth Mansions, the sixth Mansions correspond to a "dark night of the soul," in which intense psychological suffering may coexist with joy and an intense desire for union with God.[28] In the seventh Mansions, someone who may have faced inaction before now becomes engaged in the service of God (or service to humanity, as a part of God). There is a great calm, a forgetfulness of self; the ego is transcended. The interior and exterior aspects of life come into harmony.

For Caroline Myss, the fourth through seventh chakras entail "above-the-waist" concerns, and together they involve our Mystic level. She says that in the fourth chakra, the light is too bright for lower level concerns (or for the "reptiles" that tempt you to sin). God (the Ultimate Reality) comes for you and you surrender. A person may experience a calling to serve others in some way at the spiritual level.

At the fifth chakra, there is a dissolving into holiness, while at the level of the sixth chakra, it may be necessary for us *not* to attain what we want before we realize what we need; we struggle about whether we want to commit. A person must sever the connections between head and heart, allowing the heart to take over. The person may well be misunderstood by others, may become increasingly occupied in spiritual affairs, and may not want to deal with everyday, practical issues. This is similar to Fowler's Conjunctive Faith, where the person may be caught between his vision of an idealized unitive world and the harsh reality of the actual world. In contrast, at the seventh chakra, there is complete union with the Ultimate and Divine Love.

Ken Wilber's Green Altitude is conjunctive—this person ties concepts together rather than looks for divisions. He tends to reject hierarchical systems, is strongly egalitarian, and holds pluralistic values. Because Green is broadening his worldview, he begins to have more compassion for others and may become heavily involved in social causes.

He may also become more idealistic. Wilber claims his Green is roughly equivalent to Fowler's Conjunctive Faith level.

After Green in Wilber's Altitudes, we have Teal,[29] followed by Turquoise, Indigo, Violet, Ultraviolet, and, finally, Clear Light. Suffice it to say that the further up Wilber's Altitudes a person goes, the more she can include in her worldview. Teal consciousness sees how each of the previous stages reveals an important truth, pulls them all together, and integrates them. Wilber relates Teal and Turquoise to Fowler's highest level, Universalizing Faith. As for the less specific stages in this book, our Mystic level would be somewhere between Wilber's Green and Turquoise.

An important point here is that we can assume we have no idea to what level people might someday progress. While Fowler's Universalizing Faith is rare now, someday that may be the norm, and some other higher "Ultraviolet" and "Clear Light" stages may begin to emerge.

In many of his other works, Wilber elaborates a concept that is worth including here. He explains the existence of various developmental *lines*, of which spiritual development is only one. Other lines include the cognitive, the ethical, the logical, the mathematical, the musical, the spatial, etc. Because people can develop at a different rate along each line, we can easily note the existence of some people who are highly sophisticated in one respect (say, scientifically) while still operating at a much less sophisticated level in another respect (say, spiritually).

In Oser and Gmünder's fifth stage, "Intersubjective Religious Orientation," the person feels connected to the Ultimate, however that is understood. This is a stage of unconditional acceptance and complete mediation between Being and the world. This person feels at one with the universe, experiences enlightenment, or has a sense of divine illumination, depending what faith tradition he comes from. Transcendent and immanent views of the Ultimate are intertwined. The either/or orientation of the earlier stages is integrated into a broader understanding.

Each of these spiritual experts we've reviewed has outlined a path from an immature spirituality to a mature one. We can see that the path described by each shows a common spiritual trajectory, from pursuit of self-centered concerns and religious conformity as an escape from chaos (Faithful level) toward a self-transcendent universality and a submission to the will of Spirit, however that may be defined (Mystic level). Reading between the lines of these same works, we are able to flesh out the all-important, but often cryptically described, intermediary step of the Rational level—where there is a broadening of personal responsibility to include social justice toward all and a reliance upon human reasoning powers over conformity.

Other authorities have contributed to our understanding of this progression, even though they may not have addressed spiritual development specifically or may have written about it in less detail. Psychologist Lawrence Kohlberg defined stages of *moral* judgment.[30] His Pre-Conventional levels are typical in child development; but, when present in an adult, the second stage—the Self-Interest orientation—is particularly similar to our Lawless stage.

In Kohlberg's two Conventional levels, appropriate for adolescents, the emphasis is on group conformity (Stage 3) and a "law and order" orientation based on submission to "authority" (Stage 4), respectively. These correspond with our Faithful stage.

In Kohlberg's two Post-Conventional levels, morality is determined by forces within the individual (i.e., one's conscience), as opposed to being dictated by the outside force of authority. (This is roughly the same thing as saying the person is self-governing.) The fact that many adults never reach these stages leads to confusion in our society. Because they cannot imagine how anyone could live an ordered life without strict obedience to immutable rules, Conventional level adults tend to suspect and accuse Post-conventional people of anarchy.

At Kohlberg's Stage Five, rules are considered important but subject to change when necessary. Individual rights begin to take on greater importance—the person can allow that various social groups may hold different values, opinions, and rights, all of which should be respected. At Stage Six, Universal ethical principles, such as justice and truth, take precedence over rules of the current society. If a person at Stage Six perceives society's current rules as transgressing against a certain universal principle, she may be inclined to fight for change. She may be willing to put herself at risk for the sake of principle. This is sometimes exemplified in cases of civil disobedience. Kohlberg called his Stage Six a "theoretical stage," because he felt that few individuals consistently behave at that level, though Rev. Martin Luther King, Jr. is given as a possible example.

The correlation between Kohlberg's moral judgment stages and our spiritual development stages is muddied at the Post-conventional levels, but without excessive attention to the details, we can summarize that our Rational and Mystic levels relate to Kohlberg's Post-conventional levels.

In *Ego Development: Conceptions and Theories*, Jane Loevinger, a developmental psychologist, outlines nine sequential stages of ego development, representing progressively more complex ways of understanding the self in relation to the world. The stages in her system applicable to adults (her first two stages are not) begin with the Self-Protective stage, similar to our Lawless level, and progress through a conformist, group-oriented stage, like our Faithful level. Her next four stages—Self-Aware, Conscientious, Individualistic, and Autonomous—all correspond to varying points included in our Rational level. At Loevinger's final, Integrated stage, the person moves beyond seeing inner conflicts egocentrically, beyond tolerating them as in the autonomous stage, and is able to embrace them instead. Like the Mystic finding beauty in the mystery, the person at Loevinger's Integrated stage is reconciled to the fact that some answers and goals are unattainable. He can make peace with paradoxical aspects of existence and is comfortable living with unsolvable mysteries. Identity and individuality are cherished.

For a more complete understanding of the Mystic level, the reader is referred to Evelyn Underhill's *Practical Mysticism*. For finer distinctions within that level, study of Ken Wilber's *Integral Spirituality* and the writings of the great twentieth-century Indian sage Sri Aurobindo may be helpful.

Though the terms may differ, and the number of steps may vary, we can see that all these theorists describe a common trajectory in spiritual growth; each of them outline a path from an immature to a mature spirituality. They all ascribe to *immature* spirituality (our Faithful stage) these traits: reliance on forms of authority originating outside the person (tradition and religious conformity); a literal, more limited view of God; concern largely with self (one's own salvation) and one's own group; and simple black-and-white "either/or" logic about the truths of existence. Most of these works hint at an all-important intermediary "critical distance" step that must occur before a person can move beyond an "immature" faith.

In moving toward a more mature spirituality, a person will increasingly acknowledge a reliable authority that comes from within. At first, this authority will come from within the cognitive self, as at the Rational level. Later, it will come from something less definable that we may call Spirit. At the Mystic level, the person may become willing to submit to the will of this Spirit, however that may be defined.

Along the way toward spiritual maturity, a person will gain the personal strength to question and perhaps reject the literal views of God that could only apply to one specific religion. This person may leave her search at the level of outright rejection (Rational level), or she may continue seeking a way to integrate the spiritual back into her life in a postcritical manner. Like our Mystics, she may eventually choose a broader view of God that includes herself, the entire universe, and even the God of spiritual traditions other than her own. She may choose to reengage with the spiritual within a specific tradition, or she may choose a more personalized path. Nonetheless, she remains always cognizant that her choice is not the only way, but one of many equally valid choices.

Also along the path toward a more mature spirituality, a person will expand his awareness beyond concern for his own salvation or his own worldly well-being—or that of his immediate group. He may only reach a position of being able to include other humans within his perspective, as at the Rational (or humanist) level. Or he may be able to expand that perspective to include other elements: animals, plants, nature, and the mystery of the unknown. The ever-broadening worldview that accompanies spiritual growth may eventually include a sense of unity with the whole universe, as in the Mystic level. In progressing along this trajectory, a person may expand his powers of reasoning beyond the simple, black-and-white "either God is or God is not" mentality toward a position where the paradox of this mystery is not simply tolerated but welcomed.

The personal stories in parts 1 and 3 were chosen to introduce this emotionally thorny concept of spiritual growth in an appealing way. In exploring the high degree of similarity in the works of theorists from different fields and over different centuries, I have tried to provide evidence to provoke serious consideration of the merit and benefits the spiritual-development process has to offer. Wherever one might be religiously, it is worthwhile considering whether and how these stages might enrich one's understanding of spiritual truth. Awareness of the spiritual-development process may even help prod some readers toward further growth. Wherever we might be on our own journey of spiritual development, a road-map of the territory can only help shed light on our path.

Chapter 16

Two Types of Religious People

Though not well understood in our society, there are two very different categories of religious faith, independent of the details of specific religious traditions. They are called by different names, but we can see that they actually refer to the stages of spiritual development. This categorization is not widely recognized, because there is hesitation to put value judgments on people's faith. But lack of applying this language holds back a realization that could move our civilization forward. Once we divest ourselves of the need to judge people by their level of spiritual development, we can drop our emotional attachment to feeling that we have the right answer. Only then can we begin to allow this perspective to inform us about what spiritual development really is.

Abraham Maslow's "Peakers" versus "Non-peakers"

In *Religions, Values, and Peak-Experiences*, psychologist Abraham Maslow (1908–1970), father of the "hierarchy of human needs," said many organized religions tend to "develop two extreme wings: the 'mystical' and individual on the one hand, the legalistic and organizational on the other."[1] In Maslow's construct, the left wing includes *peakers*—those who enjoy "peak," mystical, or personally transcendent experiences and tend to be privately religious. The right wing includes *non-peakers*—those who "concretize the religious symbols and metaphors, who worship little pieces of wood rather than what the objects stand for, those who take verbal formulas literally, forgetting the original meaning of those words, and, perhaps most important, those who take the organization, the church, as primary and as more important than the prophet and his original revelations."[2]

Maslow noted that nearly everyone experiences transcendent personal experiences to some degree, but the non-peaker is someone who "is afraid of them, who suppresses them, who denies them, who turns away from them, or who 'forgets' them."[3] By contrast, peakers acknowledge and welcome these experiences and allow them to inform their worldview. Historically, peakers have been the people who founded religions and upon whose transcendent experiences most traditional religions are based. "Organized religion," Maslow wrote, "can be thought of as an effort to communicate peak-experiences to non-peakers . . . [a job that often] falls into the hands of non-peakers."[4] The non-peakers running our religious institutions tend to hold a superficial, legalistic, or overly pragmatic (literal) understanding of the original transcendent message. They seem prone to dismissing experiences of awe, the Divine, or the sacred that occur in everyday life and instead confine the holy to what happens in church.

In almost any church, you can find both peakers and non-peakers side-by-side. Most likely they don't even notice any difference, because things they say sound the same. Even the Mystics, if they have not studied spiritual development, may not have given enough thought to the path they have gone through and so may not recognize that some folks in their church say the same things with very different meanings.

Maslow hinted at a possible developmental distinction between the non-peakers and the peakers when conjecturing that "not having core-religious experiences may be a 'lower,' lesser state, a state in which we are not fully functioning, not at our best, not fully human, not sufficiently integrated."[5] We can clearly see how his non-peakers are more like our

Faithful and his peakers more like our Mystics. Maslow further pointed out how the transcendent experiences of mystics from religions throughout the world, including atheistic ones like Buddhism, share an intrinsic core that would seem to invalidate the differences among the religions. In this sense, the non-peakers emphasizing the literal differences among the religions are holding back this realization, causing unnecessary divisiveness among the various traditions.

Liberal versus Conservative Theology

While this is not the place to address the immense complexity of various theological variances, we can most likely agree that conservative theologies in general speak to human need for certainty and varying degrees of triumphalism about having the "right" answer. Conservative religions also speak to people's need to be comforted and the need for clear guidelines to keep them from sinning. So the conservative message is really akin to our Faithful level. The person further along on the spiritual path no longer needs such certainty.

Liberal theology, on the other hand, allows more room for mystery. In liberal theology, the words may sound the same superficially, but they lack the concrete proclamations of conservative theology; with careful attention, a listener can discern more metaphorical connotations. Liberal theology is more prone to challenge members into addressing the questions, facing their inevitable doubts, and developing a personal faith that allows room for uncertainty. Liberal religious institutions also include far less triumphalism—they do not claim to have the only right answer.

Another factor in liberal theology is inclusiveness. Where the conservative religious institution is about *us* versus *them*, the liberal church is more about *everyone*, including those with different beliefs; there is no *them*. So liberal religion is more inclusive, less ethnocentric, and more universal. Broadly speaking, liberal theology, because of its inclusiveness, its approach to the mystery, and its metaphorical interpretations, tends to be closer to our Mystic level.

But winding up in a liberal church is not at all the same as moving through the stages. Many factors influence a person's choice of church, including geographical location, the influence of other family members, social concerns, etc. For this reason, membership in a church where universal concepts are preached may have little or nothing to do with a person's spiritual stage. Similarly, participation in a church with a more literal message may not imply a Faithful stance on the part of any individual member.

Inner versus Outer God

Another distinction between the two types of religious people concerns those who see God as an entity completely external to the individual, versus those who feel God is within them (and/or see God in others or in nature). Obviously, the most traditional religious speakers refer to a wholly external God, the God of the Faithful level.

Others speak of an inner God, an entity found within the person himself. Some in traditional religion fear and reject this notion, because it sounds like self-aggrandizement. But the inner God is more like the God of unity perceived by the Mystic. In developing spiritually, a person moves from holding a wholly separate and outer God in the Faithful stage, toward a less separate, more inner God in the higher stages. Oser and Gmünder plainly state that at their highest spiritual level, a person can integrate the two concepts into one; the transcendent and immanent views of the Ultimate are intertwined. The either/or orientation of the earlier stages is integrated into a broader understanding.

Metaphorical versus Literal Interpretations

We will discuss this concept in detail later, but generally speaking, literal interpretations of religious and spiritual concepts are more typical at the Faithful level, while at the Mystic level metaphorical interpretations are more typical.

In summary, it becomes clear that the two religious "classes" discussed in this chapter do refer in a general sense to the distinction between the Faithful and the Mystic stage. It is a distinction that has been missed by much of our society. For example, the brilliant pronouncements of the New Atheist authors are quite convincing. But their arguments are largely confined to refutation of Faithful religion. In the certainty of their Rational stance, these authors and their followers disregard the all-important Mystic level, an error that could be avoided if more people understood the stages of spiritual development—and the difference between the Faithful and the Mystic stage.

Other reasons why the stages are good to know about will be discussed in chapter 18.

Chapter 17

How Does Spiritual Growth Happen?

Those who have written about spiritual development have advanced various explanations for its possible causes. Two possible factors that might occur to us intuitively must be ruled out before beginning this discussion.

Spiritual Growth Is Not a Matter of Intelligence

The first factor we must rule out as a driver of spiritual development is *intelligence*. Some highly intelligent people are traditional believers, and some are not. Some less intelligent people hold literal beliefs; some do not. Progress through the spiritual stages simply has nothing to do with intelligence—at least, not the kind that can be measured on IQ tests. Think of it this way: Some intelligent people are not good tennis players. Tennis skills can be improved by practice, but some of us, no matter how much practice we put into it, are never going to reach the highest level of performance. Some innate factor allows a person to reach top performance in tennis; call it talent, attribute it to certain physical characteristics, personal drive, or passion. But given a basic level of normal intelligence, additional levels of intelligence do not provide a tennis player with an overwhelming advantage. And so it is with spiritual development: intelligence is simply not the driver of spiritual growth.

"Spiritual Maturity" Does Not Imply Being "Better"

Ironically, the second factor we must rule out about spiritual development is how good—or how useful to society—a person might be. A higher spiritual level does not imply one is a better person or has higher value to society than anyone else. While there must be some correlation between spiritual development and moral development, we cannot even assume a spiritually advanced person is a more moral one.

Nor do we want to push everyone from the lower levels to the higher ones in hope of creating a "better" world. People from all levels are needed to comprise a balanced society. Just as one's level of spiritual development has nothing to do with intelligence, so it has little to do with one's value to society.

Different theorists have advanced notions of what drives movement through the stages. Gordon Allport implied desire is a factor when he said that maturity "comes about only when a growing intelligence is somehow animated by the desire that this [religious] sentiment shall not suffer arrested development, but shall keep pace with the intake of relevant experience."[1] He also noted, "In many people . . . this inner demand is absent. Finding their childhood religion to have comforting value and lacking outside pressure, they cling to an essentially juvenile formulation."[2]

M. Scott Peck disagreed, saying we must be careful to avoid the notion that we ourselves can direct the process of spiritual growth. Rather, he argued, "We must allow God to do the directing."[3] For Peck, grace was the necessary factor in all growth. "Grace," he said, "is a promotion, a call to a position of higher responsibility and power."[4] When intuitive hints emerge, telling us that we need to take a different direction in life (like Inés's call to enter the ministry), that is a call from grace to rise to the challenge. Peck felt that grace is available to everyone, but that many resist it out of laziness or a reluctance to grow. Grace is something we either choose to respond to—or not.

James Fowler's faith-development theory mostly attributes movement through the stages to cognitive development, reasoning power, or logic. But what Fowler calls the *logic of rational certainty*, the science and math logic that deals with what can be proven objectively can only take a person so far. To get to the upper spiritual levels, Fowler claims we need the *logic of conviction*, a more personal, more subjective cognition that includes the "necessary combination of rationality and passionality that faith involves."[5]

Heinz Streib, a later proponent of Fowler's work and a professor for religious education and ecumenical theology at the University of Bielefeld, Germany, disagreed with Fowler, saying that cognitive forces were but one of many drivers. He pointed out that a person who is brought up in a certain type of society will only be likely to adopt the faith that is typical of that society, so other factors such as family influences and life events must also have an effect.[6]

Ken Wilber and his followers insist that meditation and what he calls "state changes" are what lead a person upward. In *Integral Spirituality*, he offers a very helpful distinction between *stages of development* and *states of consciousness*, worth mentioning here because the two are often confused.[7] States of consciousness are temporary and experienced by people at all levels. Waking, dreaming, and deep sleep are normal states of consciousness. But some people also experience certain *transcendent* or mystical states of consciousness like those found in meditation, those induced by brain-altering chemicals, and those triggered by intense (peak) life experiences. Some transcendent experiences can cause a person to diverge from what most of us call reality and feel they have heard the voice of God or seen a "vision." Such an experience can happen to anyone at any stage, but each experiencer will tend to interpret it from his current level; a person at the Faithful level seeing a vision might insist she saw Jesus or heard God speak to her, while someone at the Mystic level might interpret the same experience less literally. Experiencing state changes does not imply that a person is at a higher level of spiritual development, but Wilber says the more time a person spends in the "elevated," or mystical, states of consciousness, the faster she or he can progress through the stages or the more likely they are to reach higher spiritual levels. Certainly meditation must be *one* factor that can trigger spiritual growth, but few of the Mystics in this book mention meditation; other factors must be considered.

Psychologist Mihaly Csíkszentmihályi described the transcendent state a person can reach when he is completely absorbed in an activity that uses all his skills to the utmost and the level of challenge is in perfect balance with the skills required. The activity must be neither too hard nor too easy; it must require one's full concentration so that awareness of temporal concerns such as time, tiredness, hunger, and even awareness of oneself as separate from the activity drops away.

In this situation, which Csíkszentmihályi called "Flow," a person's consciousness is completely ordered (as opposed to the psychic *disorder* that occurs with anxiety, boredom, and despair). Also, spending large amounts of time in the Flow state allows a person access to personal and spiritual growth. Described this way, flow experiences are much like Wilber's state changes; by definition, they include transcendence of self, and they are a definite factor in spiritual growth.

All the Mystics I interviewed reported significant personal trauma at some point in their lives. Jean (chapter 11), for example, lost her sister and both her parents within the same year and was forced to assume responsibility all at once for running her father's business and rearing her sister's son. Some psychologists say such trauma spurs growth. As Fowler noted, "Development results from efforts to restore balance between subject and environment when some factor . . . has disturbed a previous equilibrium. Growth and development in faith also result from life crises, challenges, and the kinds of disruptions theologians call revelation. Each of these brings disequilibrium and requires change in our ways of seeing and being in faith."[8]

Walter Clark lists six influences that inspire a person to grow spiritually, expressed in terms of progressing from *belief* to *faith*. They are 1) gradual maturation and family influence, 2) persons who serve as an example, 3) religious and educational institutions, 4) mystical experience and conversion, 5) external trauma and crisis (these could lead a person either to grow or to regress), and 6) deliberate behavior and the operation of choice—that is, doing the activities that go along with faith can reinforce the person's feeling that they believe.[9]

David Keirsey's four Temperament types (condensed from the twelve Myers-Briggs Personality Types and described in *Please Understand Me II*) neatly correspond to our four stages. The Artisan is a pleasure-seeking, sensation-seeking personality, hedonistic about the present and focused on the here-and-now (Lawless). The Guardian is a "security-seeking" personality: conformity-oriented, trusting in legitimacy of authority and hungering for membership, as in a church (Faithful). Keirsey's Rationals, like ours, are a "knowledge-seeking" group, seeking autonomy and trusting in reason above all else. Keirsey's Idealists are an "Identity-seeking" group, hopeful about the future, mystical about the past (Mystic). If temperament type corresponds with belief stage, then how could a person *grow* over time? This could pose a challenge to the validity of the spiritual stages, but perhaps one's temperament either encourages or inhibits movement through the stages.

Thus far, I have presented spiritual development through the work of others and avoided advancing my own views. At this point I will offer one personal opinion derived solely from my own studies and observation. It is known that many fundamentalists (the lower end of the Faithful group) had chaotic upbringings or difficult early lives. To them, moving up to the Faithful level, such as in a "born again" experience, is a matter of life circumstance: someone or something led them to church, something in that setting took hold, and the person was "saved" from his formerly chaotic life. Other Faithfuls were born into a given faith and never questioned it. So winding up in the Faithful group depends mostly upon *life circumstance*.

But no life experience will lead a person beyond the Faithful stage unless he is willing to dispense with outer authority and think for himself. I suggest that it is *cognition/reasoning/logic* that leads a person from Faithful to Rational.

A move from Rational to Mystic requires something quite the opposite of reasoning; one must subdue *the logic of rational certainty* in favor of Fowler's *logic of conviction.* It requires a willingness to listen to the voice of the unconscious from within or what some might call the voice of Spirit or even the will of God.

Forward movement on the spiritual journey requires that a combination of factors—reason, grace, peak experiences, and a transformative response to life trauma—all line up in a positive direction. For that to happen, I believe a single factor is responsible. For lack of an official term, I will call it *spiritual courage.* What would keep a brilliant mathematician from applying his superior reasoning skills to questions about the existence of God and the truth of his religion, if not a lack of spiritual courage? What would cause one person to rise to the challenge of responding to life trauma in the most transformative manner possible while another retreats in despair, if not spiritual courage? At the border between the Faithful and the Rational level, spiritual courage requires that the person be willing to ask the questions that could put her world in disorder and alienate her from her group. At the Rational-to-Mystic transition, spiritual courage requires the humility to subjugate reasoning powers in favor of trust and faith in an Ultimate Reality that can never really be defined. Perhaps the spiritual courage that leads a person forward in the stages is another word for *grace.*

Chapter 18

Why Do I Want to Know about the Spiritual Stages?

So if these spiritual development stages are so universal and have been written about by so many people, why are they not widely known? Even the term *spiritual development* is not common in our cultural vocabulary. Many adults are not even aware that personal growth of any kind is possible beyond adolescence.

Why Spiritual Development Is Not Well Known

One reason spiritual-development theory is not familiar to more people is the nature of the writers themselves. Texts explaining spiritual development have been written by people who live largely "above the clouds," so to speak, either academically or spiritually, so they use a vocabulary and explicate concepts most of us do not readily appreciate.

Also, research in any field tends to be carried out by people whose mind focuses on details, who try to find differences and distinctions others cannot see. Most of our theorists, each using different terminology to elucidate a different number of stages, most likely had this type of sensibility and arrived at their respective stage structures largely as a result of their own work. But as long as the theories remain separate and unrelated, no single work has sufficient

239

authority to allow spiritual development to become part of the general knowledge of our culture.

Another reason spiritual development is not more known is that each stage has a characteristic that makes its members unwilling to accept news of the stages. Mystics are enthralled with unity, and they do not want to hear of distinctions between people on any terms, much less spiritual ones. While Rationals may be interested in declaring the Faithful less mature, they will not accept the fuzzier worldview of the Mystic. And Faithful-level folks need the triumphalism of having a better answer than everyone else.

Further, the religious authorities themselves hold back appreciation of the spiritual-development stages. Apparently some seminaries encourage doubt and questioning and even teach about the stages, but others present a self-justifying mentality ("Only our church is right") such that their students never glimpse a broader view unless they begin seeking answers beyond the limits of their training. Consequently, many church leaders have not heard of the stages or do not understand them.

Also, "brand recognition"—the idea that only one particular church's message is the real "truth"—is necessary to what we might call the economic competitiveness of churches; for one church to attract lots of members, the church down the street must be seen as offering answers that are somehow not as correct. Yet a church promoting a triumphalist message holds its members back from spiritual growth; it discourages acknowledgement that in true spiritual maturity, despite stunning differences in detail, all spiritual traditions can be boiled down to essentially the same message.

Why Know about the Spiritual Stages?

Why would readers care what a bunch of theorists wrote about spiritual development? Why would they want to read stories about the spiritual paths of others?

Is this book an attempt to convert everyone to the Mystic level? Certainly not. Surely it is clear by now that 1) trying to convert others is mainly typical of the Faithful stage, and 2) movement through the stages is not a process one can direct for oneself. And if one can't direct it for oneself, one certainly cannot not direct it for others.

Also, though one level may predominate, a person will generally maintain traits from prior levels. This makes distinguishing among the stages quite muddy. So one must resist the urge to use knowledge about spiritual development as a way to judge the spiritual stage of any given person.

So, if not to judge others, not to convert them, and not to push ourselves to the upper levels, why *do* we want to know about these stages? Opining that within organized religion there is little appreciation of the difference between "great art" and that which is imitative, Abraham Maslow wrote: "Trying to teach people to paint will not make them great artists, but it can very well make them into a great audience for artists."[1]

Years ago, galleries and poster shops were flooded with a series of paintings that came to be called "Big Eye" art. Featuring mostly little girls with huge, soulful eyes and (often) tear-stained cheeks, these works were designed to pull at our heartstrings and had great emotional appeal. But does that mean they were great art? Someone who knows immediately whether a painting contains the elements of great art has no trouble distinguishing it from the commercial variety or from those works offering a facile emotional appeal. She holds no illusions that the latter will appreciate in value into the next century.

Similarly, Faithful-level preachers today promote a belief system that is useful to some and may appeal at an emotional level, but is not "great art." Religion, as a "done deal," providing strict rules about life in this world and definite answers about what happens in the next, has a very real place in society. It offers certainty, reassurance, community, and even transcendence to Faithful-level members. The pernicious effects of its ethnocentric, separatist message and its view of a limited God only big enough to love one small part of his Creation do not override the value this form of belief offers to those who need it.

But we must also recognize Faithful-level religion for what it is—and isn't. Just as Big Eye art will not find a place in the Louvre, Faithful-level religion does not represent the most advanced "art" form in spirituality. Through study of the spiritual development stages, we can begin to glimpse what "great art" in spirituality might consist of. We can teach ourselves to paint, not in hope of becoming great artists ourselves, but in hope of becoming a better audience for those who are, and to allow ourselves more tolerance of those who are not.

Let us next consider an analogy with one more art form. A person just learning to cook must follow a recipe exactly, less he risk disaster. His cooking is imitative and dependent upon the skill of "experts." The meals he produces may be useful, may provide nutrition, and may taste pretty good. But they are functional and routine—not inspired, not art.

As a cook gains more experience, he may begin to substitute one ingredient for another and may try adding ingredients just to see how the dish will turn out. More confident now in his culinary skills, he no longer avoids experimenting for fear of a poor result. No longer can someone else using the same cookbook produce the same result. His cooking takes on a more personalized, more "artful" element.

Now consider a blue-ribbon chef. He has studied under many masters and considered many different cooking methods. Given his broad exposure to varying food types, he would never proclaim that only, say, French cooking is any good or that there is only one way to make a souf-flé. He knows good meals can be produced in many different ways, from any cooking tradition.

The seasoned chef no longer needs a proven recipe to produce a good meal. Years of hard work combined with an innate talent and a driving passion for culinary excellence allow him to intuit what ingredients go well together. Driven now toward ever-higher levels of expertise, he produces meals of his own creation. The art of the master chef is no longer imitative, but inspired. No longer dependent upon the expertise of others, a topnotch chef pursues his art as an expression of himself.

The professional development of a master chef can be compared to the path of the spiritual learner. Rules, holy books, and structured messages are the spiritual cookbooks those in the Faithful stage must follow. As a person gains mastery over herself and confidence in managing her life, she doesn't so much need the structures of religion. She may begin to question and experiment a little, may learn she no longer needs the spiritual cookbooks of organized religion, and may venture into the Rational stage.

If her questioning and experimentation meet with success, her life circumstances permit it, and her spiritual ideas are not cast in stone, a person may delve further into this specialty. After years of serious study, openness to growth, and absorbing wisdom from the ideas of other cultures and religious traditions, she may approach the "master chef" level of spiritual development. Lest one suspect that just anybody can blithely discard the rules in favor of a freelance spiritual life without structure, reflection, and disciplined enquiry, the emphasis here is on the years of hard work, study, and an innate passion for the subject matter. In cooking, as in spirituality, the highest art form is reached creatively and after long, consistent effort and focus.

Most people recognize that they could further develop their own culinary skills; those at the cookbook level do not cast aspersions at master chefs. So should it be in the spiritual world. The spiritual masters should be recognized for who they are—not weirdos who have strayed from the fold, but people who have grown beyond the need for a spiritual cookbook. One of the goals for this book has been to let people become a great audience for "great art" in spirituality.

While there remains the question as to how well people can understand spiritual levels above their own, exposure to the spiritual-development trajectory holds many benefits.

When a person breaks out of the Faithful fold, perhaps out of genuine concern, and perhaps out of an insecure need to have others validate their own choices, remaining members may try in vain to manipulate the person back into the flock she or he has left. In the worst cases, the renegade may be shunned or outcast. Also, because he doesn't understand it as a growth step, a person leaving a faith group may experience guilt. So much of this interpersonal suffering would be unnecessary if it were understood that questioning and the move beyond literal belief is necessary to growth.

Studies by the various theorists suggest spiritual growth is a separate developmental line, only one of many along which humans grow. As with other lines such as intelligence, worldly accomplishment, and moral judgment, spiritual development may proceed independent of development in the other lines. Development, and the fact that some will reach higher levels than others, while commonly understood in other aspects of life, is least well recognized in spirituality. Because there is so much emotion surrounding religion, people tend to balk if any hierarchy is suggested. Perspective about spiritual development as a separate developmental line *not* connected with a person's "value" should help us be less reactive about religious differences.

Part Five

What Does It All Mean?

Chapter 19

Is There a God?

Is there or is there not a God? If this book has muddied the waters on that issue, the effect was deliberate. Spiritual-development theory—the commonalities in the work of the theorists explained in chapter 15 and the spiritual journeys of the people in the stories in parts 1 and 3—suggests the need for a new look at this question.

The God of the Faithful is a discrete entity separate from all of creation. He is father-like, invariably seen as male, and evinces some very human frailties: anger, jealousy, and favoritism. He points down from Heaven casting favor on one person or group and disfavor on another. The God of the Faithful insists that we believe in only one specific version of him and will punish those who disobey his wishes. He supposedly created billions and billions of people over the millennia—but would "save" only those who had the remarkably good fortune to be born (or "born again") into the only *true* religion. Meanwhile, countless billions born elsewhere and in different millennia would never have this chance. This is the literal, judgmental, bearded Father God in the sky. Oddly enough, this God, who is supposed to be All Good, has transmitted his wishes in a cryptic way through books written thousands of years ago and in the language of a culture that no longer exists. Would it not make sense that if that God actually existed, he would by now have sent an update on his message?

Described this way, the God of the Faithful must either exist, or not exist. There are only two possible answers: true or false, with no room for anything between. Black-and-white issues like this one, with a definite "yes" or "no" answer, respect the laws of *binary logic*.

In order to function, the simplest type of computers need their instructions to be broken down into simple steps, each expressed as a set of numbers using only two digits: either 1 or 0. (Electric current is either on or off for a given command.) So computers "reason" using binary logic. But we humans are capable of much more sophisticated reasoning than computers. We can sense that some things are only partially true, true to a greater or lesser degree, or even true at one time and false at another. Asking people whether they like their job can serve as an example. Most people probably like their job to some degree and at the same time hate certain aspects of it. They probably like it more on some days than others and over time may grow to like it more or less depending on multiple complex factors. Almost everyone can see that it would be impossible to divide people accurately into two groups, those who like their job and those who do not. Job satisfaction cannot be considered using black-and-white reasoning.

K. Helmut Reich, originally an electrical engineer and physicist who more recently focuses on theological issues, studied reasoning skills and pointed out how black-and-white logic is the least developed level of reasoning (out of five levels). As reasoning skills develop beyond the first level, people begin to be able to take in more and more angles and appreciate increasing numbers of perspectives in considering any issue.

For some reason, people seem to be able to apply more sophisticated reasoning to less crucial issues—"Is the weather good or bad today?" or "Do I have a good boss or a bad boss?" But when it comes to God's existence, these same people insist there are only two possibilities—yes or no—limiting their reasoning to the same simple binary logic computers use.

Reich actually tested this idea in one of his studies.[1] He first rated people on their level of *relational and contextual reasoning* (RCR) on nonreligious issues, then asked the same people to judge between a statement from a scientist about the world's origin (the big bang, evolution, etc.) and a statement from a minister about God as the ultimate explanation of why the universe exists. Sure enough, he was able to extract five levels of reasoning among the responses. They ranged from Level 1, binary logic, where the subject believed either the scientist or the minister to be completely right, through increasing complexity until, at Level 5, the person attempted to give a general synopsis that included both the perspective of the scientist and that of the minister. In many cases, the score for a given individual on the world-origin question was lower than his RCR level for nonreligious issues. Not a single individual exhibited higher-level reasoning on the world-origin question than his RCR level for nonreligious issues.

Clearly, intelligent people readily apply sophisticated reasoning in nonreligious matters. But when it comes to religious beliefs, the critical mass in our society—by this I mean the voices we hear in the mass media—regresses to an immature form of reasoning. Another of Reich's studies, which examined whether the Christian doctrine of the Holy Trinity is comprehensible, concluded that "an understanding of Christian doctrines requires one to transgress the limits of formal binary logic."[2] Clearly, we humans are capable of more sophisticated reasoning than the simple binary logic about God's existence that we see in much of our popular culture.

The God of the Faithful is the God of binary logic. If that God must either exist or not exist, my rational mind tells me it cannot exist. Anyone who has gone through the Rational stage must agree that this particular God is not a scientific likelihood, at least in its literal form.

The recent popularity of the best selling "atheist manifestos" by Christopher Hitchens, Sam Harris, and Richard Dawkins gives evidence that many in our society fail to relate to the God of the Faithful. Their readers were happy to reject an improbable God whose existence can't be proven scientifically—and they were grateful for the relief these books provided from the facile, fantastical, yet doctrinaire proclamations of the religiously assured.

The God the New Atheist authors refute is the mythic, magical God of the Faithful; the beliefs they denounce are the beliefs of the Faithful. But like the Faithful mindset they believe they have disproven, the New Atheists, as examples of the Rational worldview, also reduce God's existence to a matter of binary logic.

Rationals and Faithfuls see only two possibilities: God either exists or does not exist. Each group collapses the tension between these two possibilities in the direction most convenient to its worldview. But the very need to collapse this tension, the need for religious certainty (for or against the existence of God), evinces a less-than-completely-mature spirituality. It promotes an error, a logical fallacy: that the vast concept of God's existence can be reduced to the rules of binary logic. Religious certainty serves as a linchpin in an ongoing effort falsely to promote suspicion, blame, and, sometimes, even hate among us; it erroneously divides us against each other. God's existence—whether such an entity exists, and who or what that entity is—is too complex for binary logic, too big to fit into neat yes-or-no categorizations.

God as a Missed Metaphor

Mystics understand that the literal God of the Faithful cannot exactly exist in the traditional sense of the word, and yet they choose to remain spiritually involved. What can these people see that Harris, Hitchens, and Dawkins cannot see (or, given their level of scholarship, have perhaps chosen not to see)?

The word *metaphor* is worth defining here. According to *The Random House College Dictionary*, a metaphor is "the application of a word or phrase to an object or concept it does not literally denote, suggesting comparison to that object or concept." It is in the metaphorical sense that scripture and religious concepts *do* contain truth. So many in our society simply do not comprehend even the possibility that the literal God of traditional religions is supposed to be a metaphor for something else— not an actual anthropomorphic entity, but something much larger and much more difficult to define. It is in this metaphorical sense that our Mystics understand God.

Let us now look at another definition: the word *synechdoche*. The same dictionary defines it as "a figure of speech in which a part is used for the whole or the whole for a part, the special for the general or the general for the special." Thus a synechdochic metaphor is one in which a small part of the whole is used to designate a whole, which remains unnamed. A synecdoche expects the listener to fill in the gap between what is said and the actual meaning. So a teenager begging his parents for "a new set of wheels" would be most disappointed if his request were granted literally; but there is little danger of this error in our culture.

The same situation exists with respect to the God of the Faithful. However unlikely as a literal reality, the God perceived by the Faithful can have a valid, universally applicable counterpart if the word is seen as a synechdochic metaphor. The God of any given Faithful-level religion is a part of an Ultimate Reality that, from the bird's-eye view of the Mystic, applies equally to the entire universe. Let us look at what some who understand the Mystic level have said with regard to a definition of God.

To express one of his six criteria for a mature religious sentiment, Gordon Allport said, "The religion of maturity makes the affirmation 'God is,' but only the religion of immaturity will insist, 'God is precisely what I say He is.'" [3]

Contemporary rabbi Rami Shapiro, writing in *Spirituality and Health* magazine, listed three levels at which we can engage religion. At the tribal level, each faction competes with the others over whom God loves best (Faithful stage). At the worldly level, religious factions have moved beyond the need for competition and instead promote an ethic of universal justice and compassion (approaching, but not exactly equivalent to, our Rational stage). At the mystical level (very much corresponding to our Mystic stage), God is recognized by all three major religions as "the One True Reality of which all beings are a part." Although people may belong to a given religion, they see their own beliefs as pointing toward an "Absolute Reality beyond the forms and formulae . . . the One True Reality of which all beings are a part." [4]

James Fowler wrote that for those in his final stage, Universalizing Faith, "Particularities are cherished because they are vessels of the universal." [5] Put in more everyday terms, the view of God held by a particular faith tradition is a symbol, or part of, a Greater Reality that is not limited to any particular religion or tradition.

One of my favorite Mystics, Sister Joan Chittister, a member of the Benedicine monastic order, author, and speaker, said: "The real truth is that God is too great to be lost in the smallness of any single sliver of life. Truth is One, yes, but truth is many at the same time. . . . The greatest danger of them all may be in buying into too small a part of the truth. When that happens, change, growth, repentance, and development are impossible. We find ourselves frozen in the shards of yesterday. Truth is not any one truth, not any one institution, not any one way." [6] We may have to read between the lines here, but if we do it seems evident that Sister Joan is saying that the God of any particular religion is a synechdochic metaphor for an Ultimate Reality that applies equally to the whole universe.

Abraham Maslow was less diplomatic in his pronouncement that the differences between the religions amount to little more than expendable details: "[T]o the extent that all mystical or peak experiences are the same in their essence, and have always been the same, all religions are the same in their essence and have always been the same. They should, therefore, come to agree in principle on teaching that which is common to all of them . . . [and agree that] whatever is different . . . can fairly be taken to be localisms both in time and space, and are, therefore, peripheral, expendable, and not essential." [7]

John Shelby Spong pointed out how humility regarding our own powers of reasoning and a realistic evaluation of our sources of religious authority are necessary to spiritual growth: "To suggest that God and one's own understanding of God are the same is not only to stop growing, it is to die to the quest for truth." [8]

Wayne Teasdale said: "The religions are like ten blind men trying to describe the nature of the elephant; it is only when they put all their experience together that a clearer understanding of the elephant emerges. Similarly, it is only when the religions' various forms of mystical spirituality are related to one another in a larger context of truth that we will have a better idea of the shape of the absolute."[9] Teasdale borrowed this elephant concept from an old tale found in Sufi, Buddhist, and Hindu lore; the (mostly Western) spiritual development theorists are not the only ones saying spiritual development leads to a unitive view.

The clearest and boldest explication of the universality—the awareness of a Greater Reality transcending the constraints of a given religion's dogma—that characterizes continued spiritual growth comes from French philosopher Paul Ricoeur (1913–2005), who wrote mainly about interpretation of scripture. His terminology has been borrowed by some in religious circles to refer to three stages of religious growth. What Ricoeur called the "First Naïveté" corresponds roughly to our Faithful and Rational stages, respectively; his "Second Naïveté" corresponds roughly to our Mystic level. In the "Second Naïveté," the person has reconciled himself to the ambiguity and paradox of his beliefs—or, at least, is able to hold the tension between the original beliefs and the rational analysis, while still finding something of value in his faith.

Ricoeur listed two main reasons people in the First Naïveté hold on to religion: 1) Taboo—the taboos provided by religious structure help a person keep his behavior in line; and 2) Refuge—out of a desire for protection, people sometimes hunger for an all-powerful, non-local entity, someone or something stronger and better than those they find here on earth.[10] Ricoeur wrote that people must grow beyond the need for taboo and refuge—"the corrupt parts of religion"—in order to move from the First Naïveté (Faithful stage) to Critical Distance (Rational stage). But it is precisely Critical Distance, said Ricoeur, "that clears the way for a deeper type of faith—one that is purified of these baser needs and similarly purified of the *phantasm of a father figure God.*" He added: "[A]theism teaches us to renounce the image of the father. Once overcome as idol, the image of the father can be recovered as symbol. *This symbol is a parable of the foundation of love.*" For Ricoeur, an atheistic stint in the Critical Distance stage served a very valid purpose. It would allow an idol—the God of the First Naïveté—to die "so that a symbol of Being"—the small-g god of the Second Naïveté—"may begin to speak."[11] The deeper type of faith of which Ricoeur spoke is, essentially, our Mystic level.

All the above descriptions point to a perspective that only those who have climbed the highest on the spiritual-development mountain can see. None of these descriptions is blinded by obstructions from any one religious institution. None of them refers to a God who would have designated a "Chosen" people to the exclusion of all the others. None refers to a God who would love (or save) only those who hold a limited and partial view of him. None refers to a God who would harshly punish those who have not followed certain rules about dress or behavior.

The abovementioned writers all understand something many others do not: that the God of the traditional churches is supposed to be a synecdochic metaphor for the Universal Reality. God is not just the God of the Christian religion or the God of Islam; the God of each religion is a metaphor for, or a symbol of, a broader entity that applies to all religions.

We have largely missed the metaphor of God. We buy that teenager four round things with spokes connected to nothing when he asks for "wheels." We insist that the bearded old "sky God" with his rules and judgments represents the entirety of the Ultimate Reality. In much of traditional religion, "non-peaker" preachers and their congregations mistake the part for the whole.

The literal interpretations promoted by most forms of organized religion no longer make sense in our largely Rational-level society. The New Atheist authors sanctioning an intellectual escape from Faithful-level religion have had great appeal precisely because a critical mass in our culture has moved beyond the primitive needs of taboo and refuge.

What the New Atheist authors and their followers ignore is that the God they reject is but a placeholder for what was meant to be seen not as a literal entity but as a metaphor for something greater and less specific. The religion these writers deny is but a caricature of an authentic spirituality. Like the readers who have made them popular, these authors have missed the metaphor. As a culture, we have missed the synechdochic metaphor of God—that the God of each religion is just a metaphor for the less definable Universal Reality of mature spirituality. Recognizing this metaphor for what it is requires that we integrate some of the wisdom of the Mystic level.

The God of the Mystic Applies to All

So, is there or is there not a God? In *Integral Spirituality*, Ken Wilber provides a most interesting and brilliantly comprehensive exploration of this question in his discussion of the "Three Faces of Spirit."[12] According to Wilber, the God of the traditional religions comprises only one of these faces: Spirit in the *second person,* typically addressed as "You" or "Thou." This view of God is not so much false as incomplete.

Wilber then describes a Spirit in the *first person* and a Spirit in the *third person.* Wilber's Spirit in the *first person* is the "I-I" that meditators sometimes experience. During a mystical experience, there sometimes arises a feeling of unity with the whole universe. At that point, a person may experience God as the ground of his own being, may see himself as a first-person God; his own ego may dissolve into this unity. Obviously, this view of the self as God brings with it risk of narcissist misinterpretation. What could be more dangerous and more false than an ego thinking it is God without the needed spiritual growth and maturity characteristic of the Mystic level— the humility, the acceptance, the compassion, and most of all, the willingness to submit to a Spirit Authority? But this view of the self as God is not evil, as some church leaders would have you believe. It is a genuine part of human spirituality that only some people ever get to experience.

Spirit in the *third person,* as Wilber describes it, is God as the Great It, the Great Web of Life, or more simply, nature or Gaia. People who experience nature as divine (as in the earth-based religions) are simply able to access a different part of Spirit from those in churches. Neither group is "wrong." Each merely experiences one part of Spirit and not so much the others.

Wilber explains how theistic traditions emphasize the second-person God but ignore the other two, especially the first-person Spirit. Many "new paradigm" spiritual movements emphasize the third person (Gaia). Others focus mainly on the first-person concepts that can be accessed through a spiritual practice such as meditation. But these generally ignore the second-person aspect.

On a practical level, we can say that seeing God as any one of these facets, to the exclusion of the others, has the effect of distorting a person's spirituality and retarding his or her maturity. Those aspiring to spiritual maturity would do well to learn to appreciate all three persons of Spirit. Doing so forces an understanding beyond the limitations of literal belief in the parent-figure God of the traditional churches. At the same time it protects us from the facile assumptions of some of the more superficial forms of New Age spirituality.

An appreciation of all three persons of Spirit also protects us from an over-reliance on reason that leads us to reject out of hand the existence of the second-person God of the churches. Seeing that God is not limited to a specific literal entity should allow us to open our minds to the God of others. Knowing the existence of God is not determinable by the rules of binary logic should soften some of the arguments on either side. Knowing we are all subject to further growth in our understanding of these matters should serve to moderate the certainty with which we judge the religious belief (or nonbelief) of others.

What Are We All Arguing About?

If we can open ourselves to the possibilities expressed in Wilber's construct, we can begin to glimpse something truly beautiful. The Three Faces of Spirit include all beliefs and all forms of spirituality held by all people in all parts of the world in all eras. It opens up the idea that everyone's view of God is part of a whole we can never define.

Throughout this book we have been exploring the idea that people develop spiritually and that some finally reach more inclusive or more comprehensive levels than others do. The trend progresses from a limited view of God to an ever-broader one—and from concern largely with self and one's own group toward an ever-broadening perspective that eventually includes the whole universe. As people grow spiritually, they continue to include more and more of creation in their worldview.

Contemplating Ricoeur's concept of a God beyond the "corrupt parts of religion," beyond the Faithful-level need for taboo and refuge, and beyond the Critical Distance of the Rational level, we can begin to glimpse a way to appreciate an Ultimate Reality that excludes no one and no point of view.

Adding Wilber's definition of the Three Faces of Spirit to spiritual-development theory points the way toward an understanding that no matter what view of God one holds, everyone is (at least partially) right!

The Mystic view of God or the Ultimate Reality transcends the petty differences between and among the various religions. The God of the Mystic includes everyone and everything in the universe. Surely the Mystics are not wrong in their view of God. The God of the Faithful is a part of the God of the Mystic, so the Faithful are not wrong, either; their God is simply a part of the truth. And the Rationals have correctly determined that the God of the Faithful cannot exist in a literal sense. They too are not wrong. They simply are not yet able to glimpse the larger reality; they just do not yet have a full view.

Thanks to Ken Wilber, we can see that the God of the churches is a valid part of a triune Spirit, a Universal Reality with three natures. The nature worshipers have glimpsed another part, and those having episodes of unitive consciousness have experienced yet another. None of these views is wrong. None of these experiences is invalid. They all are part of a construct of which just about none of us has a complete picture.

Thus, in deciding whether to accept or deny God's existence or the validity of religion, we must ask ourselves, "Who or what is the God we are choosing to accept or reject?" Viewed through the lens of spiritual-development theory, we must consider that all the vehement debates about the existence or nonexistence of God may be a question of definition—literal anthropomorphic *being* versus metaphorical *symbol*. And all related debates on either side are applying an inadequate logic structure to the most perplexing question of our existence.

Seen in the light of the spiritual-development process, the answer each person holds to these questions is the right answer for her at the given time she holds it. Realizing that each person's beliefs are a function of her spiritual-development stage allows us to see that people at all levels have chosen beliefs that are correct and necessary to make their lives work for them.

Further, spiritual-development theory shows how every different belief system is correct because each is *part* of a whole truth, a symbol of a broader, all-encompassing Reality of which most of us are unaware. And it shows that we can recognize our own level of spiritual maturity by how much of the universe we feel a part of, how much we can include within our worldview.

What are we all arguing about? If the God of Ricoeur's Second Naïveté is but a symbol, it matters not what clothes that symbol wears or what language it speaks. A symbol does not have a Chosen People and does not stand in judgment of their actions. A symbol doesn't care if we believe or disbelieve. It does not reward or punish or require worship from us. It is up to humans to live up to the standard of Love represented by this symbol—or not. Most importantly, the symbol from one religion is no better and no worse, no more true or more false, than the symbol honored by any other religion! At the level of the Second Naïveté, the idol from each particular religion has died—and the symbol begins to refer to something universal to all of us.

It is sometimes said that a transformation is afoot in which more people are moving toward a greater spiritual awareness. When more people understand the steps on the road to spiritual maturity, there will be less opportunity for divisive factions in society to promote spiritually immature worldviews. A kinder, more inclusive society will emerge as more and more people undergo this transformation.

Chapter 20

What Transformation?

Despite the many factors suppressing appreciation of the higher spiritual levels, it seems that more people are reaching them now than in the past. In the eighteenth century, the movement called the Enlightenment marked a transformation in attitudes that basically changed the world. It began with the intellectual elite and eventually filtered down to people at all levels in the Western world. Before the Enlightenment, society was based upon unexamined superstitions and tyrannical, authoritarian social and religious hierarchies. The Enlightenment ushered in a new reliance on reason and science as well as respect for individual rights. This change has been viewed ever since as representing *progress*— growth toward a more advanced or mature form of civilization.

But Enlightenment-level thought has its limitations, which by now our civilization is beginning to realize. In science, new revelations brought to us by the theory of relativity, quantum mechanics, and chaos theory are weakening strict confidence in what we had long thought of as scientific givens: time, causality, and the properties of solid matter. Global communications and the Internet have exposed us to the crises and struggles of others and to details of their cultural and spiritual traditions. This added exposure forces us to consider ever-greater numbers of perspectives, from ever-greater numbers of often-conflicting sources.

More and more "contexts" are appearing that need to be "related," such that those of us not defensively shutting them out are getting a lot of practice in Helmut Reich's "relational and contextual reasoning." Very few factors in our existence, it turns out, are adequately determined by "either/or" binary logic. By the time all possible factors are considered, nothing is as certain as our own cultural traditions would teach; nothing is as cut-and-dried as Rational-level inclinations would have us believe.

As a general society, we are beginning to outgrow the over-reliance on reason and science of Enlightenment thought. Slowly it is dawning upon post-critical thinkers that the limits of human reason constrain a full understanding of our Ultimate Reality.

In *Faithful Change: The Personal and Public Challenges of Post-modern Life*, James Fowler compares the Enlightenment's society-wide changes to the individual transition from the Synthetic-conventional (our Faithful) level to the Individuative-Reflective (our Rational) stage. He claims, I believe correctly, that society progresses through essentially the same development trajectory that each individual must traverse in the move toward maturity. Some individuals lag behind the general society in their growth, while others parallel it and some are ahead of it. To put it bluntly, Fowler says that the Faithful mindset is comparable to that of pre-Enlightenment society; the Rational mindset is comparable to Enlightenment-level thought.

Along with a host of others, Fowler argues that a new transformation is taking place in society that will equal or surpass the Enlightenment in scope. This transformation will bring about a greater inclusiveness, less focus on material acquisition, and more tolerance—at a minimum—of those with different lifestyles and beliefs.

Just as the Enlightenment moved the critical mass of Western society from Faithful-level conformity to Rational-level individualism, the predicted transformation will move a critical mass of society beyond the independence of the Rational toward the Mystic's more open and fluid way of inhabiting the universe—toward a unitive worldview. Those not hiding from the opportunities our increasingly complex society brings us will find themselves approaching the multiple perspectives of Fowler's Conjunctive Faith, the tolerance of paradox in Reich's Relational and Contexual Reasoning, and an openness to the symbolic God of Ricoeur's Second Naïveté. In short, if there is a transformation occurring, it is hurling our society toward the universal worldview of the Mystic

Returning to the individual level of growth, Fowler's original research and the writings of the other theorists indicated that only small numbers of people ever reach the advanced spiritual stages and that growth to that level was uncommon before midlife. But most of this research was carried out over thirty years ago. If the predicted post-Enlightenment transformation is in fact occurring, and if this transformation parallels what happens at the individual level, then it must be that more and more people are reaching the Mystic level. They must be doing so increasingly earlier in life and in greater numbers than in the past.

The likely influence of this transformation on society in general explains why it may no longer be true that most people in most traditional religions are at the Faithful level. Where at one time traditional religions may have been based upon the Faithful mindset, now we have a blurring of such distinctions. For example, some formerly traditional (i.e., ethnocentric) evangelical religions now embrace social-justice causes. It may be that many in traditional religions are beginning to absorb post-Enlightenment traits from the general society and are working a more universal worldview into their faith stance.

In some circles where this transformation is acknowledged, those who have already evolved are being compared to "imaginal cells." When an ugly caterpillar goes into his cocoon, apparently his old caterpillar cells begin to disintegrate into a soup or goo, from which eventually emerge what biologists call imaginal cells. These cells, so different from the caterpillar, contain butterfly-like traits and seem to be able to "imagine" the beautiful creature that will one day emerge from the cocoon.

At first, what remains of the old caterpillar organism finds the imaginal cells so unlike itself that it destroys each one as it arises. But eventually the butterfly cells multiply faster than the caterpillar cells can kill them off. As time goes on, more and more of them survive. Soon these new imaginal cells begin to clump together and form into groups until together they comprise something completely different from the caterpillar. At that point they have transformed into a beautiful butterfly.

The imaginal cells that presage the butterfly can be compared to the few individuals in the past who have attained mystic consciousness and an awakened spirituality—Mahatma Gandhi and Rev. Martin Luther King, Jr., are two familiar examples. In many cases, traditional religious leaders found the values of these two exemplars too different from their own and failed to recognize them for what they were. These leaders often railed against Gandhi, King, and others like them, hoping to diminish their influence before it contaminated the congregation.

Now those spiritually aware individuals are said to be increasing in number—they are beginning to recognize each other and clump together into groups, just like imaginal cells do. They are even beginning to be able to share information (an activity not incompatible with the mission of this book).

Where centuries ago, people reaching this spiritual level were persecuted as heretics, their numbers are now multiplying more rapidly than our current culture can disparage their message. Spiritual imaginal cells are said to be on the verge of forming an entirely new culture that will one day no longer be the exception but rather the norm.

Traits common among those undergoing this transformation are similar to those typical of our Mystic level. They include a heightened conscience, a deeper sense of personal responsibility toward others, humility, compassion, and forgiveness. Their predominant trait is a sense of connectedness with all people, animals, nature, and even the world of spirit—with all the elements of our existence.

This type of consciousness leaves the person more inclined toward some of the other values we have discussed. An awakened spirit finds the exclusionist message (i.e., "Only those who believe as we do can be saved") offensive. She finds herself in more alignment with an understanding that includes all the world's religions as different aspects of the same Truth. A metaphorical God in whom all can share appears far more probable and appealing than an ethnocentric personified deity who limits himself to a "chosen people."

The transformed individual also exemplifies a different understanding of integrity than that held by conventional society. The dominant notions of society—time is money, profit is king, and personal gain is all that counts—are replaced by a deeper sense of personal responsibility toward others. As this transformation progresses, people will realize that in a zero-sum game where the presence of winners requires the existence of losers, *everyone* actually loses. As our society matures, people will realize that the only real wins apply to everyone.

When more people have undergone this transformation, our religious, economic, and *political* messages will have to change to accommodate this new worldview—or risk irrelevance, if not ridicule, among the increasingly larger population of the transformed. A largely transformed or post-critical society will recognize the importance of selecting political leaders with spiritually mature values. And once we have elected them, we will understand that we must work together as one to shepherd our society forward into a truly universal and transformed one.

Chapter 21

What Does Politics Have to Do with It?

A final theorist, UK psychiatrist Dr. Larry Culliford, provides one last set of descriptions for stages that correspond to our Faithful, Rational, and Mystic stages and further deepens our understanding of them. Culliford's Conformist[1] or Belonging[2] stage is characterized by a powerful urge to belong to a group and by an us-versus-them mentality in which fear of those who believe or live differently from one's group is a strong motivating factor. In Culliford's Individual or Searching stage,[3] the main drive is to think, act, speak, and take responsibility for oneself. This individuation may lead the person to break out of his tribe if necessary. In the Integration or Homecoming stage,[4] the person leaves narrow, either/or certainty behind, embracing instead a broader, both/and understanding. Here the person is driven by an altruism that makes her want to think, speak, and act not just for herself but for everyone, recognizing the responsibility we all have toward one another.

Culliford offers a particularly interesting real-life example that leads us to an important concept. He sees Barack Obama as an example of someone in transition between the individual (Rational) and Integration (Mystic) stages.[5] The crucial growth issue for Obama was not religious belief as much as personal identity. Forging beyond the Belonging level would present a particular challenge for someone whose mixed racial and cultural background provided him with no fixed group identity in the first place. Culliford discusses a dream Obama reported in his book *Dreams from My Father* as an important transition point in his growth cycle. The dream included these words from Obama's father, who had been dead about a year: "Barack, I always wanted to tell you how much I love you." [6] Here tears and sadness replaced Barack's former confusion and fear. Culliford points out a later cathartic epiphany, a moment in church when Barack was again reduced to tears by a sermon on "The Audacity of Hope": "Those [biblical tales] of survival, and freedom, and hope became our story, my story . . . until this black church . . . [seemed to be] a vessel carrying the story of a people into future generations and into a larger world. Our trials and triumphs became at once unique and universal." [7] Culliford sees this as Obama's entry into the equivalent of Fowler's Stage Five, the beginning of our Mystic stage.

Sure enough, peppered throughout both Obama's books are terms and statements demonstrating a maturing spirituality. A moment of Critical Distance, and with it the dawning of personal authority, occurred during a visit to the African town of the father he never knew. "All my life," Obama recalled, "I had carried a single image of my father . . . the brilliant scholar, the generous friend, the upstanding leader." [8] But on his visit to his ancestral homeland, Obama learned things that gave the lie to that image and suddenly saw his father as "a bitter drunk[,] an abusive husband[,] a defeated, lonely bureaucrat[.]" [9] Obama reflected on the discrepancy between his image of his father and reality: "To think that all my life I had been wrestling with nothing more than a ghost!" [10] The shock of this realization, and further reflection upon it, would spur his continued growth and maturation, including the emergence within him of a conscience authority, which he expressed clearly in his later book, *The Audacity of Hope*: "I find comfort in the fact that the longer I am in politics the less nourishing popularity becomes, that a striving for power and rank and fame seems to betray a poverty of ambition, and that I am answerable to the steady gaze of my own conscience." [11]

Several other quotes in *The Audacity of Hope* hint at a burgeoning Mystic-level spirituality and universal consciousness. Obama says he decided to join a church, not to meet his own needs, but because "I was able to see faith as more than just a comfort to the weary or a hedge against death; rather, it was an active, palpable agent in the world." The following statement almost sounds like it came from the "What is a Mystic?" chapter in this book:

> [My] religious commitment did not require me to suspend critical thinking [*it allowed him to reengage with faith* after *his Rational stage*], disengage from the battle for economic and social justice [*that is so important in the Rational stage*], or otherwise retreat from the world that I knew and loved [*a Mystic's universal love; see chart on page 90*] . . . [My selection of a church] came about as a choice and not an epiphany; the questions I had did not magically disappear [*as they would have in a Lawless to Faithful born-again experience*] . . . I felt God's spirit beckoning me. I submitted myself to His will [*Spirit Authority!*] and dedicated myself to discovering His truth."[12]

The fact that Obama later rejected the choice of church that had inspired this statement does not detract from the indication of his probable Mystic, or near-Mystic, stance (though it does seem that the leader of that church was less universal). A later comment offers confirmation: "This is not to say that I'm unanchored in my faith," Obama wrote. "There are some things I am absolutely sure about—the Golden Rule, the need to battle cruelty in all its forms, the value of love and charity, humility and grace."[13] (The faith he professes here is about values, not beliefs.) Those who accuse Obama of not being a real Christian undoubtedly fail to understand the Mystic sensibility, mired as such people are in their Faithful-level stance.

Compare the complexity of Obama's nuanced, deeply personal journey—though it may or may not involve any literal beliefs—to the simpler, more straightforward process typical of the "born-again" experience, in which the person finds life coherence by simply joining a church and taking on its beliefs *in toto* without reasoning them out for himself. This distinction gives us an opportunity to make another point about politics.

The Religion of the Religious Right

Suddenly adopting a readily available, off-the-shelf belief system without the benefit of a deep personal journey does not represent passage to spiritual maturity. Nor do the facile, absolutist answers promoted by the religious right.

With its extremely conformist orientation, the religious right in the United States promotes a worldview based upon pre-critical, literal beliefs and authoritarian social and religious hierarchies of old; as such, it represents a throwback to a pre-Enlightenment mentality. Lashing out in fear against societal changes it fails to understand, the religious right represents the antithesis of the post-Enlightenment spiritual transformation. Thus the religion of the religious right is a caricature of the Faithful stage.

The religious right limits personal responsibility to its own religion or political party (and the needs of overpaid CEOs), ignoring the needs of "the least" of our people. They reject the importance the Enlightenment/Rational level ascribes to individual human rights and scorn the emphasis a post-Enlightenment/Mystic worldview places on social justice. Viewing life as a zero-sum game, the religious right acts in fear, holding back what the other levels would consider social progress. They believe if the unfortunates in society gain something, they themselves somehow lose. Blind to the ways in which their worldview is tantamount to a game in which everyone loses, they are unable to imagine the benefits of unity.

Through the use of simplistic messages, the declamatory voices of the religious right discourage their listeners from considering our nation's most urgent issues in their full complexity. On fundamentalist radio stations especially, short, simplistic slogans reduce complex social, economic, and religious issues to binary, either/or logic. These voices tragically dumb down the reasoning power of our population, enticing rapt but unsuspecting listeners to accept immature, under-developed logic on important issues—from the teaching of evolution to fair treatment of gays in the military to our lumbering, profoundly flawed health-care system. Knowledge that spiritual maturity does not involve simplistic black-and-white reasoning—or divisive tactics—can arm listeners against manipulation by those who would control them. It would render us impervious to attempts of those who would curb our use of our reasoning power and divide us against others for the sake of their own political gain.

The religious right also obstructs development of authentic personal authority. In requiring adherents to heed an outer, i.e. biblical, author-ity (as interpreted by fallible but insistent humans), the religious right impedes discovery of an individual conscience authority.

People aware of the spiritual-development trajectory will avoid fall-ing prey to the spiritually immature worldview of the religious right and will deny these oracular authorities control over their worldview. They will see the importance of employing the most sophisticated reasoning available and applying their own conscience authority in forming opin-ions and making decisions about society's most crucial issues.

Those in the throes of personal transformation will resist capitulat-ing to a worldview that retards progress toward a more humane society. They will spread word of how these shallow voices seek to cloud our sense of personal responsibility to one another.

Whether proponents of the religious right actually believe the asser-tions they put forth, or proclaim them only as a means of controlling others, is anyone's guess. There is no guessing, however, about their use of religion as a political weapon. People aware that spiritual maturity inclines one toward unity and peace can recognize that the religious right's promotion of divisiveness, hatred, and fear stems from an imma-ture spirituality. Sophisticated thinkers will want to avoid the religious right's binary logic on important social matters, no less than on the question of God's existence.

The religious right is like the dying caterpillar cells that are threatened when the imaginal cells begin the work of transforming into a butterfly. They fear the changes the Rational and Mystic "imaginal cells" will bring about. To those who lag behind, the spiritually transformed appear so unlike themselves that they work feverishly to destroy them. But just like the beautiful butterfly that emerges from the imaginal goo, one day our society will look very different from the caterpillar stage it is leaving behind. Spiritual-development theory tells us that our current imaginal cells will eventually lead our society's emergence into the transformed butterfly world of universality. In presenting this book, I am betting that society is ready to begin this transformation. Those willing to challenge themselves to grow toward more sophisticated religious understandings can help shepherd us into a deeper humanity while providing a richer life for themselves and others.

Chapter 22

Faith beyond Belief

The personal stories you have read in this book are stories of personal empowerment; they all involve emancipation of the self. To be clear, this is emancipation of the self not for selfish purposes but rather for the ultimate purpose of endowing oneself (and, by extension, others) with the *freedom to serve*. A society with everyone in strict religious chains is not an advanced society. Where people are dependent on an oracle authority, they are likely held prisoner to divisive, ethnocentric messages that work against the universal worldview. Those who can see that we truly are all connected understand that anyone who excludes anyone else, any other group, or any other thing ultimately harms himself. And this ultimately works against the overall good of society.

In a society where people are encouraged to grow, more of its members will be called to action in service of humankind. The more people learn to stay the forces of their ego-driven immaturity, transcend the need for oracle authority, cultivate a strong conscience, and finally open their ears to the voice of a Spirit Authority, the more people there will be who stand ready to act in the service of universal good.

The personal stories in this book are also stories of trust. While the Faithful person fears the universe, God, creation, and human reality on earth and beyond, the Mystic trusts in the goodness of our existence, accepting whatever challenges and setbacks may come her way. She trusts in an unseen order that connects us all and that, by whatever name one might call it, represents the *good*. This good cannot be real unless it includes the entire universe—not just Christians, Jews, or any other religious group. People who have matured spiritually have come to trust in the Goodness of Something greater than themselves.

The stories here are also stories of freedom. Almost everyone in the Rational stories mentions a feeling of liberation that came with renouncing their literal beliefs. The Mystic-level stories incorporate even broader types of freedom. Along with Jean's spiritual growth came a freedom from the oppressive message she was brought up with about the worth of women. Nilah learned to express herself authentically and free herself from a list of trivial religious "Thou Shalt Nots." David's growth freed him to return to the basic loving nature he had had as a child. Charles became free to redefine faith as something he had always held but that had been hidden by his lack of exposure to comparative religions. Catherine's growth freed her to reframe two major life hardships as opportunities for growth. And Inés's story tells how she finally allowed herself the freedom to explore and express a powerful spirituality she had possessed since childhood.

Most of these stories display an increasing personal responsibility toward the common good. Each contributor freed himself from the shackles of religious conformity that kept him focused on his own needs and released himself instead into a greater freedom to serve others. While more striking examples of service to humankind could surely be found, each contributor in this book provides an example of a small way that an average person could serve. David serves by teaching Sunday school—in his own post-critical way, all the while respecting the pre-critical needs of his students. Catherine focuses her life around care for her disabled son while contributing to a Christian community (though most of its members are far more pre-critical than she is). Jean has devoted years to serving the environment and basically rearranged her entire life to serve the needs of a child who is not hers. And Inés reinvented herself as a

Unitarian minister, agreeing to serve at the will of a divine call she heard only at the Spirit level.

While these stories do not spell out great degrees of humility, at least they are not triumphalist proclamations about having found the "right" answer. In each one, the person moved closer to at least some of the Mystic-level traits: acceptance, forgiveness, gratitude, humility, seeking community, preferring the mystery over answers, governance by a Spirit Authority, and a more or less universal worldview.

The list of traits we attribute to the Mystic is not very different from the ones Maslow identified as those resuting when people move toward self-actualization. As people grow, Maslow argued, they press forward toward good values like serenity, kindness, courage, honesty, unselfishness, and goodness—that is, toward Love.[1]

This is not the self-serving love of romance. It is not even the more selfless, but still particular, love of, say, a mother for her child. Rather, it is something more encompassing. Where the Mystic has grown from the need for a capital-G God to an appreciation of a small-g god, that same growth step has taken him from a particular and limited small-l love to an all-encompassing Love of the whole universe.

I suggest we refer to the faith of the Mystic as "post-critical"—a spirituality that follows after a person has applied enough critical reasoning to take him beyond the literal beliefs of the Faithful stage. Doing this allows us to tease out a distinction between the "blind" belief of the Faithful and the "post-critical" faith of the Mystic, chosen deliberately in full awareness of the complexity and insolvability of the existential message.

In the words of Gordon Allport, "'Faith' . . . seems to carry a warmer glow of affection than does bare 'belief.' . . . It suggests that though the risk may be greater, still the commitment is stronger, and the outcome of the wager more precious."[2] In summary, the Mystic level entails *faith beyond belief.* The spirituality of the Mystic is faith without the need for certainties.

As a society, we do not want to leave our churches behind. Nor should we; they provide us with a rich cultural heritage and a particular sense of community not available elsewhere. They also serve as an integrating force for good and remind us to focus on issues beyond the material world.

What we *do* need to leave behind are the immature manifestations of the traditional religious message. The original "peakers" upon whose direct experiences of the Divine our world religions were founded would be horrified to learn the way so many Faithful "non-peakers" have interpreted their teachings. The triumphalist attitudes and divisive religious certainties common among many of our churches serve only to divide us from one another. These limited viewpoints run directly counter to the original intent behind any religion and work directly against the unitive worldview. They hold back a society that is trying to grow toward a more mature, more unitive community.

If the common point all religions share is about not the beliefs they espouse but following the will of Spirit toward action in *this* life (as opposed to securing one's own salvation in the next), then the goal of anyone aspiring to spiritual maturity will be a journey beyond *belief* toward *faith*. It is time we stopped allowing immature oracular authorities to shun people for lack of belief and recognize spiritual maturity for what it is. Mature faith is not so much about belief; it is recognized instead by its traits and its inclusive worldview. For those who are ready, a more meaningful faith is waiting, beyond the constraints of literal belief.

Chapter 23

Where Do
We Go from Here?

Readers for whom spiritual development theory has resonated may be wondering what comes next, or what they can do with the perspective they have gained. Some suggestions are listed below.

Things to Do

Read. This book has only barely scratched the surface of what spiritual growth might involve. Far greater depth and detail is available among the works of any of the theorists mentioned. Studying these may inspire an ever-widening and -deepening perspective.

Should a person be lucky enough for this topic to light a fire in her heart, it may keep her engaged for years to come; it may allow her to return to a tradition left behind or find a new one that fits better with her current worldview. But the main thing this knowledge should do is inform each of us that, no matter where we are on the spiritual path, there is always room for further growth.

Talk. Traditionally, the only way people learned about religion was through sources officially sanctioned by religious leaders or through personal study. This has held back appreciation of the trajectory of spiritual development. Those convinced of the benefits of spiritual growth will work to eliminate the long-standing taboo against spiritual discussion in social situations. Once we begin talking about spirituality as a dynamic topic to which we all have access, as opposed to a static list of pre-set beliefs dispensed only through a religious authority, more people will develop beyond the Faithful level.

Join. Some organizations are already set up to promote exactly this type of discussion. In particular, the Network of Spiritual Progressives is an interfaith organization that helps people from various religions and spiritual backgrounds see beyond their past distress at religion and work together to build a movement for social healing and transformation. www.spiritualprogressives.org.

Religious and spiritual paths can also be discussed in small private groups—either physically, in a given geographical area, or online. Meet-up.com has local groups that meet to discuss such issues. Meet-up also makes it easy to start one's own group on any desired topic.

Send More Stories. I have acknowledged throughout this book that the stories I presented were merely samples meant to introduce the concept to the reader, and that any one person's story would be an imperfect example at best. Additional stories would allow further exploration and deepen our understanding. I invite readers to send me a personal story that could help readers of a future book better understand any one of the spiritual levels. (Use the "Contact" button at http://www.FaithBeyondBelief—Book.com.)

Vote. Once a person understands the spiritual-development trajectory, it is hard to imagine how he could support leaders bent on taking us back to a pre-Enlightenment worldview. Enough said.

The Religion of Tomorrow

In no way do we want to leave our churches behind. Instead, we need to transform them from within—change them from institutions bent on collecting money and winning participants away from the church down the street into communities working for the good of all people. We need them to become places where spiritually mature values are understood and people are coached into adopting inclusive beliefs. We must stop tolerating so-called spiritual leaders who promote "either/or" righteousness over Reich's level five "both/and" reasoning, who favor simple, triumphalist answers over an appreciation of spiritual mystery, and who advocate ethnocentrism over universality.

If spiritual "imaginal cells" are indeed rapidly increasing in number, and if the spiritually transformed society they portend is coming, soon there will be more post-Conventional (or post-critical) people than Conventional and pre-Conventional (or pre-critical) ones. The churches of tomorrow will have to adapt in order to survive. To meet the demands of increasing post-critical thought, organized religion will have to cease dispensing absolutist answers and instead encourage people to explore the questions. Religious leaders will have to shift their role from dispensers of preordained truths to facilitators of a spiritual growth that leaves room for personal discovery and mystery. In order to appeal to the ever-increasing numbers of the "transformed," the religion of tomorrow will have to embrace the universality of a "we are all one" worldview.

To reach this point, seminaries would need to teach the spiritual stages, so their graduates could impart that wisdom to their congregations. Some 150 years after the Civil War, reasonable people now shake their heads to think that our society once permitted the keeping of slaves; society has *progressed* beyond slavery. How ridiculous it would be for an American History PhD program to restrict study of the Civil War to the Confederate viewpoint! Any seminary not teaching about the spiritual stages and not exposing the universal message will one day be equally irrelevant. And 150 years from now, society will have matured past the Faithful viewpoint. Reasonable people will shake their heads to think religion once taught about a literal sky God who only loved a small part of his creation.

Rather than keep its adherents mired in childish myths, the religion of the future will lead its members toward the more fluid form of faith that can develop *beyond belief*. It will encourage them to undertake the critical reflection required to begin the progression to mature faith. Rather than suppress diversity and self-expression in religious experience, the religion of the future will promote the spiritual exploration that is necessary to reach the Mystic level.

Where the religion of the past was exclusionist, ethnocentric, judgmental, and triumphalist, the religion of the future will be inclusive, universal, unitive, and accepting. The religion of the future will be Love!

Notes

INTRODUCTION

1. M. Scott Peck, *The Different Drum: Community Making and Peace* (New York: Simon & Schuster, 1987), 193.
2. Teresa of Avila, *Interior Castle*, trans. E. Allison Peers (Radford, VA: Wilder, 2008), 42.
3. The term *deux chevaux* (two horses) refers to the French equivalent of the American college student's Volkswagen "bug" in the 1970s.

CHAPTER 2

1. Qur'an 4:56.
2. Qur'an 22:19–20.
3. Qur'an 37:61–67.
4. Qur'an 39:67–69.
5. Qur'an 3:103.

CHAPTER 3

1. Ernest Hemingway, *The Sun Also Rises* (New York: Scribner, 2006), 251.

CHAPTER 4

1. Anonymous, "The Rainbow Bridge Poem," http://rainbowsbridge. com/Poem.htm.
2. Roger N. Walsh, *Essential Spirituality: The 7 Central Practices to Awaken Heart and Mind* (New York: J. Wiley, 1999), 6.
3. Ibid., 9.

CHAPTER 5

1. Christopher Hitchens, *God Is Not Great: How Religion Poisons Everything* (New York: Twelve, 2007), 255.
2. Ibid., 52.
3. Sam Harris, *The End of Faith: Religion, Terror, and the Future of Reason* (New York: W. W. Norton & Co., 2004), 221.
4. Richard Dawkins, *The God Delusion* (Boston: Houghton Mifflin, 2006), 248.
5. Ibid., 253.
6. Peck, *The Different Drum*, 193 (see intro., no. 1). Emphasis added.
7. M. Scott Peck, *The Road Less Traveled: A New Psychology of Love, Traditional Values, and Spiritual Growth* (New York: Simon & Schuster, 1978). 223.
8. _____, *The Different Drum*, 192.
9. Ibid., 201.
10. Ibid., 193.

CHAPTER 6

1. Lawrence Kohlberg wrote of such moral dilemmas that occur when society's rules do not provide adequate guidance on which to base a decision. This concept is further discussed in chapters 14 and 15.
2. Here the word *oracle* is used in the sense of a source of wisdom and definite answers, or a revelation from God.

CHAPTER 8

1. Matt. 5:39 (King James).
2. Matt. 18:20 (King James).

CHAPTER 9

1. The term *near-death experience* describes an event in which a person has been considered clinically dead, or nearly so, but can accurately report profound experiences from that time. Some near-death experiences include a life review in which the person sees his or her life pass very rapidly before his or her eyes. Frequently, the end result of a near-death experience is a life-changing revelation and increased spiritual focus.

CHAPTER 13

1. A censer is a vessel used in some churches to burn incense.
2. Emerson, "The Over-Soul," www.emersoncentral.com/oversoul.htm.
3. See chapter 15 for a brief summary of Saint Teresa's spiritual "mansions."

CHAPTER 14

1. Andrew B. Newberg, Eugene G. D'Aquili, and Vincent Rause, *Why God Won't Go Away: Brain Science and the Biology of Belief* (New York: Ballantine, 2001), 101.
2. Adolphe Tanquerey and Herman Branderis, *The Spiritual Life: A Treatise on Ascetical and Mystical Theology* (Charlotte: Tan Books, 2000), 716.
3. Ibid., 716–17.
4. Gordon Willard Allport, *The Individual and His Religion: A Psychological Interpretation* (New York: Macmillan, 1969), 114.

5. Ibid., 115.
6. Ibid., 139.
7. Ibid., 116.
8. M. Scott Peck, *Further Along the Road Less Traveled: The Unending Journey toward Spiritual Growth—The Edited Lectures* (New York: Simon & Schuster, 1998), 238.
9. See chapter 15 for a fuller discussion of Kohlberg.

CHAPTER 15

1. James W. Fowler, *Stages of Faith: the Psychology of Human Development and the Quest for Meaning* (San Francisco: Harper & Row, 1981), 14.
2. Ibid.,14.
3. Mary Jo Meadow, "Faith Development and Teresa's Interior Castle," *Pastoral Psychology* 41, no. 6 (1993): 377–84.
4. Tanquerey and Branderis, *The Spiritual Life*, 297(see chap. 14, no. 2). Emphasis added.
5. Caroline Myss and Lauren Artress, "Challenges and Blessings of the Mystical Path," Wisdom University seminar, 2009.
6. In certain of Wilber's works, this level is called "Beige."
7. Fowler, *Stages of Faith*, 149.
8. Ibid.
9. Ibid., 150.
10. Ibid., 149.
11. Ibid., 172.
12. Ibid., 173.
13. Teresa's "Mansions" are always referred to in the plural.
14. Tanquerey and Branderis, *The Spiritual Life*, 307.
15. The phrase *deus ex machina* is borrowed from ancient Greek and Roman theatre to describe a situation where a God would abruptly appear from out of the sky, introduced by means of a mechanical device, and suddenly determine the outcome of

the play. Oser uses it here in a somewhat derogatory sense to imply that the God at this level is a device artificially contrived to resolve life's problems.

16. In other of his works, Wilber calls this level "Blue."
17. Fowler, *Stages of Faith*, 179.
18. Ibid.
19. Ibid.
20. Oser and Gmunder use the word *ultimate* as a general term to refer to anyone's interpretation of God.
21. Fowler, *Stages of Faith*, 183.
22. Ibid.,198.
23. Ibid.
24. Ibid., 211.
25. Ibid.
26. Ibid.
27. Tanquerey and Branderis, *The Spiritual Life*, 603.
28. Keeping in mind that the word *God* can be read metaphorically can help us see correlations we might otherwise reject because they sound overly religious.
29. Elsewhere called "Yellow."
30. Lawrence Kohlberg's stages of moral development are described in chapter 7 of William C. Crain, *Theories of Development: Concepts and Applications* (Upper Saddle River, NJ: Prentice Hall, 1985), 118–136. See also www.faculty.plts.edu/gpence/html/kohlberg.htm.

CHAPTER 16

1. Abraham H. Maslow, *Religions, Values, and Peak-Experiences* (New York: Viking, 1970), vii.
2. Ibid., 25.
3. Ibid., 22.
4. Ibid., 24.
5. Ibid., 32.

CHAPTER 17

1. Allport, *The Individual and His Religion*, 59 (see chap. 14, n. 4).
2. Ibid., 60.
3. Peck, *The Different Drum*, 199 (see intro., n. 1).
4. _____, *The Road Less Traveled*, 301 (see chap. 5, n. 7).
5. Fowler, *Stages of Faith*, 102 (see chap. 15, n. 1).
6. Heinz Streib, "Faith Development Theory Revisited: The Religious Styles Perspective," *The International Journal for the Psychology of Religion* 11, no. 3 (2001): 143–158.
7. Ken Wilber, *Integral Spirituality: A Startling New Role for Religion in the Modern and Postmodern World* (Boston: Integral, 2006), 76–82.
8. Fowler, *Stages of Faith*, 100–01.
9. Walter Houston Clark, *The Psychology of Religion: An Introduction to Religious Experience and Behavior* (New York: Macmillan, 1958), 227–232.

CHAPTER 18

1. Maslow, *Religions, Values, and Peak-Experiences*, 86 (see chap. 16, n. 1).

CHAPTER 19

1. K. Helmut Reich, *Developing the Horizons of the Mind: Relational and Contextual Reasoning and Resolution of Cognitive Conflict* (Cambridge: Cambridge University Press, 2002), 126–129.
2. Ibid., 125.
3. Allport, *The Individual and His Religion*, 78 (see chap. 14, n. 4).
4. Rami Shapiro, "Can We Reconcile Faiths? Did Jesus Walk on Water?" *Spirituality & Health* 10, no. 4 (2007): 16.
5. Fowler, *Stages of Faith*, 201 (see chap. 15, n. 1).
6. Joan Chittister, *Welcome to the Wisdom of the World and Its Meaning for You* (Grand Rapids, MI: Eerdmans, 2007), 121–22.

7. Maslow, *Religions, Values and Peak-Experiences*, 20 (see chap. 16, n. 1).

8. John Shelby Spong, *A New Christianity for a New World: Why Traditional Faith Is Dying and How a New Faith Is Being Born* (San Francisco: HarperSanFrancisco, 2001), xviii.

9. Wayne Teasdale, *The Mystic Heart: Discovering a Universal Spirituality in the World's Religions* (Novato, CA: New World Library, 1999), 227.

10. Paul Ricoeur, "On Consolation," in Alasdair MacIntyre and Paul Ricoeur, *The Religious Significance of Atheism* (New York: Columbia University Press, 1969), 97–98.

11. Ricoeur, "Religion, Atheism, and Faith," in *The Conflict of Interpretations: Essays in Hermeneutics*, ed. Don Ihde, trans. Charles Freilich (Evanston, IL: Northwestern University Press, 2007), 467. (Emphasis added.)

12. Wilber, *Integral Spirituality*, 158–160, 208 (see chap. 17, n. 7).

CHAPTER 21

1. Larry Culliford, "Spiritual Leadership: The Case of Barack Obama, Part 1," *Psychology Today* online, http://www.psychologytoday.com/blog/spiritual-wisdom-secular-times/201106/spiritual-leadership-the-case-barack-obama-part-1.

2. _____, *The Psychology of Spirituality: An Introduction* (London and Philadelphia: Jessica Kingsley Publishers, 2011), 133–152.

3. Ibid., 153–172.

4. Ibid., 173–195.

5. Culliford, "Spiritual Leadership: The Case of Barack Obama, Part 1."

6. Barack Obama, *Dreams from My Father* (New York: Three Rivers Press, 2004), 129.

7. Ibid., 294.

8. Ibid., 220.

9. Ibid.

10. Ibid.

11. Barack Obama, *The Audacity of Hope: Thoughts on Reclaiming the Amercian Dream* (New York: Crown, 2006), 134.

12. Ibid., 208. Italicized comments in brackets added by MPJ.

13. Obama, *The Audacity of Hope*, 224.

CHAPTER 22

1. Abraham Maslow, *Toward a Psychology of Being* (Princeton, NJ: Van Nostrand, 1968), 155.

2. Allport, *The Individual and His Religion*, 140 (see chap. 14, n. 4).

Bibliography

Allport, Gordon Willard. *The Individual and His Religion: A Psychological Interpretation*. New York: Macmillan, 1969.

Bradley, Raymond D. *A Moral Argument for Atheism*. Essay. 1999. Available online at http://www.infidels.org/library/modern/raymond_bradley/moral.html.

Chittister, Joan. *Welcome to the Wisdom of the World and Its Meaning for You*. Grand Rapids: Eerdmans, 2007.

Clark, Walter Houston. *The Psychology of Religion: An Introduction to Religious Experience and Behavior*. New York: Macmillan, 1958.

Crain, William C. "Kohlberg's Stages of Moral Development." Chap. 7 in *Theories of Development: Concepts and Applications*. Upper Saddle River, NJ: Prentice Hall, 1985. (Chapter viewable online at faculty.plts.edu/gpence/html/kohlberg.htm.)

Csíkszentmihályi, Mihály. *Flow: the Psychology of Optimal Experience*. New York: HarperPerennial, 1991.

Culliford, Larry. *The Psychology of Spirituality: An Introduction*. London and Philadelphia: Jessica Kingsley Publishers, 2011.

_____. "Spiritual Leadership: The Case of Barack Obama, Part 1." *Psychology Today* online, http://www.psychologytoday.com/blog/

spiritual-wisdom-secular-times/201106/spiritual-leadership-the-case-barack-obama-part-1.

Dawkins, Richard. *The God Delusion*. Boston: Houghton Mifflin, 2006.

Duerk, Judith. *Circle of Stones*. Philadelphia: Innisfree, 1998.

Eisler, Riane. *The Chalice and the Blade: Our History, Our Future*. San Francisco: HarperSanFrancisco, 1988.

Emerson, Ralph Waldo. "The Over-Soul." From *Essays: First Series* (1841). Accessible online at *Ralph Waldo Emerson Texts*, www.emersoncentral.com. Site editor: Jone Johnson Lewis.

Fowler, James W. *Faithful Change: The Personal and Public Challenges of Postmodern Life*. Nashville: Abingdon, 1996.

_____. *Stages of Faith: the Psychology of Human Development and the Quest for Meaning*. San Francisco: Harper & Row, 1981.

Harris, Sam. *The End of Faith: Religion, Terror, and the Future of Reason*. New York: W.W. Norton & Co., 2004.

Hemingway, Ernest. *The Sun Also Rises*. New York: Scribner, 2006.

Hilâlî, Muhamman Taqî-ud-Dîn al- and Muhammad Muhsin Khân. *Translation of the Meanings of the Noble Qur'an in the English Language*. Madinah, Kingdom of Saudi Arabia: King Fahd Complex for the Printing of the Holy Qur'an (no date of publication given).

Hitchens, Christopher. *God Is Not Great: How Religion Poisons Everything*. New York: Twelve, 2007.

Keirsey, David. *Please Understand Me II: Temperament, Character, Intelligence*. Del Mar, CA: Prometheus Nemesis, 1998.

Lappé, Frances Moore. *Diet for a Small Planet*. New York: Ballantine, 1991.

Lerner, Michael. *Jewish Renewal: A Path to Healing and Transformation*. New York: Harper Perennial, 1995.

_____. *The Left Hand of God: Healing America's Political and Spiritual Crisis*. San Francisco: HarperSanFrancisco, 2006.

Loevinger, Jane, and Augusto Blasi. *Ego Development: Conceptions and Theories*. San Francisco: Jossey-Bass, 1976.

Maccoby, Hyam. *The Mythmaker: Paul and the Invention of Christianity*. New York: Harper & Row, 1986.

MacIntyre, Alasdair C., and Paul Ricoeur. "On Consolation." In *The Religious Significance of Atheism*. Hampton Lectures in America, no. 18, delivered at Columbia University, 1966. New York: Columbia University Press, 1969.

Maslow, Abraham H. *Religions, Values, and Peak-Experiences*. New York: Viking, 1970.

————. *Toward a Psychology of Being*. Princeton, NJ: Van Nostrand, 1968.

Masson, J. Moussaieff. *The Pig Who Sang to the Moon: The Emotional World of Farm Animals*. New York: Ballantine, 2004.

Meadow, Mary Jo. "Faith Development and Teresa's Interior Castle." *Pastoral Psychology* 41, no. 6 (1993): 377–84.

Myss, Caroline, and Lauren Artress. "Challenges and Blessings of the Mystical Path." Wisdom University seminar, Oakland, CA, February 12, 2009.

Newberg, Andrew B., Eugene G. D'Aquili, and Vince Rause. *Why God Won't Go Away: Brain Science and the Biology of Belief*. New York: Ballantine, 2001.

Obama, Barack. *The Audacity of Hope: Thoughts on Reclaiming the Amercian Dream*. New York: Crown, 2006.

————. *Dreams from My Father*. New York: Three Rivers Press, 2004.

Oser, Fritz, and Paul Gmünder. *Religious Judgement: A Developmental Perspective*. Birmingham, AL: Religious Education, 1991.

Peck, M. Scott. *The Different Drum: Community Making and Peace*. New York: Simon and Schuster, 1987.

————. *Further Along the Road Less Traveled: The Unending Journey toward Spiritual Growth—The Edited Lectures*. New York: Simon & Schuster, 1998.

————. Introduction in *People of the Lie: The Hope for Healing Human Evil*. New York: Simon and Schuster, 1983.

————. *The Road Less Traveled: A New Psychology of Love, Traditional Values, and Spiritual Growth*. New York: Simon and Schuster, 1978.

Rachels, James. *Created from Animals: The Moral Implications of Darwinism*. Oxford: Oxford University Press, 1990.

"Rainbow Bridge Poem." Author Unknown. *Rainbows Bridge Home Page.* Web. 16, Nov. 2010. http://rainbowsbridge.com/Poem.htm.

Read, Donna. *Women and Spirituality.* New York: Wellspring Media, distributed by Winstar TV & Video. VHS video, 1999.

Redmond, Layne. *When the Women Were Drummers: A Spiritual History of Rhythm.* New York: Three Rivers Press, 1997.

Reich, K. Helmut. *Developing the Horizons of the Mind: Relational and Contextual Reasoning and Resolution of Cognitive Conflict.* Cambridge: Cambridge University Press, 2002.

Ricoeur, Paul. "Religion, Atheism, and Faith." Translated by Charles Freilich. In *The Conflict of Interpretations: Essays in Hermeneutics.* Edited by Don Ihde. Evanston, IL: Northwestern University Press, 2007.

Shapiro, Rami. "Can We Reconcile Faiths? Did Jesus Walk on Water?" *Spirituality & Health* (Nov.-Dec. 2007): 16.

Spong, John Shelby. *A New Christianity for a New World: Why Traditional Faith Is Dying and How a New Faith Is Being Born.* San Francisco: HarperSanFrancisco, 2001.

_____. *Resurrection: Myth or Reality? A Bishop's Search for the Origins of Christianity.* San Francisco: HarperSanFrancisco, 1995.

Stone, Merlin. *When God Was a Woman.* New York: Mariner Books, 1978.

Streib, Heinz. "Faith Development Theory Revisited: The Religious Styles Perspective." *International Journal for the Psychology of Religion* 11, no. 3 (2001): 143-158.

Tanquerey, Adolphe, and Herman Branderis. *The Spiritual Life: A Treatise on Ascetical and Mystical Theology.* Charlotte, NC: Tan Books, 2000.

Teasdale, Wayne. *The Mystic Heart: Discovering a Universal Spirituality in the World's Religions.* Novato, CA: New World Library, 1999.

Teresa of Avila. *The Interior Castle.* Translated by E. Allison Peers. Radford, VA: Wilder Publications, 2008.

Underhill, Evelyn. *Practical Mysticism.* Columbus, OH: Ariel, 1942.

Walsh, Roger N. *Essential Spirituality: The 7 Central Practices to Awaken Heart and Mind.* New York: J. Wiley, 1999.

Wilber, Ken. *Integral Psychology: Consciousness, Spirit, Psychology, Therapy.* Boston: Shambhala, 2000.

_____. *Integral Spirituality: A Startling New Role for Religion in the Modern and Postmodern World.* Boston: Integral, 2006.

Wise, Steven M. *Drawing the Line: Science and the Case for Animal Rights.* Cambridge, MA: Perseus, 2002.

_____. *Rattling the Cage: Toward Legal Rights for Animals.* Cambridge, MA: Perseus, 2000.

Women and Spirituality. Wellspring Media, 1999.

Zeitgeist: The Movie. Directed by Peter Joseph, 2007. (See ZeitgeistMovie.com.)

Index

Related Quest Titles

Becoming a Practical Mystic, by Jacquelyn Small
Beyond Religion, by David N. Elkins
Commentaries on Living, by Jiddu Krishnamurti
Finding Faith in the Face of Doubt, by Joseph S. Willis
The Fundamentalist Mind, by Stephen Larsen
The Spectrum of Consciousness, by Ken Wilber
The Transcendent Unity of Religions, by Frithjof Schuon

MORE PRAISE FOR MARGARET PLACENTRA JOHNSTON'S
FAITH BEYOND BELIEF

"An excellent, wise, and important contribution to vital contemporary discussions about spiritual development at every level: personal, social, and global. As the future of humanity may be at stake, how wonderful it is that this book puts us so firmly back on the right course."
—Dr. Larry Culliford,
author, *The Psychology of Spirituality*

"A welcome and much-needed humanization of the psychological and spiritual conflicts that beset humankind. What rings with a strong clarion call in this book is the *psychological truth* of the individual stories."
—R. G. Kainer, PhD,
analytic psychologist and
author of *The Collapse of the Self and its Therapeutic Restoration*

"Postmodern humanity is hungry for a postmodern faith, and Margaret Placentra Johnston offers us just that. Blending the insights of James Fowler and Paul Ricoeur with the stories of real people grappling with their own spiritual maturation, she offers us a map and a model for our own wrestling with truth. This is an important book."
—Rabbi Rami Shapiro,
author of *Rabbi Rami's Guide to God*

"This book will undoubtedly be considered one of the contributing factors in advancing our understanding of evolving human spirituality. By acknowledging the emergence of mysticism in ordinary lives, Margaret helps to outline a way of living that is relevant, wise, and healing."
—Reverend Karen Tudor, senior minister,
Unity Church of Practical Christianity, New Braunfels,
Texas, and cohost of "Biblical Power for Your Life"
on Unity Online Radio